THE PARTISAN DIVIDE: CONGRESS IN CRISIS

BY TOM DAVIS, MARTIN FROST AND RICHARD E. COHEN

PUBLISHED BY PREMIERE

Published by Premiere
307 Orchard City Drive
Suite 210
Campbell CA 95008 USA
info@fastpencil.com
(408) 540-7571
(408) 540-7572 (Fax)
http://premiere.fastpencil.com

Manufactured by Courier Corporation – 33128001 2014

First Edition

DEDICATIONS

Tom Davis – "To my wife and trusted advisor Jeannemarie."

Martin Frost – "To the women in my life – my wife JoEllen and my three daughters Alanna, Mariel, and Camille."

Richard Cohen – "To my insightful and non-partisan wife Lyn."

"TO THE MANY MEMBERS OF CONGRESS AND JOURNALISTS WHO HAVE ENHANCED OUR UNDERSTANDING OF CAPITOL HILL."

❧

ENDORSEMENTS

"Martin Frost and Tom Davis are uniquely qualified to examine how constant conflict in Washington keeps too many good things from happening. The Partisan Divide is a smart book that asks the right questions and offers some intriguing solutions."

- President Bill Clinton, 42nd President of the United States

"Put plainly, this is the most significant political book I have read in a decade or longer. Our system of self-government is manifestly in crisis and the stakes could not be higher. For over a decade, the public has awaited explanations and recommendations, which are provided by the book."

- David Eisenhower, Pulitzer Prize Finalist, Public Policy Fellow, Professor at the University of Pennsylvania

"Democrat Martin Frost and Republican Tom Davis knew how to work together effectively as congressional leaders. In this important book, they describe how the decline of bipartisanship has brought about a government that seems incapable of addressing the serious problems that affect our nation, and they suggest how this might be reversed."

- President Jimmy Carter, 39th President of the United States

"Tom Davis and Martin Frost are two true Washington insiders who care more about the institution of Congress than their respective parties. Here's hoping that every CURRENT member of Congress reads this book and uses it as a blueprint of how to get the institution to work again on behalf of the American public."

- Chuck Todd, Moderator of "Meet the Press," Political Director at NBC News

"This book by two veteran politicians - one a Democrat and one a Republican - shows just how broken our political system is and how difficult it is going to be to get it back on track."

- Bob Schieffer, Moderator of "Face the Nation," Chief Washington Correspondent at CBS News

"Martin Frost, a Democrat, and Tom Davis, a Republican, are two thoughtful former members of the House of Representatives who headed each of their party's campaign committees. They know what they are talking about. There are major problems in the Congress today. We need some changes; and they have recommendations that will make a difference."

- Sen. Trent Lott, Former Senate Majority Leader (R-MS)

"Tom Davis and Martin Frost are two men who have been in the pits of the great partisan battles of the past yet were able to join with their leaderships to bridge the politics and get real things done in the legislative arena. Their book brings unique insights and answers on how our nation's political discourse can begin to yield positive results."

- Rep. Dennis Hastert, 59th Speaker of the House (R-IL)

"As bipartisan progress becomes ever scarcer in Washington, Frost and Davis have come together to present thought-provoking ideas and insights from four decades of collective experience in Congress. In their powerful insiders' account of the road into political gridlock, readers will find both the full extent of the problem and new possibilities for a way out."

- Rep. Nancy Pelosi, Democratic Leader, 60th Speaker of the House (D-CA)

"Tom Davis and Martin Frost, along with Rich Cohen, have written a book that desperately needed to be written and arguably no other three people are better qualified to write it. Not a textbook or a 'tell-all' book, but really a firsthand, behind-the-scenes account and explanation of what has gone terribly wrong in Washington and politics, and why."

- Charlie Cook, Editor and Publisher of the Cook Political Report, Columnist for National Journal

"Martin Frost and Tom Davis are two of the savviest members of Congress to have served in recent decades, comfortable with both politics and policy, and immersed enough in our recent political turmoil to have great perspective on causes and consequences. One doesn't have to agree with all their viewpoints and recommendations to appreciate their terrific contribution in this book to our understanding of Congress and political dysfunction."

- Norm Ornstein, Resident Scholar at the American Enterprise Institute, Contributing Editor and Columnist for National Journal and The Atlantic

"It doesn't take a Washington insider to know that Congress is broken right now. In The Way Forward (final chapter), Martin and Tom identify the primary causes of and potential solutions to this dysfunction. From campaign finance to the 24/7 news media to demographic trends, their explanation of congressional gridlock is wide-ranging and comprehensive."

- Donna Brazile, Political Strategist at CNN and ABC, Vice-Chairwoman of the Democratic National Committee

"Republican Tom Davis and Democrat Martin Frost have teamed up to explain in lay terms the macro trends that have contributed to the polarized political environment in the U.S. today. Drawing on their experience as congressional leaders and campaign chairs for their respective parties, this is a must read for the politically curious."

- Rep. Darrell Issa, Chairman of the House Oversight and Government Reform Committee (R-CA)

"Martin Frost and Tom Davis have offered their readers an insight into our nation's current crisis in the 21st century - our system of governance. Their thoughtful analysis and recommendations will provide the American people with solutions in restoring faith and confidence in today's political climate."

- Dick Gephardt, Former House Minority Leader (D-MO)

Acknowledgments

Tom Davis

Let me acknowledge the help of my wife, Jeannemarie, who constantly edited my drafts and made many useful comments in formulating my conclusions. As a 10-year veteran of both the Virginia House and Senate, she offered a distinctly feminine and state perspective, as well as organizational expertise, to my drafts.

Also, to my Amherst College classmate David Eisenhower and political science professor Hadley Arkes, many thanks for challenging and inspiring my interest in politics.

To Charlie Cook of the Cook Report and Rhodes Cook (no relation), many thanks for your slides and insights into the political process.

Many thanks to Bruce Butterfield, my college roommate, for suggesting I write a book about the changing nature of politics, and to our editor, Elizabeth Wallingford, who made our initial draft much more readable.

And, finally, many thanks to Greg Walden, Chairman of the National Republican Congressional Committee, and his staff for their continuing insights into the evolving nature of the electoral system.

Martin Frost

I want to start with my wife, JoEllen, and my three daughters, Alanna Bach, Mariel Sala, and Camille Wight, all of whom at various times have urged me to write a book about my experiences as a member of Congress.

Next, I owe special thanks to three of my former staffers who provided invaluable help in recalling parts of my career – Matt Angle, Susan McAvoy, and Kristi Walseth.

And then I would like to thank the following individuals who spent time discussing various aspects of this book with me: former House Speaker Jim Wright; House Democratic whip Steny Hoyer; former House Democratic leader Dick Gephardt; Al From; University of Texas government professor Sean Theriault; election law legal expert Ken Gross; my law partner and former Senate staff member Jim Davidson; Dr. John C. Fortier, co-director of the Bipartisan Policy Center's Commission on Political Reform; George Kundanis, longtime director of the House Democratic Policy Committee; Yale Law Professor Heather Gerken; the staff of Congressman Marc Veasey; Gerry Hebert and the staff of the Campaign Legal Center; the staff of the Democratic Congressional Campaign Committee; and the staff of the Federal Election Commission.

Finally, I would like to thank Garrett Lamm, my assistant at the Polsinelli law firm, who helped immeasurably with the organizing and formatting of much of this material.

CONTENTS

Preface xiii

Chapter 1   The Mess We're in: How Did We Get Here, and Where Do
We Go From Here? 1

Chapter 2   Qualifying the Expert Witnesses 7

Chapter 3   The New Normal: Divided Government 31

Chapter 4   The Continuing Role of Race in American Politics 47

Chapter 5   Redistricting and the Art of Gerrymandering 61

Chapter 6   Moneyball 75

Chapter 7   All Politics Is No Longer Local 95

Chapter 8   Do Independents Matter?, and the Collapse of the Middle 147

Chapter 9   Relying on Base Voters Makes Compromise Much Harder 159

Chapter 10   The New Media: Polarized and Segmented 171

Chapter 11   House Elections: A Science Unto Themselves 183

Chapter 12   Senate Elections: Voters Still Matter 199

Chapter 13   When Congress Was Fun ... and Productive 219

Chapter 14   Committee Selections and Leadership Elections 235

Chapter 15   The Big Punt 253

Chapter 16   The Way Forward 271

Endnotes 287

About the Authors 293

Index 299

PREFACE

By David Eisenhower

As an observer of the American political scene for over 50 years, I have witnessed many changes in our political system. But like most Americans, I was taught to best appreciate the durable features of our national system of self-government which have provided a framework for American freedom and the prosperity we have historically enjoyed. Our system of checks and balances has been one such enduring feature; another has been a political climate of optimism and moderation characteristic of much of American history.

Our democratic foundations were forged out of compromises made during a sweltering summer in Philadelphia in 1787, and the basic principles have endured for over two and a quarter centuries. In two centuries, Americans have cumulatively built the greatest nation in history; provided a haven for the persecuted and oppressed; led the world in scientific and technical innovation; and provided leadership and strength when the world has become threatened. Yet despite these accomplishments, Americans today seem more divided, our government appears less effective, and our leadership appears more challenged than at any time in the past century. As the authors point out authoritatively, today we face a serious political crisis, a crisis of governmental effectiveness, a crisis centered on Congress but affecting all branches and levels of government; in short, a crisis that threatens the structure of our system as we have known it.

That good old American democratic value of compromise has gone dormant. Budgets have become elusive; solutions have been kicked down the road; and the political system has become more rancorous. To the average American, these changes have been confusing and frustrating. To the casual observer, it often appears the system is coming apart, as pessimism about America's future grows. In a word, national politics have become "polarized" and characterized by a hyper-partisanship not seen since the Civil War. The main impact of this polarization has fallen on the operations of Congress, the "first branch of government," which has always been the citizens' most direct link to the national government.

Yet the current political crisis is paradoxical in some ways. America remains a powerful and prosperous nation. Though the American economy mends slowly, we have safely navigated our way past the financial crisis of 2008 which threatened the return of a great depression. Americans are deeply involved in problems overseas, but there is no Vietnam War to set generation against generation. Racial problems remain, but the real civil rights turmoil is history and the peaceful revolution it brought forth is a matter of law, thanks to a visionary and compromise-minded Congress 50 years ago. And ironies abound. Partisanship thrives, but as the authors show, national political parties are weakened. Because election considerations are and always have been the primary determinants of congressional behavior, more and more non-competitive districts rob members of Congress of incentives to court the middle, which effectively disenfranchises the largest single group of Americans – independents. The rise of what Davis calls "nationalized elections" actually produces results that segment and fragment America.

But the key point made by the authors throughout this book is that the political crisis Americans face has causes that must – and can – be remedied.

Authors Davis and Frost – former congressional campaign chairmen for the House Republicans and Democrats, respectively – draw on their cumulative years as congressional leaders and campaign chairs to explain why this has happened to our system of government. Drawing on a wealth of experience, they explain in readable prose how the "macro" events shaping our political system have emerged and how they and lesser causes have combined to bring us to the current impasse.

The authors describe and analyze the ideological sorting of the parties and the resultant polarization and ineffectiveness of Congress, which have not happened in a vacuum or as the result of any single set of political events or decisions. They describe the marginalization of "moderate voters," which underlies hyper-partisanship in Congress. They look carefully at the emergence of non-competitive districts, a phenomenon due partly to the "residential sorting process" (in which people of like-minded values live in enclaves) and partly to the 1965 Voting Rights Act (which has had the effect of packing minority members in districts and bleaching the districts around them). As they explain, non-competitive districts have also come about thanks to the sophisticated gerrymandering of House district lines. And as the number of non-competitive districts has risen, so has the importance of primaries and the partisans and interest groups that gravitate toward the poles of American politics and have the effect of driving policy right and left, punishing compromise and rewarding intransigence.

Another "macro" factor is the commonplace new media business model – whether 24/7 cable news, talk radio, or the Internet – which aims at attracting traffic by playing to the more passionate political participants, rather than by offering filtered and unbiased news reporting to the population at large. Campaign financing law has strengthened ideologically-oriented interest groups while greatly undermining the national parties – historically moderating influences on political behavior. It is likewise startling to read in this book how much candidates have lost control of their election campaign messaging due to the expenditures of "independent" groups.

Put simply, the macro factors itemized in this book have proven combustible and have essentially eliminated any meaningful center to an American political system. Polarization underlies the "nationalizing trend" so evident in congressional affairs, upending Tip O'Neill's famous adage that all politics are local. This nationalizing trend applies both to elections and to House and Senate practices, which have taken on the features of what Davis calls a "parliamentary style" that is unsuitable – at best – in a "checks and balances" system. A looming potential future consequence of the resulting impasse is presidential government. But the authors show that the situation is reversible and recommend measures – large and small – that can and will change recent patterns.

I have known and worked with Tom Davis since our days as Amherst classmates in the late 1960s. He draws on his experience from the White

House political office to Fairfax County, Virginia, politics to two successful terms (in 2000 and 2002) as chairman of the National Republican Congressional Committee (NRCC), the campaign arm of House Republicans, in explaining the changing nature of the electorate and the changing pressures on our elected leaders that make compromise so difficult. Often called the "Michael Barone" of the House, Tom is a certified genius on the subject of elections and politics, but he is also one of the greatest political practitioners of his generation. Tom was a prodigious legislator, authoring over 100 bills that became law and spearheading hearings on controversial issues – such as steroid use in baseball – from his perch as chairman of the House Government Reform Committee. Indeed, with an encyclopedic knowledge of politics, Tom's most important traits are his ability to make friends of political rivals, his ability to advance his principles while getting things done, and his profound reverence for the Congress and the American way of government he has served since high school.

I have observed Martin Frost and Richard Cohen from afar. Frost's record as Tom's counterpart as chairman of the Democratic Congressional Campaign Committee (DCCC) in 1996 and 1998 made history. He was rewarded by his Democratic House colleagues by being elected as chairman of the House Democratic Caucus and has the vantage of presiding over hundreds of Democratic Caucus meetings. Cohen's *Almanac of American Politics* has been an indispensable source on American politics for years. It is evident in this book that both Martin Frost and Rich Cohen share Tom's spirit of generosity, pride in the significance and history of America's "first branch" of government, and commitment to finding ways to meet the current crisis and serving the system which has served America so well.

The fact that Tom Davis, Martin Frost, and Rich Cohen can come together to explain the changes afoot in national politics and to present various solutions makes this book a "must-read" for both avid and casual followers of our political system. In an era where partisans talk over each other with prepackaged messaging points, it is rare indeed that two experienced congressional partisans from opposite ends of the spectrum can write candidly about our political system, share their insights and experiences, and concur on the steps that need to be taken to restore Congress and the federal government to effectiveness. But the authors are more than experienced partisans and friends. They are accomplished professionals who as congressmen made political history, and they represent the best in politics.

Put plainly, this is the most significant political book I have read in a decade or longer. Our system of self-government is manifestly in crisis and the stakes could not be higher. For over a decade, the public has awaited explanations and recommendations, which are provided by this book.

Again, the polarization of American politics has happened over the course of several decades, and it will not go away all at once. It can be addressed meaningfully with steps ranging from the restoration of discarded customs in Congress to legislation reforming the redistricting process. As the authors show, it will require political will on the part of officeholders as well as greater involvement of independents and moderates of both parties before and after Election Day. But the political stories told in this book remind us of the good things that can be recaptured and what is to be gained by restoring the spirit of compromise and optimism to national politics. In changing the tone and effectiveness of our national political institutions, Americans have everything to gain.

I'm convinced by this book that the goals set forth are attainable. It is also clear that time is of the essence. So, as the authors say, let's get started.

*David Eisenhower, grandson of General and President Dwight D. Eisenhower, is an historian and the Director of the Institute for Public Service at the Annenberg Public Policy Center. He serves as a senior research fellow at the University of Pennsylvania's Annenberg School of Communication and is a fellow in the International Relations Department at the University. Eisenhower is the author of*Eisenhower: At War, *which was a finalist for the Pulitzer Prize in history in 1986. He and wife Julie Nixon Eisenhower are co-authors of* Going Home to Glory.

1

THE MESS WE'RE IN: HOW DID WE GET HERE, AND WHERE DO WE GO FROM HERE?

By Tom Davis and Martin Frost

We are both longtime baseball fans, so we honestly feel Casey Stengel's famous quote about the inept 1962 New York Mets provides an ideal summary and query for this book. The Mets were in the midst of their first year as an expansion team, when they ultimately lost 120 games. Stengel was their manager and in an exasperated moment he said, "Can't anyone here play this game?"[1] The same can be said about the woeful 113th Congress, derided as one of the least productive in the history of our country.

Martin grew up in Ft. Worth, Texas, listening to Harry Caray broadcast the St. Louis Cardinals on radio. The Cardinals were the southernmost major league team at the time and had the South tied up on radio. One of Martin's earliest memories was listening to a Cardinals game as a seven-year-old in 1949. His first World Series game as a spectator was the fifth game of the 1964 Yankees-Cardinals World Series, which the Cardinals won in ten innings at Yankee Stadium on a home run by Tim McCarver.

Martin's greatest stress in baseball occurred in 2011, when the Cardinals played in the World Series against his home district Texas Rangers. He will only say that his American League team is the Rangers and his National League team is the Cardinals.

Tom has spent most of his life in the Washington, D.C., area and has been a regular at Washington Nationals baseball games since the team moved from Montreal to the District of Columbia in 2005; prior to that, he followed the Washington Senators, who moved to Martin's district in 1972 to become the Texas Rangers. During the three-decade interval in between, he enjoyed Baltimore Orioles games at Camden Yards.

Tom's interest in baseball led to his chairing the now-famous baseball steroid hearings detailed in Chapter 13 of this book. This hearing resulted in Tom's being listed by *Sports Illustrated* as one of the 50 top figures in sports that year. His greatest pride, however, is having gotten a hit in five straight years of the annual congressional baseball game played between Democrats and Republicans.

This book is written for the millions of people who follow politics and who have thrown up their hands in dismay at the current state of our national government. It is also written for young people – high school and college students – who are studying the American system of government and who plan to participate in the political process someday, either as candidates or just as informed voters. It is the book we wish had been available when we were first studying American government.

It's a book about what has happened to American politics in recent years and the implications of all this for the ability of the two parties to restore some degree of bipartisan cooperation in dealing with the major problems facing our country.

Neither one of us is a political scientist, though we were practitioners and observers of national politics during our combined 40 years in Congress. We were both political moderates – a disappearing breed in both political parties. Each of us also headed our party's House campaign committee. In another time, either or both of us might have become Speaker of the House. But our parties moved away from us, Tom's to the right and Martin's to the left.

Like much of the public today, we are appalled by the current state of politics in America. It hasn't always been like this and it doesn't have to be like this in the future. The purpose of this book is to discuss how we reached this point in our history and to offer some suggestions for a better, more bipartisan government. It contains our personal observations about the challenges Congress has faced in recent years and some of the institutional and political problems that have led to this current extreme deadlock.

We will start with our own stories – how we each became involved in politics and some of the things that made it both interesting and productive for the people we represented. We don't pretend to have all the answers, but we believe our perspectives are both accurate and helpful as we try to chart a path forward.

We will then chronicle the various developments that have occurred during our political lifetimes and led to the gridlock Congress faces today. These include chapters on the "new normal" in American politics that has led to divided government, the continuing role of race in American politics, the insidious role of highly partisan gerrymandering, evolution in campaign finance laws that started out as reforms but have further corrupted the system, the new media, and times when Congress was both fun and productive.

Each of us has witnessed huge changes in our party and our home state. Texas is a microcosm of what has happened to the two parties in the House. In Martin's office, there is a picture of the Texas Democratic congressional delegation that was taken in 1989, on the day Speaker Jim Wright resigned from Congress. The delegation on that day consisted of 19 Democrats and eight Republicans. Many of the Democrats were political moderates. In 2014 (25 years later), the Texas delegation had 24 Republicans and 12 Democrats. Of the people in that picture, only one – Ralph Hall – remained in Congress, though he had switched parties and become a Republican. In May 2014, at age 91, he lost the Republican nomination for an 18th term.

Texas has gained nine seats since 1990 as a result of population growth and reapportionment. Many of these growth areas have been in suburban Republican districts. Democrats have lost seats as rural and small-town whites moved en masse to the Republican Party because of race and social issues like abortion and gun control. New Deal seniors have died off and been replaced by Reagan seniors. Many of them have lost their connection with the Democratic Party. The remaining Democratic seats exist in parts of the state where blacks and Hispanics are packed together because of housing patterns and clever redistricting by Republican legislators. This is a recurring pattern in the South, where there are almost no white Democrats still holding congressional seats (except in Florida, which does not really qualify as a southern state). As a result, the Democratic Party in the House has moved farther to the left.

Virginia, too, has experienced huge political change in recent decades. In the early 1960s, the state and its elected officials remained firmly committed to the South's "massive resistance" to the federal government's civil rights initiatives. Its senior members of Congress – mostly Democrats – included arch-segregationists who held powerful positions on Capitol Hill. They included Senate Finance Committee Chairman Harry Byrd and House Rules Committee Chairman "Judge" Howard Smith. Change came in the 1980s, when both senators and most of the House delegation were Republicans. In recent years, several House seats in Virginia have competitively switched back and forth. In 2014, Republicans held 8-to-3 control in the delegation, but both senators were Democrats, as were the three elected statewide officials in Richmond. In presidential politics, Barack Obama won the state twice, becoming the first Democrat to win Virginia since 1964. His vote share in that state in both 2008 and 2012 matched his national vote performance. Virginia voters have rejected strongly conservative candidates who might have won a decade or two prior.

Two of the corners of the South, Texas and Virginia, have shown the growth of the Republican Party in that region. Much of the party's national leadership has been drawn from conservative southerners. As the religious and social right continue to play a major role in state and national politics, pushing Republicans farther to the right, little place has been left for moderate Republicans – who once played a significant role in Congress. So, too, the decline of moderate southern Democrats – who not long ago were a dominant force in Congress – has weakened the political center and the potential for coalition-building. We have experienced a major "sorting" of the two political parties such that the threat of a party primary challenge from an extreme member of one's own party leaves little incentive for either Democrats or Republicans to seek compromise in the legislative process.

There is a great irony in all this that extends far beyond who controls Congress: presidential politics are also being shaped by these trends. Bill

Clinton was elected president in 1992 by creating a majority based in the political center. Barack Obama, on the other hand, was elected in 2008 and reelected in 2012 by putting together a liberal coalition of blacks, Hispanics, gays, Jewish voters, upper-income whites, union members, young people, and suburban women turned off by Republicans' stance on women's health issues. This coalition worked because of changing demographics and the fact that Obama was able to increase traditional turnout levels among blacks and young people. It is possible that a future white Democratic presidential candidate would not be able to replicate Obama's success, particularly if the Republican Party ever connects with Hispanics and suburban women.

There clearly are other forces at work – money spent by outside groups, a more partisan media, the state of the economy – which continue to have a heavy influence on Congress's partisan shape and ability to function. All this and more will be explored in the chapters that follow.

We are both optimists who believe in our system of government and hope that there is a path forward to a better, more productive legislative body. We also both know some very competent, highly motivated members of Congress who hold hope for the future. Toward that end, we offer a few suggestions for the future in our last chapter.

In writing this book, we have been joined by Richard Cohen, a longtime congressional reporter, book author, and former co-author of *The Almanac of American Politics*. As a Massachusetts native, Rich suffered through decades of woeful performances by the beloved Boston Red Sox. Their success in winning three World Series championships in the past decade – twice against Martin's Cardinals, no less – has been a welcome change. Like the Sox, Congress too has had its shining moments along with its dismal performances. As Rich has learned, there's rarely a dull moment. Change has become inexorable – and more frequent than ever in recent years.

As students of politics who have had diverse congressional experiences, we have decided to combine our perspectives into this book on the changing forces in American politics. Our goal is to make this book understandable to the average reader and supply some depth and insights to students of politics as well. We hope readers will find this book interesting and helpful. In the meantime, we anxiously await the arrival of pitchers and catchers at baseball's next spring training.

2

QUALIFYING THE EXPERT WITNESSES

By Martin Frost, Tom Davis, and Rich Cohen

MARTIN'S STORY

Getting elected to Congress requires hard work and more than a little bit of luck. As the old song goes, "You can't have one without the other."

For me it all began in 1957, when I was 15 years old. I spent that summer with my maternal grandfather, Mose Marwil, in the small east Texas town of Henderson. My grandfather had served two terms as mayor of Henderson in the 1930s and was still very much the small-town politician. Virtually everyone we passed on the street would greet him by name, and he took me to his old political haunts, like the local domino parlor. I was transfixed.

During that summer I learned about my great uncle, Charlie Brachfield, who had been Rusk County judge from 1898 to 1902 and a state senator from 1903 to 1911. Uncle Charlie, who had died some years before my visit, had even run for the Democratic nomination for Texas attorney general in 1926. He had run a close third, barely missing the two-person runoff. My family insisted that he'd lost not because he was Jewish, but because he was a "dry" from a county where alcohol sales were banned and had been out-voted by the "wets" in south Texas. I have serious doubts about this since 1926 was the heyday of the Ku Klux Klan in Texas.

About this time I started winning statewide elections to various offices in my religious youth group, the Texas Federation of Temple Youth, so I clearly was hooked on politics. Following my graduation from high school, I was elected to a national office in this same movement. However, I also figured out that I could write and was co-editor of my high school newspaper in Ft. Worth. Ultimately I decided to pursue a career in journalism and hoped to cover politics in Washington someday.

Following graduation from the University of Missouri School of Journalism, I spent a year working for a newspaper in Wilmington, Delaware, covering county government, and then spent two years in Washington covering Congress for *Congressional Quarterly*. As I now often tell students, I met a lot of congressmen during that time, figured out they were not so smart, and decided I could do that job. Most journalists think that; but few, if any, act on it.

I did. I enrolled in Georgetown Law School with the intention of someday running for Congress.

That's where luck came in. My parents had been students at the University of Texas at the same time as Bob Strauss, who by 1969 was starting his climb up the ladder of national Democratic politics. My family had stayed in touch with Bob and his wife Helen and let them know I would be coming through Dallas looking for a job. I got off my flight at Dallas Love Field, walked straight to a pay phone, and called Bob. I remember his words to this day: "Martin, if you can get your ass down to my office in 30 minutes, I'll be happy to see you."

I did. Bob, who later would become chairman of the Democratic National Committee, told me he would talk to his former law partner, Irving Goldberg, who had been appointed to the U.S. Fifth Circuit Court of Appeals by President Lyndon Johnson, and ask Judge Goldberg to put in a good word for me with the local Democratic federal district judge, Sarah T. Hughes. Judge Hughes hadn't hired her law clerk for the following year and I was qualified – I was law review at a good school. I ultimately got the job with Judge Hughes.

If Bob Strauss hadn't helped me, I might never have gotten the position and might have wound up taking a job in Houston or Los Angeles, where I was being considered by major local law firms. I honestly believe Dallas is the only city where I could have won a congressional seat, especially within eight years of arriving, as I did.

And then there was some additional good luck. Even though I didn't realize it at the time, the year I clerked for Judge Hughes (1970-71) was about the exact time when Texas was in the process of converting from a one-party Democratic state to a two-party state. As a result, many of the old-line conservative Democrats who controlled the Texas Democratic Party started moving over to the Republican side, and there were opportunities for someone younger that would have not been there ten or even five years earlier. Judge Hughes was a good friend of a local newspaper reporter, Jim Lehrer, who was also a Missouri J-School grad. Jim had recently started a public affairs program on the local public television station, KERA, that had a wide audience of opinion-makers in town. Several years later he would move to Washington to co-anchor the widely-acclaimed "McNeil-Lehrer Report" on PBS. Jim hired me to be on his show, and I suddenly became a known commodity to many of the political activists in Dallas.

My luck didn't end there. Texas had gained one additional congressional seat as a result of the 1970 census: the new 24th district in the Dallas-Ft. Worth area. It was drawn by the Democratic-controlled Texas legislature to elect a Democrat and was won in 1972 by Dale Milford, the well-known weather forecaster on the number-one-rated local commercial television station. Milford was more conservative than the new district, which contained a significant black population; but after he won his initial race, no one would run against him because of his great TV name recognition. I volunteered to run and got him one-on-one in the 1974 Democratic primary. I didn't win but was the beneficiary of all the anti-Milford vote and received 42%, a respectable showing for my first-ever race.

I considered running again, but then presidential politics intervened. I was impressed with the then-little-known ex-governor of Georgia, Jimmy Carter, and signed on to his campaign early in 1976, ultimately becoming his north Texas coordinator. It was a hard-fought race and Carter became the last Democratic president to carry Texas.

My involvement in the Carter campaign basically changed my life. I'd had some lingering doubts about my ability to win an election after my 1974 loss, but strategic decisions I made during the Carter campaign that fall confirmed in my mind that I could play this game.

There are two key examples. First, the campaign had decided to bring Carter to Dallas in mid-September and my mentor Bob Strauss, by then chairman of the Democratic National Committee, wanted him to speak to a group of white ministers. I felt that there was already enough religion in this campaign and overruled Strauss by scheduling Carter to speak before a group of young professionals. In between the time when that decision was made and Carter's actual appearance in Dallas, *Playboy* published an interview with Carter in which he said he "had lusted in [his] heart." Had he spoken before the ministerial group, that quote would have dominated the news and we would have had a disaster on our hands; but it never came up in his talk to the young professionals.

The second example occurred when polls in Texas were very close and the Carter campaign decided to come to the Dallas-Ft. Worth area two days before the election. The national campaign staff wanted a Dallas-only stop. I was a 34-year-old local operative who told the national staff members they were wrong. They couldn't just bring Carter into the then-Republican city of Dallas and ignore the neighboring Democratic city of Ft. Worth, represented in Congress by Jim Wright. After some back and forth, they decided I was right. We did a 2,000-person Sunday morning breakfast in Dallas followed by a noon 10,000-person rally in Ft. Worth at the downtown convention center. Jim Wright arranged for local supporters to donate 10,000 fried chicken boxed lunches for the event and bused hundreds of people in following services in black churches. The rally made for great television. I had grown up in Ft. Worth and understood the bitter civic rivalry between Dallas and Ft. Worth better than some people in the Atlanta campaign headquarters.

I briefly considered taking a mid-level appointment in Washington in the new administration but decided I really wanted to be a congressman, so I took Milford on again in 1978 (again one-on-one) against the advice of Bob Strauss, who thought I couldn't win. This time I won 55% and was on my way to Washington.

Had I not wound up in Dallas and not had the chance to run against a congressman who was relatively junior and out of sync philosophically with his district, I certainly would not have gotten to Congress so quickly and maybe wouldn't have gotten there at all. Don't get me wrong, there was a lot of hard work involved in my two campaigns; but luck played a role too.

When I arrived in Washington to begin my first term, good fortune smiled again. By that time, the local congressman from my hometown Ft. Worth, Jim Wright, had become House Majority Leader. Wright went to Speaker Tip O'Neill and asked that I be appointed to the powerful House Rules Committee to replace a Texas congressman from another part of the state who had been defeated in 1978. O'Neill replied that he didn't put freshmen on this committee because he didn't know if they could be trusted to withstand pressure and vote with the leadership on important issues. Wright pressed the matter and O'Neill asked the Rules chair, Dick Bolling of Kansas City, Missouri, to check me out. It turned out that Bolling's late wife had been from the Dallas area and her best friend in the world was U.S. District Judge Sarah T. Hughes. Bolling called Judge Hughes, who gave me a glowing recommendation; and, as they say, the rest is history.

Getting on the Rules Committee my first term was important because it immediately made me a player in the House. Other congressmen routinely came to the Rules Committee seeking permission to offer amendments to pending legislation on the floor, and this was an opportunity for me to help my colleagues early in my career. It also helped me gain backing for matters important to my own district from committee chairs who needed favorable Rules Committee treatment for their bills. Chairman Bolling told me my main assignment during my first term was always to be in my chair when the committee met since the Rules Committee required a live quorum to act (proxies were permitted in other committees, but not Rules). I took his advice and was always there when the gavel fell. In return, Chairman Bolling helped me with some matters key to my district.

I then spent the next 16 years biding my time, taking assignments that other members didn't want or didn't think were important. These included helping draft the Democratic Caucus issues book, which became the foundation for the new centrist Democratic Leadership Council (DLC)$_2$; chairing the Democratic Caucus Rules Committee, which, among other things, changed the rules to make the whip position elected rather than appointed so that current leadership could not select the next person to be on the first rung of the ladder to be Speaker; chairing the Democratic Party's redistricting committee, IMPAC 2000; and chairing a special House Task Force to help the parliaments of Eastern and Central Europe after the Berlin Wall fell.

And then we lost the House in the sweep of 1994. During the 1988 presidential campaign, I had taken responsibility for Wapello County for my friend Dick Gephardt during the Iowa Caucuses. Dick won the Iowa caucuses and rolled up a big vote in Wapello County. Dick was now House Democratic leader and remembered my organizational abilities. He asked me to be chair of the Democratic Congressional Campaign Committee, a post only a handful of people wanted at that time. One of the first congratulatory calls I got was from my old mentor Bob Strauss. "Martin, I know why you took the DCCC job," he said. "Why is that, Mr. Strauss?" I asked. His reply was typical Strauss: "Democrats have just lost the House for the first time in 40 years and expectations are low. If you don't accomplish anything, no one will be disappointed. If you do well, you will be a hero."

I almost made hero status. We gained nine seats in the 1996 election and five seats in the 1998 election for a total of 14 seats. This kept us close enough to the Republicans that we could take the House back in a good year. That good year happened in 2006. Our five-seat pickup in 1998 was the only time in the 20th century that the party of the president had gained seats in the sixth year of a president's eight-year term. And it led directly to the resignation of Speaker Newt Gingrich, who took the fall for his party's losing seats in a year when it should have won.

Chairing the DCCC taught me quite a bit about congressional election politics.

I remember getting a call one day from then-Vice President Gore about efforts by the DCCC to win back the 1st district in California. Vice President Gore had a candidate – the granddaughter of one of his longtime supporters, Mayor Joe Alioto of San Francisco. The 1st district covered an area north of San Francisco that was agricultural and conservative. Gore's candidate was a liberal who was to the left of the district. It was my job to tell the vice president that she couldn't win and that we needed a more moderate candidate. We found one – State Senator Mike Thompson, who was a Vietnam War veteran. Mike won the election and, as of 2014, is still serving.

And then there was the case of an open seat in Madison, Wisconsin. Three candidates wanted to run – two men (a county commissioner and a state representative) and one woman (a state representative). The woman was openly gay, and local politicians were concerned that she couldn't win. I invited all three candidates to Washington and arranged for them to be grilled by a room full of Washington political pros. After an hour of intense questioning, I walked out of the room and told my chief of staff, Matt Angle, that the woman was clearly the superior candidate. That candidate, Tammy Baldwin, won the congressional seat and ultimately became a senator.

Also, for years we had been trying to win a congressional seat in Mississippi that was 35% black. No state in the country was more racially polarized than Mississippi. Each year, a black candidate would win the Democratic Primary and lose the general election. I approached Bennie Thompson, the state's only black congressman, and asked if he could help find a white candidate who would be acceptable to members of the black community so that they would stand down and not field a black contender that year. Bennie, at some significant political risk to himself, did exactly that; and Ronnie Shows won the Democratic Primary and the general election.

My favorite story from my years chairing the DCCC involved an incident in the fall of 1995. Speaker Newt Gingrich and I had both been part of the U.S. delegation to the funeral of Israeli Prime Minister Yitzhak Rabin. Shortly after we got back, Gingrich was threatening to close down the government in a budget dispute with President Bill Clinton. Gingrich said at a press breakfast that he was going to teach Clinton a lesson since he had been treated so poorly on that trip. He complained about having had to exit through the back of the plane and not having gotten enough time with the president.

It just so happened that the House Appropriations Committee chair, Bob Livingston of Louisiana, appeared before the Rules Committee that day in support of a continuing appropriations bill to keep the government open. My Rules Committee assistant handed me an AP story about Gingrich's comments about the Rabin funeral. I then posed a question to Livingston in the hearing, which was being carried live on cable TV. I said something to this effect: "Bob, I have this AP story about how Gingrich is threatening to close down the government because of his mistreatment by Clinton on the trip to the Rabin funeral. I was on that trip and know that Gingrich was actually treated very well. He was the only politician who was permitted to take his wife along. Bob, don't you think the Speaker is acting like a crybaby?"

The next day the *New York Daily News* ran a full-page, page-one cartoon of Newt in a diaper with a baby bottle and the headline of "Cry Baby: Newt's Tantrum." That was the beginning of the end for Newt's Speakership.

I left Congress at the end of 2004 – thanks to Tom DeLay's highly partisan gerrymandering of the Texas delegation – but politics was not completely out of my blood. I took over the presidency of America Votes, a central coordination hub of the progressive community, for the 2008 presidential campaign and coordinated Democratic turnout efforts of a collection of outside groups including organized labor, the civil rights community, the environmental movement, and the pro-choice community. We helped Barack Obama carry a number of Midwestern battleground states and some key states in the Rocky Mountain West, where the Hispanic vote was key.

Chairing a party's political committee and working in presidential politics are not for the faint at heart. But the results speak for themselves and the experience gave me great insight into how we should move forward in trying to make politics work again in this country.

Tom's Story

I agree with Martin that getting elected to Congress is combination of a lot of hard work and a little luck. As the old saying goes, "the harder you work, the luckier you get." I was lucky in the sense that what many consider the "hard work" of campaigning for office, I found fun! My paternal grandfather, who was my role model, often noted that if you find a profession you love, you'll never have to work a day in your life. He had been elected attorney general of Nebraska in 1918, when he was 25 years old and fresh out of Harvard Law School. He'd come to Washington in 1953 to serve in the Eisenhower administration and my parents had followed.

My first exposure to politics was as a seven-year-old boy in 1956, when I wore an "I Like Ike" campaign button to school. I was the only one in my second grade class with the button, and as I procured more, my classmates wanted to wear them as well. Although I can't take credit for President Eisenhower's victory in Virginia or even in Arlington County that year, I believe I helped the ticket in the Cherrydale precinct! More importantly, at the ripe old age of seven, I caught the political bug.

In 1958, as the Democrats swept to a midterm victory, I woke up the morning after the election to see how the Republicans had performed in California, as my mother had made me go to bed too early to witness the results on election night. I remember being encouraged when Rockefeller won the governorship in New York and Ken Keating the Senate seat. In retrospect, that was about all the Republicans won, but I remember vividly following the races.

This love affair with politics began a grand journey that took me to the Capitol Page School, where I served my four years in high school as a Senate page, and then on to Amherst College, where I majored in Political Science, writing my senior honors thesis in 1971 on "Political Realignment in the Outer South," using my home state of Virginia as a model.

During my Amherst years I developed a lifelong friendship with David Eisenhower, Ike's grandson and son-in-law of President Nixon, which led to summer jobs and, later, employment with Harry Dent in the White House. Dent had been Senator Strom Thurmond's chief of staff, headed the political office in the White House, and been dubbed "the chief southern strategist." The work there meshed well with my senior thesis, and my political love affair was in full bloom.

After some active duty in the Army, I enrolled in the University of Virginia Law School, where, in the fall of 1972, I simultaneously attended classes and covered five states for the Nixon presidential campaign. I confess that law school was my secondary concern as I became active in Republican politics in both Fairfax County, where my mother had moved and which was now considered home, and the UVA campus (referred to as "the Grounds" by the university community), where I was elected president of the Law School Young Republicans and first vice chairman of the State Young Republicans.

I also became active with the Fairfax County Republican Committee, commuting from Charlottesville to Fairfax for party meetings and campaign events. Upon graduating from law school, I turned down offers from New York law firms to return to Fairfax and practice law and, more importantly, to prepare to run for public office.

I came within a whisker of filing for the State Senate in 1975, the year I graduated from law school. Fortunately, a couple of the more experienced party hands took me aside and advised me that that year did not look very good for Republicans and that the incumbent in the state senate district, Abe Brault, was the Senate majority leader and would be impossible to take down. They suggested I wait a few years, get active in my local community beyond party activity, and get to know some of the financial gurus I would eventually need to help finance a campaign.

On their recommendation, I waited four years. I joined a startup Rotary Club, bought a home, was elected president of my neighborhood civic association, and became active in the community I wanted to represent. I basically grew my Christmas card list to several hundred families and stayed active in GOP circles.

By 1979, I was ready to go! Again, luck played a role, as the chairman of the Fairfax County Board of Supervisors suggested that I run for supervisor of my magisterial district. The district was half the size of a State Senate district (about 100,000 people), the salary was double, and the supervisor was allocated four staff members (as opposed to one), with a nice office located a mile from my house. The County Board of Supervisors met once a week and was higher profile than the state legislature. To me, it made sense. It was a chewable bite and included nearly everyone on my Christmas card list.

Gaining the Republican nomination for Mason district supervisor was not a problem, as the district was heavily Democratic and the party usually had a hard time finding a candidate for this district. My activities within the party made me a consensus candidate.

The incumbent was a young two-term supervisor named Alan Magazine. He had been reelected with 61% of the vote four years before and was considered a shoo-in. I announced in January 1979 my candidacy for the November election (Virginia state and local elections are in odd-numbered years) and received good press coverage in the local papers. I procured the voter lists from the State Board of Elections and had them indexed by street (for door-to-door campaigning) and alphabetically (for looking up phone numbers and for phone banks). A local Republican activist, Dorothy Norpel, volunteered as a full-time campaign manager, and one of my fellow Rotarians donated the space for a campaign office.

With my first few campaign dollars, I had a few thousand campaign brochures printed and proceeded to go out every afternoon from five to eight and ring the doorbells of registered voters. I also did this on Saturdays from ten to seven, with a break for a Big Mac at lunch. At each door I would notate something about the people I met – where they were from, where they went to school, where they worked, their children's schools, their dog's name, ... anything that would give me a chance to find a connection.

A huge snowstorm hit in January, and people couldn't get out of their driveways for three days. Other candidates were snowed in, but I walked street after street and met voter after voter. Everyone was at home and after a couple of days hanging around the house, the husbands and wives were stir-crazy. They were delighted to have someone new to talk to! They would invite me in to spend a few minutes and it gave me a wonderful chance to connect. Two weeks later they would receive personal letters from me, thanking them for their time and noting our "connections." One voter's children had gone to school with my brother. Another voter was also a UVA Law School alumnus. Another voter was from Nebraska, my family's home state, and we bonded over that.

My favorite story takes place soon after that election. I was inside a local 7-Eleven when a woman approached me and said, "Mr. Davis, Football died." I wasn't sure what the heck she was talking about until she went on to say, "Our little dog, Football, died right before the election. We received a personal note from you, after you rang our door, saying 'Give Football a pat for me.' We usually vote for the Democratic candidates, but anyone who cares about our dog must be a good person. So, we voted for you!"

At another house I thought everything was going well. The woman said, "Mr. Davis, we go to church with your in-laws and our daughter is at Jeb Stuart High School with your sister-in-law Kate. And we know your mother from her work with the blind." I told her I appreciated her support, but was immediately corrected when she said, "But we are Democrats and always vote Democratic." I replied, "I'm just running for supervisor, and there is no

Republican or Democratic way to pick up the trash." She noted that her father and grandfather were Democrats and they felt compelled to vote for the Democratic candidate. I responded that if her father was a thief and her grandfather a thief, that wouldn't necessarily make her a thief. She replied, "No it wouldn't. It would make me a Republican!"

In late January I caught a break when Alan Magazine decided he was not going to run for reelection. (More luck!) The Democrats had a nominating fight between Betsy Hinkle, who ran a Board-centered newsletter, and Nancy Shands, a Democratic activist and Planning Committee member from the Lake Barcroft neighborhood. They had a contentious primary and Hinkle, supported by Alan Magazine, won the primary. I appropriated a copy of Nancy Shands's support list and went door-to-door enlisting their support with some success.

As I rang doors, I picked up volunteers; and in July I held a fundraiser that attracted 150 local people. Thirty attendees was the norm, but my campaigning was paying off and I was raising money from my Rotary Club colleagues as well.

The Democrats, meanwhile, put their usual organization – "The Mason Mafia," we called it – into play. Tenant groups, labor organizations, and civic activists kicked into gear and money poured in from developers and business groups that were strategically giving to the perceived winner – the Democrat. Fortunately, I cobbled together enough money to stay competitive, and with the political establishment and newspaper endorsements going against me, I made up in hustle what I lacked in every other aspect.

The weekend before the election, I was working the crowd at a local high school football game when a Democratic leader whispered to me that she thought the race was "too close to call." I was elated! Our informal phone banks showed me substantially ahead, but history was against us.

On election night, the first precinct to come in showed I had won 70% of the vote. The Tripps precinct was swing; but my mother lived there, had followed up at the houses I had previously visited, and had worked the precinct polling place all day. But other precincts followed and at the end of the night, I was heading to the County Board of Supervisors with 63% of the vote!

The key to our victory was turnout. The Mason district was heavily Democratic with substantial minority and tenant populations. In off years, the usual turnout was 33%, with Democrats getting out their known voters and Republicans reading about the election the next day, having failed to vote. But with my going door to door twice; following up with those I met with personal letters; and utilizing volunteers, direct mail, and phone banks to reconnect repeatedly, the turnout swelled to 46% – the highest of the nine magisterial districts in the county.

I had contacted all the Republicans I could find and turned them out to vote. While they were there, they voted straight-ticket, bringing in a GOP sweep in the Mason district. In the past cycle we'd been swept; this time we won nearly everything, with me leading the ticket by a wide margin.

As an historical fact, I do remember hitting the door of a military officer who told me he voted only in presidential elections. He was not one of the 46% who showed up on Election Day. His name was Oliver North, and our paths would cross again later.

Once elected to the County Board of Supervisors, I worked my base hard by attending every civic association meeting, baseball opening day, school event, and block party I could find and was subsequently reelected with 78% and 84% of the vote. It was often said – not so inaccurately – that "Tom Davis would go to the opening of an envelope."

In 1991, the Democrats controlled the board seven to two, including the chairmanship, which was elected at large and a position equivalent to that of a city mayor. The Democratic chairman of the board was Audrey Moore. She had been elected in 1987 with 59% of the vote, beating the Republican incumbent by running on a no-growth platform. Voters had been fed up with the growing traffic and ousted three incumbent Republicans. I had survived easily and felt I had earned the right to the nomination to oppose her. However, the former board chair wanted a rematch and he was closely aligned with the party leaders outside my district. The party devised a convention for the nomination process, which was designed to attract the more conservative element in the party. This was neither my natural base nor a good platform on which to win the general election in an urban county of 900,000 people.

I hired a professional team to help me, worked 24/7 for months, and ended up outfiling my opponent for convention delegates five to one. He graciously dropped out and I became the Republican nominee, ready to run against Audrey Moore.

Our first poll, in June, had me behind only 42% to 38%, and Moore's unpopularity was rising due to budget pressures brought on by a recession. The county was way too large for a door-to-door campaign, so we had to win strategically. Focusing on a pro-business message, we put together a coalition of groups upset with the status quo. I was moderate enough to be acceptable to a broad group of dissonant Democrats, public employees who couldn't get a raise, business groups that were hurt by Moore's no-growth strategies, and Republicans who wanted control of county government. My base in the Mason district helped me sell to a growing minority population as well, including the president of the NAACP. Even the *Washington Post* endorsed me, citing the need to attract businesses.

On election night I won with 66% of the vote, carrying 119 of 120 precincts. On my coattails were four new board members, giving the county a GOP majority for only the second time in history (and probably the last).

The county was broke. Our commercial tax base had fallen by 30% in one year, and our AAA bond rating was in jeopardy. Fortunately, I was able to work with both the Republican and Democratic members to put things back together, and I did it immediately. I gave committee chairmanships to both Democrats and Republicans. I met with all the members to understand their priorities and we all worked together, shoulder to shoulder. Not every vote was unanimous, but ultimately we created a budget surplus, maintained our AAA bond rating, and were, for the first time, labeled Best Financially Managed County in America by *City and State* (now *Governing*) magazine.

Having accomplished what I'd set out to do, I set my sights on Congress. A new Virginia congressional seat had been created in 1992 as a result of the post-census reapportionment, and a Democrat, Leslie Byrne, had won it in a close race. She had been a state delegate from the Mason district prior to her election; so we shared the same base, the same neighbors, and the same set of friends.

Once again the local Republican Party apparatus chose a convention system for the nomination and chose to hold the convention in Woodbridge, in Prince William County, which accounted for about 25% of the congressional district's population. However, I prevailed by a wide margin and turned my sights on running against Leslie Byrne.

Leslie was a tough competitor and fully backed by the unions. I got my first taste of how different a national race would be from my local races when the Professional Firefighters, a group that had remained close through our county budget battles, endorsed Leslie. Several of my Mason district contributors informed me that they thought I was a great Board of Supervisors chairman, but that this was a national race and more about Newt Gingrich – who would be one step closer to becoming Speaker of the House of Representatives if I won – than about my abilities.

The final shoe to drop was when the Republican Party of Virginia convention nominated Oliver North, now a national figure, to head the ticket as the Republican candidate for the Senate. He would be my running mate and although he was a hero in the exurbs and rural areas, he was radioactive in the 11th congressional district.

North had long since moved from the Mason district to rural Clark County. Fortunately, my campaign team discovered early on that although he was wildly popular with the Republican Party committee members and other conservatives, he was a polarizing figure for many other voters. In fact, John Warner, Virginia's senior senator, made a public pronouncement that he could not support North, instead opting for Independent candidate and former Republican attorney general Marshall Coleman. I opted not to follow his lead, but I also needed to ensure voters would not mistake us for twins, so I repeatedly stated, "I support the Republican ticket."

I took great care to run a separate campaign. When Oliver North came to Fairfax, you couldn't find me with a search warrant. Meanwhile, the Byrne message was twofold: Tom Davis has been a bad chairman, and he is Oliver North's twin. My general retort at our debates (and there were over 30 of them) was, "If I am such a bad chairman, you can get rid of me by sending me to Washington! But, if you feel I've been a good chairman, don't I deserve a promotion?"

Although the bulk of Byrne's money was spent on television ads morphing me into Oliver North, I got a break the Monday before the election when the *Washington Post* gave me a 12-paragraph endorsement with the headline, "He's No Oliver North." The final tally in the 11th congressional district at the end of Election Day was Davis 54% and North 34%. I received the ticket split I needed to win, but the most gratifying election night victory was my 57% win in the Mason district. Although I had lost some ground there, it was still home base.

As a freshman congressman, I was appointed to a high-profile subcommittee chairmanship, that of the District of Columbia Subcommittee. This was ordinarily a nondescript assignment, but the city's bond rating went to junk status and its deficit boomeranged right after I was named chairman. Something had to happen and as I was chair it fell to me, a newly-sworn-in member, to draft legislation that could pass, be signed by the president, and work for the city. Fortunately, my partners were Alice Rivlin (President Clinton's Office of Management and Budget Director) and Eleanor Holmes Norton (D.C.'s non-voting delegate to Congress). They stepped up to the plate, and with the backing of Speaker Newt Gingrich, the Control Board Bill passed both chambers and was signed into law ten days after it was introduced.

Long-term, the bill was a success; but short-term, passing a tough bill with a minimum of political friction brought me near rock-star status with the local media and made me bulletproof in my congressional district. It was difficult for a white Republican from a suburban county sponsoring legislation that stripped power from the black Democratic mayor! With all of that positive press coverage and a lot of hard work, I was able to win reelection with 66% of the vote in 1996, while Bill Clinton carried my district.

The year 1998 brought a new opportunity. The GOP lost seats in the House and it was only the second time in modern history that the party of the president picked up House seats in a midterm election. Martin Frost, who was the Democratic Campaign Committee chairman at the time, made lemonade out of the lemon he'd inherited when Monica Lewinsky came forward with the infamous stain containing Bill Clinton's DNA on her blue dress. Republicans overplayed their hand and nearly lost the House.

This outcome set off a firestorm in the House Republican Conference. Members had been led to believe that the GOP would add up to 20 additional seats to its majority. They had given millions of dollars from their personal campaign accounts to the National Republican Campaign Committee to help the cause. They felt angry and betrayed.

Gingrich was in trouble with the conference, so he decided to make the NRCC chairmanship an elected leadership position. It had previously been the Speaker's appointment. John Linder, the NRCC chair, was being thrown to the wolves to save the Speaker. In hindsight, it was not fair to Linder, who represented a district adjacent to the Speaker's district in Georgia. It was not Linder, but the Speaker, who had called the errant strategic shots that had lost the GOP five seats. Linder had simply raised the money (and lots of it!). He decided to try to keep his post.

However, this was politics, and it was clear to me that Linder was on thin ice with the other Republican members. I spent three solid days calling around; and after I had a critical mass of support and the tacit support of Tom DeLay, the GOP whip, I jumped into the race for NRCC chair. I utilized DeLay's whip team after it was clear no one else would enter the race.

It was a perfect match – DeLay, the conservative firebrand, and Davis, the moderate, against an opponent who had not delivered. The secret ballot vote was 130-77. I'm not sure why Linder took the vote to a full ballot, but possibly he thought he might win. He had the open support of the National Rifle Association, the National Right to Life, and other conservative groups. And I suspect that members he called wouldn't tell him they weren't with him. After all, in a secret ballot, who knows who voted for whom?

I learned one lesson from this caucus fight: if a member says "Yes, I am with you," it means they maybe are. "Maybe" means they are not. The only members you can truly trust are the ones who will publicly endorse you or who look you in the eye and tell you they are against you.

In this rebellious caucus, Gingrich withdrew when it was clear he couldn't win another term as Speaker and was replaced by Bob Livingston. The conference chair, John Boehner, was unexpectedly defeated for reelection by J.C. Watts. In another shock, two weeks before the start of the new Congress, Bob Livingston resigned his newly-obtained Speakership and Denny Hastert, DeLay's chief deputy whip and a popular member, was elected Speaker. Hastert was well-respected and the caucus was looking for some healing. He was the right pick for the time.

Still, we were heading into the 2000 presidential election with what was to be a five-seat margin. The Republican brand was in the trash can after the Clinton impeachment vote and I had 26 open seats to defend in tough districts versus nine open Democratic seats. Nearly every political pundit in D.C. predicted the Democrats would win back the House. The Democrats in early 2001 picked up the majority in the Senate when Republican senator Jim Jeffords of Vermont switched to Independent. And the Democrats won the plurality vote for president.

It was a five-to-four Supreme Court decision that gave Florida and the country to Bush, even as Gore polled 537,179 more votes nationally. The Supreme Court called the election for Bush by 537 votes, an 0.01% margin out of nearly six million votes cast in Florida. But when the final tallies came in, we had kept the House majority with no net loss.

The story of how we prevailed is a book unto itself, but it revolves around spotting vulnerable districts the Democrats didn't recognize, recruiting the best candidates possible, and running great campaigns against headwinds in some states.

Due to the 2000 House victory, I was unanimously reelected chairman of the NRCC for the 2002 cycle, at which time we picked up seven seats while still holding the White House; and for only the third time in American history, the party of the president picked up House seats in a midterm election.

The 2002 cycle was unique from others in a few ways. First, the GOP controlled more seats at the once-a-decade redistricting than at any time since 1920. This allowed us to actually pick up seats at the gerrymander table and, more importantly, to strengthen our weaker incumbents by adding Republicans to their districts. Secondly, because of 9/11, the president's popularity did not suffer the midterm blues that most presidents have experienced after their honeymoon period. And finally, control of Congress was split. Because Jim Jeffords of Vermont had left the GOP, the Senate was ostensibly "controlled" by the Democrats. This gave way to a Republican narrative that whatever the problems in the country, it was not "our" fault, but the Senate's fault, for holding up the agenda. This gave pause to a "balance the government" narrative that House Democrats were peddling. The government was already balanced by a 51-49 Senate. (As an Independent, Jeffords had decided to caucus with the Democrats.)

So Republican control of redistricting, the incumbent president's relative popularity, and a divided Congress gave us the opportunity to pick up seats as the president's party for only the third time in history. We understood that opportunity and executed a campaign strategy that controlled the redistricting process, limiting our downside and creating new GOP districts where possible; utilizing the president where he was popular; and attacking the Democratic Senate for inaction.

I went on from there to chair the House Committee on Government Reform and Oversight and to win reelection to Congress three more times. But running the Campaign Committee was by far the best job I ever had, and it put me front and center in the political history books.

RICH'S STORY

My interest in writing about government and politics started early in my high school years. In my hometown of Northampton, Massachusetts, I had an admittedly peculiar interest in attending the meetings of the local city council. The issues were mostly the routine topics of budgets and property rights. A major controversy was the mayor's decision to remove the United Nations flag that had flown over City Hall in some sort of Cold War protest. But the national headlines that resulted were an embarrassment to many townsfolk – not least because of civic pride over the home-state roots of the president at the time, John F. Kennedy.

When I went to Brown University in Providence, Rhode Island, I quickly immersed myself in writing and editing for the *Brown Daily Herald*. The newspaper work became an apprenticeship of sorts. I reported regularly on news, both on campus and beyond – which soon began to focus on protests of the Vietnam War. And I learned the routine of assembling the daily paper, including a weekly assignment as "night editor" that required me to spend several hours at a downtown print shop where we put the paper to bed – usually between 2 and 5 AM. Those experiences, and my pattern of pushing deadlines, launched my lifelong behavior as a night owl.

I combined my campus newspaper activities with the university's encouragement of "independent studies" to pursue various national news stories –

especially with the tumultuous and often tragic events of 1968. In March, a small group of *Herald* reporters drove to New Hampshire to cover the Democratic presidential primary, which Eugene McCarthy famously "won" with 42% of the vote that placed him second to President Lyndon Johnson. Two days later, we published a 16-page glossy edition with feature stories and analysis. Two weeks after that, LBJ announced that he would not seek reelection. That spring, I wrote an academic paper that described journalistic coverage of the search for the assassin of Martin Luther King, Jr. My premise was that the one-sided coverage illustrated the tensions between "free press vs. fair trial." The *Columbia Journalism Review* published lengthy excerpts. On another academic project that allowed me to reduce my classroom time, I spent a week in early October with the Independent presidential campaign of Alabama governor George Wallace. I flew on Wallace's plane as he made multiple stops each day and spent time interviewing the candidate as well as many political reporters who followed his tumultuous campaign. That experience furthered my desire to become a national political reporter.

My next step was Georgetown Law School, which I entered while Martin was in his final year. I had little interest in the core law classes, though I enjoyed the school's many courses that were related to legislation and public policy. My chief outside interest during my three years of law school was serving as a staffer to my home-state senator, Edward Brooke. I got the job chiefly because one of Brooke's top aides was a longtime friend of my father in Northampton. Observing the activities of a congressional office and, occasionally, the Senate floor was more useful to my career interests than was law school. I got my law degree, but I had no interest in practicing law.

After Brooke was reelected, I applied for journalism jobs in Washington. My limited experience as a professional journalist might have been a handicap. Fortunately, the editors of *National Journal* – a weekly magazine that was three years old – decided to take a chance on my background in the law and as a junior legislative aide. I served as a reporter there for more than 37 years, mostly covering Congress. That included a wide range of stories, ranging from the impeachment of Richard Nixon (memorably, I was in the House Judiciary Committee room during the bipartisan votes to impeach him) to the enactment of Obamacare. What I enjoyed most about the job were the opportunities to spend time with the usually helpful members of Congress – including my eventual co-authors of this book – and explain to our magazine readers the legislative and political dynamics of Capitol Hill. I worked hard and contributed more than my share of the workload. It was a great job! Among other topics, I interviewed and wrote about many prominent lawmakers, including seven House Speakers and seven Senate majority leaders. I especially enjoyed identifying junior members – from Democrats Dick Gephardt and Nancy Pelosi to Republicans Newt Gingrich and John Boehner – who were "rising stars" before they became prominent public figures.

While staying busy with my day job, I spent a growing amount of my time writing books for a variety of audiences. I authored a textbook for political science students on how the Democratic-controlled Congress worked with the senior President Bush to enact the 1990 Clean Air Act. The title was *Washington at Work: Back Rooms and Clean Air.* I wasn't then, nor am I now, an environmental expert. But the book remains relevant to current debates – for example, those on steps to deal with climate change. A few years later, I wrote a trade-book biography of Rep. Dan Rostenkowski of Illinois, who chaired the House Ways and Means Committee for 13 years, but ended his career with an indictment – and eventual conviction – for a series of crimes dealing with his office and personal finances. A memorable experience for that book was interviewing him for eight hours in the cafeteria of the federal penitentiary at Oxford, Wisconsin.

In addition, for ten years I was co-author of the biennial *Almanac of American Politics,* which has been widely regarded as the "bible" of Congress and national politics. For those editions, I wrote the profiles of most House members. Writing the *Almanac* and the other books while continuing with my magazine work was often a grueling pace. But I discovered that time usually expands in response to the demands and that the various writing assignments often became synergistic.

I left *National Journal* in 2010 – as did most of the editorial staff at the time – following some management changes. Subsequently, I spent a year each with *Politico* and *Congressional Quarterly,* where I continued to cover Congress. The pace of those publications, and of journalism generally, became faster. Often, I was writing one or two stories daily. I could maintain that pace and write shorter stories, though I prefer "long-form" writing.

Spending four decades as a Washington-based reporter – most of it with the same publication – has become an unusual accomplishment in the demanding news business, where the coverage now devotes less attention to analysis and places more of a premium on "breaking news." My reporting and writing about Congress became, in many ways, an extended seminar on vital parts of our national politics. I remain fascinated by the countless facets of Congress and its members – not unlike the city council in Northampton. Whether they are good, bad, or indifferent, they "represent" and reflect the nation that they serve. I am grateful for the insights that I gained from the numerous lawmakers and their aides with whom I had regular contact – plus outsiders from various interest groups and academic experts. Along with occasional travel to states and congressional districts across the nation, where I learned from the grassroots, I gained a continuing education about our nation and public attitudes. Even the many moments of relative inaction, or failure, by Congress offered opportunities to explore the political interactions.

The demands on a writer can be stressful and they ultimately require a team to complete a finished product. I am grateful to my journalistic colleagues – other reporters, editors, photographers, production staff – who encouraged my career interests and helped me to craft and communicate my stories for our readers.

Aside from my writing, I kept busy for many years as an elected member – including several years as chairman – of the Executive Committee of the congressional Periodical Press Gallery, which is one of four congressional press galleries. This assignment gave me additional insight into the operations of both the Capitol and Washington's press corps. Although our committee operated independently of congressional authorities, we had the responsibility to enforce rules that were written decades ago by the House and Senate. Given the great changes in journalism in recent years, it's often been challenging to determine who should be credentialed as legitimate reporters and who should be excluded as special-interest advocates or others who fail to meet journalistic standards. That activity increased my appreciation for the challenges that members of Congress and other elected officials face as they make decisions and seek consensus.

Given the growing dysfunction on Capitol Hill and elsewhere in American politics, as this book will describe, it's not surprising that journalism has less appeal than was the case during the Watergate scandal, when I started work. But I firmly believe that the responsibility is greater than ever for impartial observers to communicate how our political system functions. I have especially enjoyed the opportunity to serve as a co-author of this book with two knowledgeable former members of Congress who also are skillful writers and communicators – and happen to be from separate parties. It's an unusual combination. We hope that the results will be instructive.

3

THE NEW NORMAL: DIVIDED GOVERNMENT

By Tom Davis

Two "new normals" in electoral behavior have emerged over the past 20 years. The first is the tendency of the electorate to divide government between the parties. The second is the evolution of the American voters' thought from "all politics is local" to "all politics is national," with less ticket-splitting and more straight-party behavior on the part of the electorate. Although these two tendencies may seem incongruent to the casual observer (straight-ticket voting equals divided government), they are indeed highly compatible and engrained in recent trends.

Consider that over a period from 1980 to 2014, a total of 34 years, 26 years have seen divided government and only eight have witnessed one party controlling both the House and the Senate as well as the presidency. Moreover, in the three midterm elections where the voters had an opportunity to either change control and balance government or maintain party control, the voters overwhelmingly opted to throw the president's party out of power in the House of Representatives.

I was a beneficiary of that trend in 1994, when voters elected me and dozens of other new Republicans to the House of Representatives as a pro-test to the leftward drift of the Democratic Party and the Clinton administration. For the first time in 40 years, Republicans took a majority of the House. However, the GOP over-read its mandate and the voters in my congressional district, who had elected me to protect themselves from Bill Clinton in 1994, reelected Clinton two years later to protect themselves from me – a kind of balancing act in and of itself. Although straight-ticket voting as a "normal" was just beginning to emerge in 1996, swing voters opted for a divided, or balanced, government.

It is in the off-year elections when voters tend to take their vengeance out on one-party control of government. Presidential years have witnessed a greater propensity for straight-ticket balloting, probably because those years bring out larger turnouts and a higher proportion of voters who are more passionate than strategic in their electoral behavior.

The Senate is more complicated because of its staggered elections, with only one-third of the body facing reelection at a given time, but the facts are indisputable. In the 1994 cycle, for example, President Clinton's Democrats lost 44 House seats and nine Senate seats, which gave Republicans control of both the House and Senate for the first time in 40 years. That flipped 12 years later during President George W. Bush's second term. Democrats gained 31 House seats and six Senate seats, taking back control of each chamber. In President Obama's first midterm election in 2010, Republicans took back House control with a 63-seat gain; their six-seat Senate gain was not enough to retake the Senate.

This tendency to divide government has now been the rule nearly 80% of the time since 1980. At first, divided government was a good thing, in the sense that bipartisan government – *shared* responsibility for governing – produced many new laws, from tax reform to immigration reform (Simpson-Mazzoli, 1986) under the leadership of Ronald Reagan to budget deals and welfare reform under President Clinton. Shared responsibility for outcomes and governing brought out bipartisan compromises on the issues of the day. Under President Clinton, a bipartisan balanced budget compromise actually produced four years of surplus revenues!

It wasn't always easy. There were government shutdowns (several under President Reagan and two lengthier ones under President Clinton) and an impeachment, but along the way both parties saw it in their interest to produce a work product and tackle tough issues together. And when one party tried to do the heavy lifting all by itself, in a one-party government, it usually over-read its mandate and was punished by the voters in the next midterm.

There has been a tendency in off-year elections for swing voters to vote against the president's party. Balancing government is certainly one consideration independent voters have in making their off-year choices. There is a reason for this: certain segments of the electorate do not get their first choices in general elections, so they must opt for the lesser of two perceived equals. And not giving one party total control of the legislative process is one way to do it.

In my opinion, voters were concerned about the direction of the country in the huge election changes of 1994: a record tax hike, gun control, and national health care (then known as "Hillarycare").

However, for many voters, the agenda of the Newt Gingrich House – shutting down the government twice, cutting entitlement benefits, and passing abortion restrictions – proved to be too much change. So they clipped the Republicans' wings a bit, shaving their majorities while reelecting Bill Clinton in 1996, and reducing GOP majorities in 1998 with Clinton still in the White House. That set up a 2000 match that remained closely contested for the House, the Senate, and the presidency.

In the pre-Bush, pre-Obama days, the minority party acted as a minority shareholder in government. It tried to have an impact on outcomes, sometimes limiting damage to its constituencies and sometimes winning policy battles by attracting enough of the majority party's votes to change or mitigate an otherwise unsatisfactory outcome.

But along the way, things started to change. The parties began to sort themselves out ideologically. Liberal Republicans became rare and conservative Democrats all but disappeared. Along the way, the minority party began to act less as a minority shareholder in government and more like an opposition party. Compromises became rarer and bipartisanship a dirty word.

Surprisingly, although the pundits decried the decreasing civility and cooperation between parties, voters doubled down and became more parliamentary in their voting habits, opting for less ticket-splitting and more straight-ticket behavior. Politicians responded by going back to their partisan corners and behaving in a more parliamentary manner, compromising less and opposing nearly everything the other side wanted. Redistricting or gerrymandering – manipulation in the drawing of the legislative district lines – became both a cause and a manifestation of this new normal.

I say divided government is a new normal in part because the House of Representatives has a decidedly Republican edge in the way votes are distributed throughout the various districts. In 2012, Democrats posted a 1.4-million-vote edge$_3$, in total votes cast, for the House of Representatives nationwide, but they came up short of control by 17 seats. It would have taken a swing of another three to five percent to bring Democrats to a majority because of the alignments of the districts and the disparate distribution of Democratic votes.

Despite President Obama's substantial victory nationwide, with a plurality of nearly five million votes and a 51.1% to 47.2% margin, he carried only 209 congressional districts, while Governor Romney carried 226.$_4$

In that presidential election, the distribution of GOP and Democratic votes had a very different impact.

In 18 states, plus the District of Columbia, Democratic presidential candidates have now won in six straight elections! These states account for 242 electoral votes, which puts a candidate well on track for the 270 needed to win elections. The GOP has 13 states that have been consistently Republican over the same period, but these states only yield 102 electoral votes, far short of what is required to be elected president. Thus, given the trends that have developed over the past 25 years, Democrats start off with a nearly two-to-one advantage in the Electoral College.

Whether by design, the unfolding of historical patterns, or just plain luck, the playing fields for the House and the presidency carry different institutional advantages for the two parties, resulting in a strong bias for divided government.

As presidential voting patterns have become clear and relatively consistent, and residential sorting patterns have emerged to establish solidly blue and red states, the congressional vote pattern has followed suit. The following chart indicates that the 18 "blue wall" states (plus the District of Columbia) with consistent Democratic presidential patterns have also reflexively voted Democratic for the Senate. They also have elected nearly twice as many Democrats to the House, and more than three times as many

Democratic governors. The reverse is true for the 13 "red wall" states (voting six straight elections for the same presidential party's candidate). In 2010 the GOP saw its largest off-year wave since 1938, and Republicans significantly over-performed throughout the country.

Presidential Voting by State (1992-2012)

This chart shows the frequency with which each state has voted Democratic and/or Republican in the six presidential elections from 1992 to 2012:

VOTED DEM 6x	VOTED DEM 5x	VOTED DEM 4x	VOTED DEM 3x	VOTED DEM 2x	VOTED DEM 1x	
	VOTED GOP 1X	VOTED GOP 2X	VOTED GOP 3X	VOTED GOP 4X	VOTED GOP 5X	VOTED GOP 6x
19 states, 242 EVs	3 states, 15 EVs	2 states, 24 EVs	2 states, 38 EVs	7 states, 61 EVs	5 states, 56 EVs	13 states, 102 EVs
California (55)	Iowa (6)	Nevada (6)	Colorado (9)	Arkansas (6)	Arizona (11)	Alabama (9)
Connecticut (7)	New Hampshire (4)	Ohio (18)	Florida (29)	Kentucky (8)	Georgia (16)	Alaska (3)
Delaware (3)	New Mexico (5)			Louisiana (8)	Indiana (11)	Idaho (4)
D.C. (3)				Missouri (10)	Montana (3)	Kansas (6)
Hawaii (4)				Tennessee (11)	North Carolina (15)	Mississippi (6)
Illinois (20)				Virginia (13)		Nebraska (5)
Maine (4)				West Virginia (5)		North Dakota (3)
Maryland (10)						Oklahoma (7)
Massachusetts (11)						South Carolina (9)
Michigan (16)						South Dakota (3)
Minnesota (10)						Texas (38)

New Jersey (14)							Utah (6)
New York (29)							Wyoming (3)
Oregon (7)							
Pennsylvania (20)							
Rhode Island (4)							
Vermont (3)							
Washington (12)							
Wisconsin (10)							

SOURCE: Cook Political Report

Following is our summary of the voting patterns – including electoral votes (EVs) – in the blue, red, and swing states:

Parliamentary Voting Patterns

	19 states*	3 states	2 states	2 states	7 states	5 states	13 states
President	Voted D 6x	Voted D 5x	Voted D 4x	Voted D 3x	Voted D 2x	Voted D 1x	
		Voted R 1x	Voted R 2x	Voted R 3x	Voted R 4x	Voted R 5x	Voted R 6x
EVs	242 EVs	15 EVs	24 EVs	38 EVs	61 EVs	56 EVs	102 EVs
Senate**	32D, 4R	4D, 2R	2D, 2R	3D, 1R	7D, 7R	4D, 6R	3D, 23R
House	134D, 69R	6D, 3R	6D, 14R	13D, 21R	10 D, 37R	16D, 30R	16D, 60R
Gov	13D, 4R, 1Ind	2D, 1 R	1D, 1R	1D, 1R	4D, 3R	1D, 4R	0D, 13R

* Includes the District of Columbia, which has no Members of Congress.
** Independents Angus King of Maine and Bernie Sanders of Vermont caucus with Senate Democrats.

THE HOUSE OF REPRESENTATIVES REPUBLICAN INSTITUTIONAL BIAS

The House of Representatives, as lines are currently drawn, has a significant (but not insurmountable) bias in favor of the Republicans. This bias is due to three unrelated but interconnected factors: the Voting Rights Act, residential sorting patterns, and political gerrymandering and redistricting (the GOP had the upper hand in drawing state lines after the 2010 census). This is exacerbated by the second "new normal" that has evolved over the past 40 years: the propensity of voters to vote straight-party and not split their tickets in federal elections. Voters' thought has mutated from the old adage that "all politics is local" to behavior indicating that "all politics is national." Nowhere is this clearer than in the makeup of Congress today.

In 2013, of the 234 GOP House members, 94% were from districts that Mitt Romney carried in 2012. Of the 201 Democratic seats, fully 96% were from districts carried by Obama. The number of split-ticket districts is the lowest in nearly a century and has been decreasing over the past decade.

In the Senate, those 18 "blue wall" states that have voted six straight times for presidential Democrats have a Senate lineup of 32 Democrats (including Independents Bernie Sanders and Angus King, who caucus with the Democrats) and four Republicans. Three of the four Republicans were swept into office in the GOP tidal wave of 2010 and potentially face difficult reelections in 2016. They are Ron Johnson of Wisconsin, Mark Kirk of Illinois, and Pat Toomey of Pennsylvania. The fourth, Susan Collins of Maine, has the most moderate record of any Republican and is an 18-year Senate veteran from a small state where personal politics still matter.

Of the 13 "red" states that have a solid Republican presidential performance, the 2014 Senate lineup was 23 Republicans out of 26 seats. Entering the 2014 election campaign, Democrats were projected to lose two of their three seats (Alaska and South Dakota). Only Heidi Heitkamp of North Dakota breaks the mold, having won an open seat by less than a percentage point in 2012. The governorships in these states follow a similar pattern, but I would note that in voters' minds, a state election is different from a national election.

A generation ago, ticket-splitting was a time-honored American tradition that advanced the idea that all politics is local. Throughout the second half of the 20th century, American voters would go to the polls in presidential years and often vote for one party for president and another for their congressman. Columnist Ron Brownstein has observed, "Voters used to vote for the name on the back of the jersey. Today, they vote for the color of the jersey."

That's not to say that straight-ticket voting and coattails didn't have their place. In some states, it was so institutionalized that a voter could pull one lever and vote a straight-party ballot for every office. The Connecticut legislature shifted from heavily Republican in 1956 to heavily Democratic in 1958. But that was an exceptional outcome, and the pattern ended a few years later when the state eliminated the straight-party lever in voting.[5]

Residential Sorting and Straight-Ticket Voting

Perhaps the easiest way to explain how residential sorting patterns benefit Republicans is to examine Obama's top-performing districts against Romney's top-performing districts.

As districts within states must represent equal populations (but not equal numbers of voters), the chart below illustrates how much more Democratically the Obama districts voted in 2012, compared to the percentage who voted for Romney in the GOP's best districts:

Top Ten Obama Districts	Obama %	Top Ten Romney Districts	Romney %
NY-15 Serrano	97	TX-13 Thornberry	80
NY-13 Rangel	95	UT-3 Chaffetz	79
NY-5 Meeks	90	TX-11 Conaway	79
PA-2 Fattah	90	UT-1 Bishop	78
NY-7 Velazquez	89	GA-9 Collins	78
NY-8 Jeffries	89	TX-8 Brady	77
FL-24 Wilson	88	AL-4 Aderholt	75
CA-13 Lee	88	OK-3 Lucas	74
NJ-10 Payne	88	TX-19 Neugebauer	74
IL-7 Davis	87	AL-6 Bachus	74

Many of Obama's top districts are contiguous, indicating that partisan gerrymandering is not the cause of the high Democratic voter distribution. In fact, only two of the top ten Obama districts were subject to Republican redistricting plans (FL-24 and PA-2). On the Republican side, all ten top-heavy Romney districts were in states where the GOP had drawn the lines! A partisan redraw would not waste so many extra Republican votes if it could be avoided. This is clearly the result of residential patterns. For each of the 20 districts shown above, the neighboring districts show a similar, but less intense, partisan pattern.

To more clearly demonstrate how residential sorting contributes to a Republican institutional advantage, consider that Obama scored over 80% of the vote in 27 congressional districts, while Romney scored over 80% in just one: the Texas Panhandle district (adjacent to TX-19, TX-11, and OK-6 – all three of which are among Romney's top ten performing districts).[6] In other words, Democrats have more wasted votes in House races, as there is no prize for running up the score.

Moreover, the Voting Rights Act is *not* the sole cause of packing Democrats in many of these districts. California's 12th and 13th districts (contiguous; San Francisco and Berkeley) have infusions of large white liberal constituencies. MA-8 has the same with MIT and Harvard. (Martin has a different view about how Republicans used the Voting Rights Act to pack black districts in the South, as he sets out in the next chapter.)

As demonstrated earlier, this is a new normal. Compare the 2012 outcome with the 1988 presidential race between George H.W. Bush and Michael Dukakis. Bush won the race 53.4% to 45.6%, but only 21 Democratic districts produced Dukakis percentages of over 70%, while nine districts produced Bush percentages of over 70%. Democratic members of Congress were reelected in four of the nine supermajority Bush districts! Today, no Democrat would be remotely competitive in such districts.

Democrats prevailed in all 21 of the 70%-plus Dukakis districts. New York's Bill Green was the best-performing Republican (61%) in a highly Dukakis district (66%). All of the aforementioned Democratic districts were in large northern cities (Chicago had three, New York had six, and Detroit and the Bay area had two, plus Cleveland, Pittsburgh, Philadelphia, St. Louis, Newark, Baltimore, and Los Angeles). The only exception was Houston's Mickey Leland, who represented a black district in Houston's core. But these districts were mostly African American enclaves within major cities. Today, many large Bohemian and academic communities produce Democratic majorities rivaling those of ethnic communities.

Today, as a rule of thumb, urban areas belong en bloc to the Democratic Party while most rural areas belong to the GOP. Suburbs are the new battlegrounds for political control, with inner suburbs (with closer ties to the cities) being more Democratic and outer suburbs (exurbs) exhibiting strong Republican tendencies.

In my congressional district I saw my voter percentages drop precipitously as suburban areas revitalized and new "town centers" were developed. In the 2004 election I saw my reelection percentage drop compared to the 2000 election, despite the fact that redistricting had removed several heavily Democratic parts of my district (such as Reston and Dumfries) and added heavily Republican sections of exurban western Prince William County. President Bush ran better nationally in 2004 than in 2000, so what could explain my drop from 62% of the vote to 60% of the vote?

The late political scientist Robert Wood (later the president of the University of Massachusetts) published a book in 1958 entitled *Suburbia: its People and Their Politics.* He was opining on the suburban movements out of cities following World War II. He observed that young families were moving to the suburbs, not to be near the city but to be away from the city. He believed suburbanization was an anti-urban phenomenon.

Fast-forward 60 years and Dr. Wood's thesis is still relevant. But most political observers miss the point when they call Nassau County or Arlington, Pasadena, Bethesda, Merrifield, or Evanston "suburbs." The people flocking to these former suburbs are in fact moving to what have now become cities. Their value set, their densities, their diversity, and, yes, their politics are thoroughly citified. The new "suburbs" as envisioned by Professor Wood are now the outer suburbs, the exurbs, that attract young families moving away from the city – not because housing is cheaper, but because of the values they represent. These voters flee the rapid urbanization that is taking place in older suburbs for megachurches, gun shops, Walmarts, and youth sport centers. As cities spread into suburbs, the stereotypical suburbanite moves further out.

The explanation for my 2004 percentage drop came to me at a post-election dinner I had with Democrat Gerry Connolly, who was, at the time, the chairman of the Fairfax County Board of Supervisors, and later became my successor in Congress. He asked me if the results in the Merrifield precinct surprised me. I was surprised at the question, but it was revealing. Merrifield had been a small precinct sitting just outside of the Capital Beltway with a

mix of modest houses, apartments, and an older, established black community. It has always had a Democratic flavor but had always given me solid
support, even in the most Democratic years.

The county had decided to put a Metro rail stop nearby, and the county
board had decided to revitalize this depressed area with higher-density
office and upscale, high-rise residential development. My instinct told me
that the new owners and renters would be higher-income whites who relo-
cated to be near the subway line for their commutes into high-paying jobs in
the city. In my periodic visits to the area during my reelection campaign,
that view had been sustained, with the caveat that a substantial professional
ethnic population was also moving in.

What I hadn't noticed was that the national GOP and President Bush
were failing to connect with these new voters. Although I had met many of
them in my travels to their local schools or shaking hands at the subway
stop, these voters had not been integrated into the larger community. Many
were single and others were DINKs (double income, no kids). Their politics were decidedly not Republican and on Election Day, I was their target
for sending a message. I lost the precinct, decidedly, even while I carried
everything around it.

These newcomers were *not* suburbanites, as we traditionally view them.
They would have been comfortable in the city, where their jobs were. But
Fairfax had brought the city to the suburbs. Shopping, mass transit, dense
living patterns – all within a five-minute walk. With higher numbers of sin-
gles, ethnics, and folks with alternative lifestyles, the values in Merrifield
were far different from those in the Merrifield of a decade prior. The newcomers were decidedly unhappy with the Bush administration and its social
views. They were higher-income, upwardly mobile, and certainly not part of
the progressive politics one finds in inner cities, but they voted solidly Democratic. Merrifield was lost for the GOP. These new voters identified more
with the characteristics of a city than those of a suburban county.

At the same time, I noticed in picking up new precincts in western Prince
William County that a counter-change was taking effect. In outer suburbs,
the GOP vote was increasing. And in Appalachia, once a Democratic
stronghold, Republicans were on the rise.

The following charts illustrate the growing dominance of the GOP in Appalachia along with diminishing voter turnout, against turnout models in Democratic urban areas:

Democratic Performance in Appalachia

Candidate	Year	% of Appalachian Counties Won*
Carter	1976	68%
Clinton	1996	47%
Obama	2008	13%
Obama	2012	7%

* 428 counties classified by Appalachian Regional Commission covering 13 states

Democratic Presidential Vote

County	1976	1996	2012
Winston, AL	52.5	36.2	13.2
Pike, KY	70.1	60.1	23.9
Harlan, KY	69.4	58.0	17.2
Swain, NC	57.0	50.2	45.7
Meigs, OH	50.9	45.2	39.4
Washington, PA	59.2	52.7	42.6
McMinn, TN	51.1	40.5	25.8
Buchanan, VA	54.0	63.4	32.1
Logan, WV	76.5	72.0	29.0

Although these mountain counties were losing population and electoral strength, they were moving rapidly away from the Democratic Party. Environmental politics (coal), guns, gay rights, abortion – issues that were helping to move Fairfax into the Democratic column were transforming Appalachia into a solid GOP bastion.

I remember asking West Virginia's Nick Rahall, a 38-year Democratic member of the House of Representatives, if he saw the movement to Bush in 2000 as a permanent or temporary realignment. Congressman Rahall, a native of southern West Virginia and a survivor of West Virginia politics, replied, "I'm afraid the movement away from the Democrats is permanent." Although he had worked the coalfields for a generation, he faced political extinction in 2014, just as his neighbor to the south, 28-year Democrat Rick Boucher of southwest Virginia, had been defeated in 2010 by a Republican who didn't live in his district.

Politics was no longer personal. It was no longer local. It was national. In the case of Appalachia, it wasn't changing demographics driving the electoral outcomes, it was a changing set of issues; and the Democrats were now on the other side of the issues that mattered.

More importantly, these were no longer competitive areas. They had become overwhelmingly Republican areas, where gerrymandering couldn't change outcomes. Except for a few college towns and art colonies scattered around the 428 counties of this mountainous region, these areas were now in solidarity with the GOP.

Unfortunately for Republicans, Appalachia is not growing, but the suburban counties are. These growth patterns portend a real problem for the GOP.

Gerrymandering – combined with residential sorting, the Voting Rights Act, and straight-ticket voting – was taking voters out of the equation. Instead of the voters picking their leaders, the leaders were picking their voters, and the resulting polarization and institutionalization of divided government were taking hold.

The net result has been a Democratic presidential advantage and a Republican House electoral advantage. The Senate is likely to be a battleground in the years to come, with no party likely to clear the 60-vote filibuster-proof majority in the next several cycles. Thus, divided government is the likely continuum. Institutional realities limit the ability of voters, particularly nonaligned voters, to meaningfully affect the result. While many of us proudly vote in November and leave the polling place with an "I Voted" sticker on, we are reluctant to admit that the real election was in the spring or summer primary where the candidate of the pre-drawn majority party was nominated.

It is the emergence of both of these trends simultaneously that makes them significant. One-party districts, without parliamentary straight-ticket voting, would *not* produce an institutionally Republican-biased House alignment. In the past, massive ticket-splitting would have tempered this bias, as it did in GOP presidential landslide years 1956, 1972, and 1984. And with more competitively-drawn districts, the House would be in play every two years, dependent on voter moods, much as the Founding Fathers envisioned. But ideologically-sorted parties confine the House of Representative's playing field to fewer than 20% of the seats in theory and, in practice, fewer than 10% per cycle. This helps account for the unusually high reelection rates every two years, even in times of massive voter discontent.

In roughly 80% of the House districts, where the partisan outcome is predetermined by the district's lines, incumbent members cater to their party bases, and not to the independents or the other party, because their party bases determine their futures; those folks are the participants in the defining primary or nominating convention. And both parties have been moving in opposite directions: Republicans to the right and Democrats to the left.

Primaries, in these 80% of districts, are the incumbents' chief and often only concern. Primary voters tend not to reward moderate candidates who compromise. They prefer hardliners who will not stray from party orthodoxy. Moreover, as will be discussed later, the organized interest groups that dominate the respective parties serve as an enforcement mechanism for toeing the party line.

The end result is that the new normals make it difficult to achieve consensus and undermine efforts to compromise. Divided government and party-line voting have established themselves as the norms. Even bad legislative outcomes fail to shake the underlying foundations of these factors.

MARTIN'S RESPONSE

While Tom makes a number of excellent points, his analysis does not necessarily mean that the Republicans have a lock on the House of Representatives. The GOP margin in the House entering the 2014 elections was relatively small (17 seats), and Democrats could retake the chamber, particularly in a presidential year when turnout among base Democratic constituencies (minorities, young voters, single women) is high. Thus, straight-ticket voting is a two-edged sword. It generally favors Democratic congressional candidates in presidential years and generally favors Republican congressional candidates in midterm elections. Recent exceptions to this were 2006, when a "wave" election swept the GOP out of the majority, and 1998, when Democrats picked up five seats after then-Speaker Newt Gingrich overplayed his hand with the impeachment of President Bill Clinton.

As the *Economist* pointed out on May 17, 2014, off-year voter turnout in the United States is whiter and older than in presidential years. Both of these groups currently favor the GOP.[7]

The *Economist* noted that whites constituted 77% of the vote in the 2010 midterm elections; the white percentage of the overall population is currently 72%: "Racially, mid-term voters lag the changes in the voting-age population by about 20 years and the country as a whole by nearly 30 years." On the subject of age, the *Economist* further pointed out, "Mid-term voters are disproportionately old: a quarter of those who told the Census Bureau that they voted in 2010 were over 65, though only 13% of Americans have that distinction."[8]

The results in 2012 (+8 for House Democrats) were particularly noteworthy because the general consensus is that the 2011 redistricting favored Republicans nationwide. It is certainly possible that Democrats could retake some state legislatures in 2020 and redraw enough districts to tip the balance in a subsequent election.

Additionally, Hispanics are moving into close-in suburbs in many areas, and their votes could tip the balance in some congressional districts – particularly if Republican hardliners continue to block any significant immigration reform in Congress.

Our country remains closely divided, so every election will be a challenge. However, there is no question that straight-ticket voting does make our Congress much more into a parliamentary-type system, with bipartisan compromise more difficult to achieve. This all cries out for strong leadership on both sides.

4

THE CONTINUING ROLE OF RACE IN AMERICAN POLITICS

By Martin Frost and Tom Davis

MARTIN'S VIEW

Very few people are willing to address the continuing role of race in American politics. I am.

I come to this subject with a long history. In 1974, when I first ran for Congress, many young Democratic politicians were inspired to seek office because of opposition to the Vietnam War or because of the Watergate scandal. That was not my motivation. I ran largely because of a deep commitment to civil rights.

I grew up in the segregated South and attended segregated schools in Ft. Worth, Texas, which were not integrated until eight years after my high school graduation. As a teenager, largely because of my involvement in the youth movement of Reform Judaism, I became committed to civil rights and decided I wanted to help promote racial progress in our country if I ever had the chance.

When I first won my congressional seat in 1978 and in every election thereafter, I had the strong support of the black community in north Texas. Without that support, I would not have won my initial race and would not have remained in Congress for 26 years. Twenty years later, in 1998, I was elected chairman of the House Democratic Caucus with the support of black members like Charlie Rangel, John Lewis, Jim Clyburn, and Bennie Thompson.

With this in mind, I am now able to take a step back and seriously examine the role that race still plays in American politics.

We have now reached a point in our history where both parties may make significant miscalculations when it comes to the effect race will play in future presidential and congressional contests.

Let's start with the Republicans. By design or otherwise, the GOP has become the clear majority party of white America, and it has bet the ranch on winning a big enough share of the white vote to elect a president. Karl Rove on election night in 2012 couldn't believe that his turnout model had been wrong. Rove and others in the Republican Party had been convinced that President Obama could not replicate the high turnout among blacks and young people that had carried him to victory in 2008. Obama did just that, and Rove, on FOX national television, basically dissembled.

As can be seen in the chart below, the Democratic share of the white vote for president has dropped from a high of 44% in 1996 to a low of 39% in 2012. Conversely, the Republican share of the white vote peaked at 59% in 2012. The three-way contest in 1992 does not give a complete picture of the racial vote because Ross Perot won 21% of the white vote as a third-party candidate.

That's the good news for the Republicans. The bad news is that white voters as a share of the electorate decreased from 87% in 1992 to 72% in 2012. All indications are that the white percentage of the electorate will continue to decline in future years because of demographic change.

Republicans understand this dilemma, and that's why they are doing everything possible to make it more difficult for minorities to vote. This has included passing voter ID laws that require a government photo ID (something many minority individuals don't possess) to vote and shortening the period for early voting in many states they control by eliminating voting on weekends and cutting down the total number of early voting days. Democrats are right to fight these changes, but so far Republicans have succeeded in making them in some states with a high concentration of minority voters.

These changes have implications for both presidential and congressional elections.

Presidential Election

Year	White Vote as % of Electorate	White D Vote	White R Vote	Third-Party White Vote
1992	87%	39%	41%	21%
1996	83%	44%	46%	9%
2000	81%	42%	55%	3%
2004	77%	41%	58%	1%
2008	74%	43%	55%	
2012	72%	39%	59%	

Source: Roper Center, University of Connecticut[9]

Thus, Republicans are fishing in an ever-decreasing pond and must expand their share of the white vote even further if they can't figure out how to appeal to the fastest-growing portion of the electorate – Hispanics. The GOP's share of the white vote has been propped up by its strong showing among white men and white seniors. Also, despite all the noise about Democratic gains among women, Republicans still win a majority of the total white female vote despite losing among college-educated women in the suburbs.

When I was chair of the DCCC and pollsters would come into my office and tell me how we were making gains among seniors and women, I would always ask for the percentages among white seniors and white women. They would then sheepishly provide numbers that were not nearly as impressive.

The most dramatic shift away from Democrats in recent years has occurred with white seniors. According to a study released by the Gallup organization on March 26, 2014[10], Gallup's polling data in 2013 showed that Democrats trailed Republicans by 13 points among white seniors (40% to 53%). Gallup further observed that seniors were overwhelmingly white (85%), whereas other age cohorts contained a larger number of minorities (though not constituting a majority). Romney defeated Obama among all seniors by 56% to 44% in 2012.

Gallup put it pretty succinctly in the study: "Race appears to be a signifi-cant factor in seniors' Republican realignment, because whites have become more solidly Republican in recent years, seniors are overwhelmingly white, and white seniors today are Republican-aligned, while white seniors in the past were Democratic-aligned." Gallup concluded with a suggestion that the change in white seniors may be due to Obama's race. It noted, "Once Obama leaves office, his influence on party preferences among racial and age groups may become clearer, if he is succeeded by a white president from either party. Should the current trends in party preference persist, it sug-gests a political realignment among seniors has taken place. If the current trends by age shift in the other direction, it suggests the shift was temporary, likely tied to the Obama era."

As the white share of the electorate has declined, the minority share has increased. The black share of the electorate increased from 8% in 1992 to 13% in both 2008 and 2012. The growth of the Hispanic share of the elec-torate was even more dramatic, increasing from 2% in 1992 to 10% in 2012. The Asian share increased from 1% in 1992 to 3% in 2012.

Minority Vote as Percent of Votes Cast for President

Year	Percent Black	Percent Hispanic	Percent Asian
1992	8%	2%	1%
1996	10%	5%	1%
2000	10%	7%	2%
2004	11%	8%	2%
2008	13%	9%	2%
2012	13%	10%	3%

SOURCE: Roper Center, University of Connecticut[11]

Republicans have a chance to win the presidency in the short term by playing out the same hand if minority Democratic turnout falls off, but long-term this is not a winning strategy.

That brings us to the clear challenge for Republicans – can they increase their share of the Hispanic vote? As can be seen from the next chart, the Republican share of the Hispanic vote peaked at 44% in 2004 (George W.

Bush's second election) but then settled back down to 31% and 27% in 2008 and 2012, respectively.

Hispanics could be allies of the GOP. They are patriotic, family-oriented, entrepreneurial, and pushed toward the GOP because of their Catholic faith and the abortion issue. However, the Republican Party has given them the stiff-arm with its consistent anti-immigration-reform rhetoric, refusal to invest in public education, and opposition to raising the minimum wage. Some key individuals in the GOP understand this, but so far they have not prevailed and the GOP remains the Grand Old White Party. Interestingly, Asian voters who started off as Republicans have now drifted to the Democratic Party for the same reason.

Presidential Results among Hispanic Voters – Key Demographic

Year	D Percent	R Percent	Third-Party Percent
1992	61%	25%	14%
1996	73%	21%	6%
2000	62%	35%	3%
2004	53%	44%	3%
2008	67%	31%	
2012	71%	27%	

SOURCE: Roper Center. University of Connecticut[12]

That brings us to the Democrats, who have bet the ranch in recent elections on a combination of higher-than-normal turnout among blacks and young people and the votes of gays, Jews, Hispanics, and college-educated, single suburban women. This coalition held for Barack Obama's two successful elections in 2008 and 2012. However, it might not hold for a white nominee in the near term, though it is possible that Hillary Clinton could keep it together if she is the nominee in 2016 because of strong voter identification with the Clinton brand and the chance for her to become the first female president. However, this is not guaranteed.

Bill Clinton in 1992 and 1996 was able to put together a coalition of blacks and middle-class whites concerned about economic issues. The Democratic presidential share of the white vote (44%) peaked in 1996 with Clinton's reelection. It dropped in both 2000 (Gore) and 2004 (Kerry), bounced back temporarily in 2008 with Obama's appeal to some higher-income whites, and then dropped to a low of 39% in 2012. The trend line clearly is going in the wrong direction for Democrats.

If Democrats cannot maintain higher turnouts among blacks and young people moving forward, then things could get dicey, particularly if Republicans can ever figure out how to get well with Hispanics. Should the Republicans make inroads with Hispanics, Democrats would need to cut Republican margins among white voters. To pretend that this is not the case and to run the same playbook as Obama ran in 2008 and 2012 is to risk defeat, at least until Republicans are overwhelmed by demographic changes. Democrats' best options with white voters are to take a leaf out of Bill Clinton's playbook by emphasizing basic economic issues to middle-class voters and to make an all-out effort to win back white seniors by hitting on GOP plans to reduce Social Security and Medicare benefits. To date, Republicans have out-messaged Democrats on senior issues, but that doesn't mean that Democrats should quit talking to seniors.

Many Democrats see the path to the party's salvation as continuing to campaign against the GOP's record on matters important to women, thus running up the gender gap numbers. This clearly worked for Virginia governor Terry McAuliffe in his successful race in 2013. However, not all of America is northern Virginia (large numbers of college-educated, white women), where this strategy was successful against a Republican candidate with a bad record on women's issues. Furthermore, white women as a group still vote Republican, and Democrats win a majority of the female vote only when minority women are added to the equation. An overemphasis on women's issues while not adequately addressing economic issues for all members of the middle class may not be a winning strategy. Relying heavily on issues important to women, while strategically a good idea, will not make up for the votes lost if black turnout drops and the GOP makes inroads among Hispanics.

Tom's View

Before the 1964 Civil Rights Act, public opinion polls showed little differentiation between the Republican and Democratic parties on race-related issues. Indeed, the major differentiation was within the Democratic

Party, with a southern wing that supported segregation and obstacles to black voting, and a northern wing – particularly in northern cities – that had incorporated black voters into its coalitions and fought for civil rights.

The first African American elected to Congress in the 20th century was Oscar De Priest, a Chicago Republican, in 1928. Prior to the Depression, nearly all black voters identified with the party of Lincoln, who had of course freed the slaves. The Democratic Party was reliant on a southern block of voters to win presidential elections and Congress. These southern Democrats were united on one issue – race.

As the great V.O. Key noted in his classic *Southern Politics*, published in 1949,

In the American South, the discipline necessary to maintain sectional unity on the race question ... has first crushed and then prevented the rebirth of political parties. The potent unifying force of the threat of external intervention on the race issue ... caused the South to close its ranks in a national politics and thereby removed the possibility of a dual party system in state and local affairs ... . Voting a Republican ticket in the general election came to be regarded, not as the erraticism of a mugwump, but as a desecration of the memory of Robert E. Lee, disrespect for one's gallant forebears who fought at Gettysburg, and an open invitation to boycott one's grocery business.[13]

However, with the passage of the Civil Rights Act in 1964 and the Voting Rights Act of 1965, the entire segregationist, one-party system began to unravel. Introducing new voters into the electoral system, African Americans set off a chain reaction of partisan realignment over the South and the nation over the next 40 years.

As newly-registered blacks entered Democratic primaries in droves, many Democrats who had been aligned with segregationist policies were defeated in Democratic primaries by the huge infusion of African American voters. Senators A. Willis Robertson of Virginia, B. Everett Jordan of North Carolina, and Ross Bass of Tennessee were such casualties, as were Representatives John McMillian of South Carolina and Howard W. Smith of Virginia.

The lesson was clear for southern Democrats – move to the center to attract black voters, who were now major factors in Democratic primaries, or face political extinction.

It also paved the way for conservative southern Democrats to switch to the GOP. Black voters were proportionately more potent in restrictive primaries than in general elections. As a result, many white, heretofore Democratic voters began voting for Republicans, who more approximated their views, in statewide elections.

Southern party switches included both Senator Strom Thurmond and Congressman Albert Watson of South Carolina. Senator Harry F. Byrd, Jr., of Virginia, after narrowly winning his Democratic primary in a special election in 1966, opted to run as an Independent in 1970, facing a larger electorate where he was not as likely to be ambushed in a primary by a nearly solid black turnout.

It took decades for these coalitions to realign, with each state having its own timetable as an older generation left office and new leaders emerged. What is clear, however, is that the tandem of the Civil Rights Act and the Voting Rights Act set a series of forces in play that realigned American politics forever.

Ironically, neither act would have passed without the strong support of Republicans in Congress. In fact, in both chambers, a higher percentage of Republicans than Democrats voted for the Civil Rights Act. For example, 20 of the 21 southern Democratic senators voted against final passage. Only Texas Democrat Ralph Yarbrough voted for it, and he lost his seat in a Democratic primary in 1970.

But what brought the race issue to center stage in the partisan realignments was its championing by the Democratic president Lyndon Johnson and its opposition by the 1964 Republican presidential nominee, Barry Goldwater. Black votes were scarce for Goldwater in 1964, even as he carried four deep South states that had never, ever voted Republican (Mississippi, Alabama, South Carolina, and Georgia) plus Louisiana, which had only voted once for the GOP, in 1956 – although in the disputed presidential election of 1876, the Special Electoral Commission, on an 8-7 vote, awarded Louisiana's and South Carolina's disputed electoral votes to Republican Rutherford B. Hayes.

Black voters held a strong allegiance to the Republican Party after the Civil War. After all, it was Republican Abraham Lincoln who had issued the Emancipation Proclamation, freeing slaves in Confederate states. And it was Republicans who had pushed the 13th, 14th, and 15th Amendments to the United States Constitution, abolishing slavery and guaranteeing both equal protection and the right to vote, regardless of race. It was Democrats who had introduced Jim Crow laws in the South, run the Ku Klux Klan, and filibustered every pending civil rights law for the first half of the 20th century.

But as blacks left the South and migrated to northern cities, Democratic machine bosses greeted them as they arrived, and they were gradually absorbed into the city Democratic machines. The economic policies of Franklin D. Roosevelt made it acceptable for Northern blacks to join the Democratic Party. As previously noted, in 1928, Oscar De Priest became the first African American elected to Congress in the 20th century, winning a seat in Chicago's Loop and Southside as a Republican; and he was reelected in 1930 with 58% and again in 1932 with 55% of the votes cast.[14]

As the only African American in Congress, De Priest proposed a reduction in the number of House seats for states that disenfranchised southern blacks and introduced a bill to provide monthly pensions for former slaves more than 75 years old. He also introduced anti-lynching legislation.[15]

But De Priest's refusal to support Roosevelt's remedial economic measures alienated many voters in his inner-city district. In 1934, another African American – Arthur Mitchell, a former Republican lieutenant in Chicago's political machine who switched to the Democrats to become an ardent supporter of the New Deal – defeated De Priest. The race reflected a larger trend occurring in northern cities, as blacks were changing their allegiances in favor of the Democratic Party.[16]

Even as the Democratic Party in the South doubled down on segregation, the Democratic Party in the North became reliant on African American voters to win elections in Illinois, Pennsylvania, Ohio, Michigan, and New York. So on the eve of the 1964 election, President Johnson, who was a native of the South but feared a primary challenge from Robert F. Kennedy, pushed through the Civil Rights Act.

The following chart illustrates the direction of the black vote in the North, from 1956 to 1964, in presidential elections:

Presidential Vote in 1956-1964 Among Selected African American Precincts[17]

	1956		1960		1964	
	Stevenson	Eisenhower	Kennedy	Nixon	Johnson	Goldwater
Baltimore (Ward 10)	1,540	1,403	2,035	578	2,854	130
Detroit (Ward 12)	22,035	7,822	21,790	4,283	24,062	1,247
Cleveland (Ward 10)	6,351	5,057	9,007	3,187	11,135	259
Chicago (Ward 6)	17,398	13,572	24,837	7,701	34,000	1,034
Chicago (Ward 20)	17,572	11,281	21,641	6,645	35,016	807
Philadelphia (Ward 32)	13,562	3,600	12,611	2,505	15,853	542
New York (Ass. Dist. 11)	17,895	8,025	18,857	5,161	25,295	933
Brooklyn (Ass. Dist. 6)	13,554	8,968	14,340	6,395	21,768	1,036

As Ron Brownstein of *National Journal* has noted, "The initial fissure between Democrats and many whites over Civil Rights widened over an array of other racially infused wedge issues, such as school busing and affirmative action, and by the emergence of new social disputes, such as abortion rights and gun rights that further divide the white electorate along social lines."

Richard Nixon, an ardent opponent of segregation, won the presidency in 1968 against both Johnson's vice president, Hubert Humphrey, and Alabama's governor, George Wallace. Wallace's famous phrase "segregation now, segregation forever" won him the electoral votes of five southern states – four that had voted for Barry Goldwater plus Arkansas.

Southern whites, particularly the less affluent and less educated, were reluctant to embrace their country club, Mountain Valley Republicans; but they were put off by a Democratic Party that was, with the passage of the Voting Rights Act, rapidly becoming dominated by blacks. Over the next 30 years, these Wallace voters, socially conservative but economically more populist, became the balance of power in southern elections. They voted overwhelmingly for Nixon's reelection against the culturally liberal George

McGovern, but in the aftermath of Watergate gave support to Georgian Jimmy Carter against the Yale-educated Gerald Ford. Carter carried 10 of the 11 southern states (losing only Virginia), only to lose 10 of 11 Dixie states four years later, carrying only his native state, as Reagan's campaign emphasized conservative social values.

Martin observes that the overwhelming movement of blacks to the Democratic Party really started with the presidential race in 1960, when Martin Luther King, Sr., endorsed Kennedy following Kennedy's expression of sympathy after the jailing of Martin Luther King, Jr.. It was accelerated by Barry Goldwater's opposition to civil rights legislation during the 1964 campaign. By the time Martin finished law school and returned to Texas in 1970, Democratic candidates in his state were regularly receiving between 85% and 90% of the black vote.

Republicans lost any chance of winning significant black votes in the South with the prominence of leading anti-civil rights southern GOP politicians such as Senators Strom Thurmond and Jesse Helms during the 1970s, as Martin also notes.

The racial stratification in the South and nation overall continued, as since 1976 no Republican president has won more than 12% of the African American vote nationally; and during this period, only Reagan in 1984 and George W. Bush in 2004 carried more than 30% of the Hispanic vote. As blacks moved solidly into the Democratic column, especially after the Voting Rights Act encouraged their registration and voting in the South, many conservative southern and working-class whites moved to the Republican Party. This ideological and racial resorting of the parties worked to the Republicans' advantage from 1968 to 1988, allowing them to win the White House in five of six elections, with only southerner Jimmy Carter breaking the spell.

Another southerner, Bill Clinton, won in 1992 and 1996, but failed to get a majority in either year. Southerner Al Gore narrowly won the popular vote in 2000, but failed to carry a single southern state (though Florida, thanks to the Jewish Joe Lieberman, was a dead heat), while 2004 saw George W. Bush narrowly win the presidential majority against the more liberal John Kerry.

This led strategists like Karl Rove to proclaim that the Republicans would become the permanent majority. No Democratic candidate since Lyndon Johnson has carried the white vote and no Democrat since Carter has received over 43% of the white vote; and Democrats, despite nearly unanimous black support, were in trouble. Between 1964 and 2008, a period of 44 years, the only Democrats who could win national elections were southern Democrats who could hold the votes of less-affluent southern whites.

Southern Democrats, it seemed, could culturally identify with enough whites to cobble together a winning coalition. While southerners Johnson, Carter, Clinton, and even Gore could muster pluralities, McGovern, Mondale, Dukakis, and Kerry all fell short – usually way short. It appeared Rove and others had it figured out. The racial and cultural alignments that had attracted southern and working-class whites to the GOP would endure. Democrats could only win by going after the swing "Reagan Democrats." In fact, in 1994, Republicans reached majority status in Congress as well.

But underneath, a near-mirror image realignment was taking place, not just among African American voters, but also among Hispanics, Asians, and higher-income, well-educated whites.

The Obama candidacy threw out the playbook on racial voting by doubling down on minority voters. The campaign ran massive registration and get-out-the-vote drives among voters of color. The following chart illustrates the overwhelming support for President Obama in heavily African American districts in selected cities and counties in 2012:

Support for Presidential Candidates in 2012 in Select Heavily African-American Districts

Jurisdiction	Ward/Precinct	Obama	Romney
Cleveland	1	13,544	101
Cleveland	4	10,436	207
Detroit	1	34,120	571
Detroit	7	30,632	563
Philadelphia	10	13,315	101
Harlem	AD 79	33,286	586
Brooklyn	AD 57	50,332	928
Brooklyn	AD 32	39,932	676
Chicago	6	25,918	137
Richmond, VA	310	737	7
Richmond, VA	602	1,272	7
Clayton County, GA	Lake City	1,175	181
Clayton	Oak	5,341	170
Baltimore	District 10	1,757	11
Washington, D.C.	8	31,980	237

The one factor that has been clearly demonstrated is that blacks today are a solid block of the Democratic vote. Although President Obama is clearly a revered figure in the African American community, that population's propensity to vote a straight ticket is palpable.

African American Republicans cannot win African American districts under today's dynamics, though. Successful black Republicans, like Senator Tim Scott of South Carolina or Utah's Mia Love (who is also a Haitian immigrant), can win in deeply conservative white areas. Conservative whites are willing to vote for conservative blacks who hold their economic and cultural views, but there is little indication that blacks will support anyone with the Republican label in a national race. Republican outreach efforts into the black community have had little success with black voters, though there is anecdotal evidence that it may help them with moderate whites. Note our discussion on Thad Cochran's reelection primary in Chapter 12 for a further window into racial dynamics and the Republican Party.

Moderate black Republican candidates, like Michael Steele in Maryland, have made few inroads into the black community against white Democrats. Nevertheless, as Barack Obama leaves office, there is no reason for the GOP to quit trying. Gaining just 10% to 15% of the African American vote can be enough to create majorities in some blue states, such as Michigan and Pennsylvania, that have been out of reach at the presidential level.

5

REDISTRICTING AND THE ART OF GERRYMANDERING

By Martin Frost

In the 2012 elections for the House, Democratic candidates received about 1.4 million more votes nationwide than Republican candidates, and yet Republicans won a 17-vote margin in the House.[18] How did this happen?

It's a long story and not quite as simple as some pundits believe.

It started with the 1962 U.S. Supreme Court decision in *Baker vs. Carr* that redistricting for congressional seats must be on a "one man, one vote" basis (equal population within a state).[19]

It became real for me in 1990. My state of Texas would pick up three seats in 1992 as a result of population growth reflected in the 1990 census. The new lines would be drawn by the Texas legislature in 1991 during its regular session, and there was a significant (and justified) push for the creation of a new black district in my home base of the Dallas-Ft. Worth area. Creation of this district would dramatically affect the shape of my 24th district, which at that time contained much of the black population of Dallas.

And so I started asking the question, "Who is doing redistricting for the Democratic Party?" I wanted to talk to that person. I was stunned by the answer: "No one."

I quickly determined that there was one group, which was called IMPAC 2000 and headed by my House colleague Vic Fazio of California. However, the mandate of that organization was very limited – raise money for state legislative candidates who would be drawing the lines for their states during 1991 and 1992. This would later become a central issue (fast-forward to what the Republicans did in the 2000 and 2010 elections), but that was far from everything that needed to be done.

Congressman Fazio had just been named chair of the Democratic Congressional Campaign Committee, so there was no one to take the helm of IMPAC 2000. I volunteered, and we quickly broadened the scope of the organization to include providing legal and technical (line-drawing) help to Democratic congressional delegations and Democratic state legislators. The issue confronting line-drawers in Texas was one faced by every southern state: the black community was entitled to much greater representation because of the Voting Rights Act.

It was in Democrats' interest to come up with plans that created new black districts in the Deep South while at the same time preserving as many neighboring districts held by Democratic incumbents as possible. Republicans, on the other hand, saw an opportunity to eliminate a number of white southern incumbents by packing as many black voters as possible into a few districts, thus bleaching the surrounding districts held by Democrats. The survival of white southern Democrats would be determined by how many black voters were left over for their districts after the new majority black districts were created. Similar fights would also occur in northern states, where the issue was how to preserve existing black districts in city centers that were losing population without harming surrounding districts held by white congressmen. Again, the GOP response was to pack as many blacks as possible into these districts, thus bleaching the surrounding districts.

Like everything in politics, nothing was completely straightforward. The tide in the South had already started turning against white Democrats, and a number of them were older members near retirement in districts that were much harder to hold without a popular incumbent on the ballot. Moreover, Republicans' efforts to make their districts less hospitable to Democrats clearly would encourage some of these older members to retire.

REDISTRICTING AND THE ART OF GERRYMANDERING...

How out of racial balance were southern congressional districts at that time? As hard as it is to believe today, in 1991, none of the following southern states (all with significant black populations) had a single black member of Congress: Virginia, North Carolina, South Carolina, Florida, Alabama, and Arkansas. Texas, Tennessee, Louisiana, Mississippi and Georgia only had one black member each.

Members of the black community, loyal supporters of the Democratic Party nationally, justifiably clamored for representation. By the end of 1992, the following new black districts had been created in the South: Virginia (1), North Carolina (2), South Carolina (1), Florida (3), Alabama (1), Georgia (2 additional), Louisiana (1 additional), and Texas (1 additional). Of the 11 states of the Confederacy, only Arkansas was left without a black congressman. Hispanics also made some gains, but not nearly to the magnitude of those made by the black community.

Republicans followed a very shrewd strategy (made successful by Democratic disunity in some states) of trying to work in concert with local black politicians. Their pitch was simple: work with us and we will help you draw districts that a black cannot lose by making the black population so large that a white cannot win.

This had appeal to some black leaders who feared that state legislatures would draw majority black districts but without a sufficiently large black population, such that a black candidate could lose because of turnout differences between whites and blacks. Also, in some states there was resentment against white Democratic legislators who had failed to draw black districts in the past, either out of lingering prejudice or because they were trying to protect incumbent white Democratic congressmen by spreading the black vote around among several districts.

Some black leaders understood the games Republicans were playing and supported an "all of the above strategy" that created new winnable black districts while at the same time protecting surrounding white incumbents so that the national Democratic Party would still have a majority in Congress. Others didn't care about the national party and only wanted a guarantee of new black seats.

Since most southern legislatures were still controlled by Democrats in 1991, this was the only strategy Republicans could realistically pursue. A

New Yorker article cited Republican redistricting strategist Ben Ginsburg as calling this GOP strategy to work with blacks to eliminate white Democrats "Project Ratfuck."[20] Republicans also used court challenges in some instances (and threatened court challenges in others) as leverage for what they hoped to achieve.

IMPAC 2000, initially operating with a team of volunteer lawyers and software provided by Mark Gersh and the National Committee for an Effective Congress (NCEC), drew districts state by state that accomplished both objectives – creating new minority districts and preserving as many white Democratic surrounding districts as possible, thus minimizing Democratic losses. Some delegations and legislatures took our advice and some others didn't. Without this effort, Democrats could have been shut out in the South during this cycle. IMPAC 2000 – with the help of its vice-chair, Alan Wheat, a black congressman from Missouri – was able to convince black politicians in some southern states of the need to maximize total Democratic representation while at the same time creating new minority seats. Georgia's Congressman John Lewis was also very helpful in carrying that message.

A major issue during the 1991-92 round of redistricting was the black percentage necessary to create a "minority opportunity" district under the Voting Rights Act. Black leaders felt a demographic that was 65% black was necessary to elect a black candidate. Republicans pushed for such districts because it packed black voters and bleached adjoining districts. Democrats generally took the position that the percentage should vary from state to state, based on past turnout patterns and the amount of racially polarized voting. For instance, there was little dispute that 65% should be the standard for Mississippi because of racial polarization and voter turnout differences in that state. But in other states, like Texas and North Carolina, a hard and fast 65% was not required.

This issue was litigated throughout the decade. It is now generally accepted that an effective black district can be less than 65% black, but the standard remains higher for Hispanic districts because of low turnout and non-citizen issues among Hispanic voters. The minority percentage is critical because the higher the minority makeup of "minority opportunity" districts, the fewer minorities there will be available for surrounding districts.

After a monumental effort by both sides, redistricting was basically a partisan draw in 1991-92. However, the retirement of senior conservative white Democratic incumbents in the South and a growing GOP tide in that region tipped some districts to the GOP during the decade. Also, the South gained some additional seats as a result of population shifts during that time, and the new seats tended to be in GOP suburban growth areas.

The next two rounds of redistricting – following the 2000 and 2010 censuses – were a different story. Republicans won both those rounds for several reasons.

Firstly, states such as Florida, Ohio, and Pennsylvania, which are narrowly divided in statewide elections, had congressional delegations that tilted heavily toward Republicans. In both cycles, they had partisan control in several battleground states. By 2011, the McCain-Feingold campaign finance reform law, enacted in 2002, eliminated soft money from party committees. The Democratic redistricting vehicle, IMPAC 2000, which functioned through the 2011-12 redistricting cycle, had been largely funded with soft money, whereas the Republicans wisely brought their redistricting effort in-house at the Republican National Committee, where they had adequate funding for the fights ahead. Democrats did not take this approach with the Democratic National Committee and had a harder time putting together the necessary resources for these battles. Also, the GOP put its hard-charging attorney, Ben Ginsburg, in charge of its redistricting strategy and he did a masterful job for them.

Secondly, Republicans had made significant gains in state legislative seats in both the South and the Midwest. They basically took no prisoners and used their newly-won majorities to the maximum extent possible. Democrats, on the other hand, wasted their majorities in states like California and Illinois because of pressure from Democratic members of Congress to enter bipartisan incumbent protection deals preserving the status quo between the two parties. The Democrats clearly left seats on the table in those two states. By the time they corrected this in Illinois following the 2010 census, it was too late. Democrats in California never agreed to change their approach but ultimately won some additional seats as a result of a statewide referendum (pushed by Republican governor Arnold Schwarzenegger) that took redistricting away from the state legislature in the post-2010 round and put it in the hands of a nonpartisan commission.

During both the 2001 and 2011 rounds of redistricting, Republicans used their legislative majorities in Pennsylvania, Ohio, Michigan, and Florida to redraw maps to their advantage. During the 2001 round, they cut their margins pretty thin, trying to absolutely maximize the total number of seats they would gain. This came back to bite them in the good Democratic year of 2006, when Democrats retook the House and Republicans lost some of these newly-gained seats. It does not appear that they made the same mistake during the 2011 redistricting round.

Also, once Republicans started winning control of southern legislatures, they drew maps maximizing their advantage with the not-too-subtle objective of eliminating every white Democrat in the South. They have largely accomplished this. As of 2014, the only white Democratic congressmen from southern states are two from northern Virginia, one from North Carolina (who represents the Research Triangle district), three from Texas (all of whom represent majority Hispanic districts), one from Georgia, two from Tennessee (one of whom represents a majority black district), and six from Florida (four of whom represent districts with significant Jewish populations). The effect of minimizing white southern Democrats with districts containing 20% to 30% black voters was to eliminate moderates who needed to vote with the Democratic Party in the House on some issues to be responsive to their black constituents.

This brings us to ground zero – the redistricting fight in Texas that directly affected me. This battle, which was divided into three parts, illustrates the creativity employed by Democrats and the tenacity expressed by Republicans on the issue of congressional redistricting.

The first round occurred during 1991. The Texas population had grown by enough in the previous decade to merit three new seats, increasing the size of the delegation from 27 to 30. There was little disagreement over the fact that one of these new seats would be an African American district in the Dallas-Ft. Worth area and another would be a Hispanic district in south Texas. At that time, Democrats occupied a majority of the Texas districts – 19 out of 27. Republicans felt they were entitled to a greater proportion of the state's seats since the last Democratic presidential candidate to carry

Texas had been Jimmy Carter in 1976 and Republicans were very competitive in statewide offices. The governor, Ann Richards, was a Democrat and Democrats controlled both houses of the legislature. After considerable controversy, the legislature adopted a plan that drew a new black district in the Dallas area (won in 1992 by Eddie Bernice Johnson) and also drew the 24th district, which I represented, around the new district in such a way that it would continue to be Democratic.

The drafting of the plan that both created three new minority districts in Texas and preserved the existing districts of all of the white incumbent Democrats was a classic example of what could be done when all members of a state Democratic delegation worked together for the common good. Unfortunately, we could not get other southern delegations to cooperate in the same manner. It is worth telling this story.

The delegation spent months putting together a plan that achieved these objectives. There was a lot of give and take before it was over. The plan created three new minority districts – the 28th (a Hispanic district in south Texas), the 29th (a Hispanic district in the Houston area), and the 30th (a black district in Dallas). In order to create these three new minority districts, a number of incumbent white Democrats had to give up some favorable territory and run in new districts that were not as favorable toward them. They included John Bryant of Dallas, Pete Geren of Ft. Worth, Chet Edwards of Waco, Charlie Wilson and Jim Chapman of east Texas, Jack Brooks of Beaumont, and me. All were reelected in 1992, though Brooks ultimately lost his seat in the GOP sweep of 1994. Charlie Wilson, one of the most colorful Texans ever, told a key Democratic staffer, "I just took one for the team."

The plan yielded 21 Democrats and nine Republicans. Republicans were floored when the Republican Justice Department (under President George H.W. Bush) pre-cleared the plan, thus making it harder to attack in the courts. As it turned out, all three of the new districts for Texas were minority districts (two Hispanic and one black), and the districts of a number of rural white conservative Democrats were protected. Some of the white Democrats' seats ultimately switched to the Republicans after the incumbents retired, but those changes were not caused primarily by redistricting.

Fast-forward to 2001. Texas gained two seats as a result of population growth; however, by then, all the statewide offices were held by Republicans and the legislature was deadlocked, with Democrats controlling the House and Republicans controlling the Senate. The legislature was unable to agree on a plan, and a race to the courthouse ensued. Democrats won the procedural battle and the case wound up in a favorable federal court in east Texas. The court ultimately adopted a plan that resulted in a 17-15 advantage for Democrats, much to the consternation of national Republicans. The 24th district that I represented was once again preserved as a Democratic district, and white conservative rural Democrats who survived the 1994 GOP sweep had their districts protected.

Republicans were livid and determined to take seats away from Democrats. The Republicans swept the Texas legislature in 2002, which set the stage for House Majority Leader Tom DeLay to convince the legislature to take the unusual step of re-redistricting Texas congressional seats during the 2003 session. There was virtually no precedent anywhere in the nation for this action – redistricting historically was only done once in a decade unless the courts compelled districts to be redrawn. Democrats did not go down without a fight. First, Democratic House members and then Democratic senators fled the state to break a quorum so the Texas legislature could not pass a new plan. Ultimately they lost their fight during a special session called by Republican governor Rick Perry.

The very partisan gerrymandered plan passed by the legislature radically changed districts held by Democrats Max Sandlin, Jim Turner, Chet Edwards, Charlie Stenholm, Ralph Hall, Nick Lampson, and me. Sandlin, Stenholm, Lampson, and I were all defeated in the next election. Turner retired and was replaced by a Republican, and Hall switched parties, netting the Republicans six seats. Only Edwards survived, though he eventually lost his seat to a Republican after the next round of redistricting. This represented the largest single swing in the nation between Democrats and Republicans and laid the groundwork for Republicans to hold the House until the Democratic sweep in 2006 and to recapture the House in 2010. Texas lost political clout as a result of the 2003 re-redistricting. DeLay's plan cost the Texas delegation three important committee chairmanships when the party retook the House in 2006: I would have chaired Rules, Stenholm would have chaired Agriculture, and Turner would have chaired Homeland Security.

The plan pushed through the legislature by DeLay still had to face pre-clearance by the Justice Department, again controlled by a Republican administration. The key professional staff in Justice wanted to reject the plan, but they were overruled by political appointments. DeLay assured nervous members of the Texas legislature that his plan, which clearly diminished the clout of minority voters in Texas, would get Justice Department approval. He had it wired, he told them. And apparently he did.

An internal memorandum by the Justice Department subsequently revealed that its voting rights experts had firmly concluded that DeLay's plan illegally reduced minority voting strength to advance the partisan goals of DeLay and Texas Republicans.[21] They found, among other things, that the new redistricting map was "an impermissible retrogression in the position of minorities with respect to their effective exercise of the electoral franchise," and that the state failed to follow in two congressional districts – including mine – its traditional redistricting principles preserving communities of interest.

"Even though all seven of the Voting Rights lawyers who examined the Texas map found grounds to file an objection based on south Texas and north Texas, they were overruled by the DOJ political appointees," concluded my longtime chief of staff, Matt Angle, a Ft. Worth native. The Supreme Court, on a 7-2 vote, subsequently upheld the basic plan. But a separate majority ruled that the west Texas district held by Republican Henry Bonilla needed to be redrawn because it unlawfully harmed Hispanic voters. In the next election, under a redrawn district, Hispanic voters replaced Bonilla with Democrat Ciro Rodriguez. That left the delegation with 19 Republicans and 13 Democrats.

DeLay, meanwhile, suffered his own downfall. In the midst of the legal challenges to the redistricting map, he was indicted by the Travis County (Austin, Texas) prosecutor on criminal charges related to corporate campaign contributions to Texas Republicans in the 2002 election. That forced him to step down as House majority leader in September 2005, and he resigned from the House nine months later. He was convicted in 2011, but an appeals court subsequently threw out the jury's verdict.

From my perspective, the Texas redistricting battle was reminiscent of the French and Indian War's exhausting 1759 Battle of Quebec, in which both the British general (Wolfe) and the French general (Montcalm) were killed. DeLay and I – after leading our forces in combat – made our separate and painful departures less than two years apart. With their partisan advantage in Texas, Republicans retained disproportionate control of the congressional delegation. But in the long run, the huge increase in Hispanic voters and other demographic changes seem likely to produce a Democratic comeback.

Following another round of redistricting in 2011 that netted the state four additional seats, one of which was a second minority opportunity district in the Dallas-Ft. Worth area, Republicans held a 24-12 margin in Texas congressional seats, which was critical to their slim 17-vote margin in the House after the 2012 elections. In both 2003 and 2011, Republicans used their redistricting muscle in the Texas legislature to pick up most of the new seats gained during these two cycles. Thus, as of 2014, Democrats hold only 33% of the congressional seats in a state where statewide Democratic candidates routinely win in the range of 44% of the vote.

Texas Democrats fought the good fight in Texas, but they were eventually overwhelmed by a relentlessly aggressive partisan effort by the GOP.

This chart[22] shows comparable dramatic shifts in partisan and demographic control of House seats throughout the South during the past three decades:

Southern House Seats

Year	GOP	White D	Black D	Hispanic D
1982	34	76	2	4
1992	49	54	17	4
2004	84	26	18	5
2012	98	16	18	6

The effect of all this partisan redistricting nationwide has been to create districts where the real action is often in the primary rather than in the general election. Republican incumbents live in mortal fear of challenges from the right in their own primaries, and Democrats face the same fear from the left. The effect of this is to drive the two parties to the extremes and make it difficult for members of either party to reach a compromise position in the middle. Less partisan districts (i.e., less gerrymandering) would have resulted in more truly swing districts, resulting in more moderates in both parties.

There are observers who feel that the partisan nature of districts is driven somewhat by housing patterns in addition to redistricting. Racial minorities tend to live together and create districts that vote overwhelmingly Democratic, and white suburban Republicans tend to live together among people of like political philosophies who vote Republican – but not in as large percentages as the residents of Democratic districts. They point to these patterns as one reason that Democrats can outvote Republicans nationally and still not win a majority of seats.

The difficulty with this analysis is that partisan redistricting that draws a circle around large numbers of Democratic minorities, thus leaving surrounding districts mixed but not as heavily Republican, limits the number of districts that Democrats can win, no matter how many people vote Democratic. There is an exception to every rule and it is conceivable the Democrats could still win a majority of unfairly-drawn districts if they could be the beneficiaries of a massive national sweep. But it won't happen very often, and thus the electoral process remains distorted because of partisan redistricting.

This brings us full circle. Were the 2012 elections results, which found one party winning the popular vote and the other party winning control of the House, the product of gerrymandering or housing patterns?

Let's look at history as a guide in answering that question.

In the 36 elections for the House since the year I was born (1942), there are only four examples of one party winning the popular vote but losing the election.

The first was in 1942, when Democrats won 222 House seats while the Republicans won 50.7% of the vote for the House. This was the midterm election during FDR's third term, when the outcome of World War II was still in doubt. The second example was in 1952, when Republicans won 221 House seats and yet the Democrats won the popular vote 49.8% to 49.3%. The third time was in 1996, when Republicans won 227 seats and the Democrats won the popular vote 48.22% to 48.15%. The final time was in 2012, when the Republicans won 234 seats and the Democrats won the popular vote 48.8% to 47.6%. There was not a single case of one party winning control of the House and the other party winning the popular vote in consecutive elections. If this phenomenon occurs again, we may have a pattern that can only be explained by gerrymandering.

CONCLUDING NOTE BY TOM AND MARTIN

In our final chapter, we recommend that Congress pass legislation to end partisan gerrymandering by requiring states to use bipartisan commissions when redrawing congressional lines.

Shown below are two pieces of supporting evidence:

1. A chart demonstrating how partisan redistricting in three states controlled by Republicans and carried by President Obama produced a number of Republican congressional districts that far exceeded the Republican percentage of the vote statewide in each of these states in the 2012 elections. Democrats have done similar things in states where they controlled the process in previous redistricting cycles.

Vote for Congress (2012) – Three States in Midwest[23]

	Pennsylvania	Michigan	Ohio
D	2,793,538	2,487,243	2,412,451
R	2,710,070	2,238, 540	2,620,251
House D Seats	5	5	4
House R Seats	13	9	12

Three-State Totals

	Total Votes	Percentage of Votes	Number of Seats	Percentage of Seats
D	7,693,232	50.4%	14	29.9%
R	7,568,861	49.6%	34	70.8%

2. Maps showing extreme examples of gerrymandered districts.[24]

Illinois 4th

Illinois 7th

North Carolina 12th

Ohio 9th

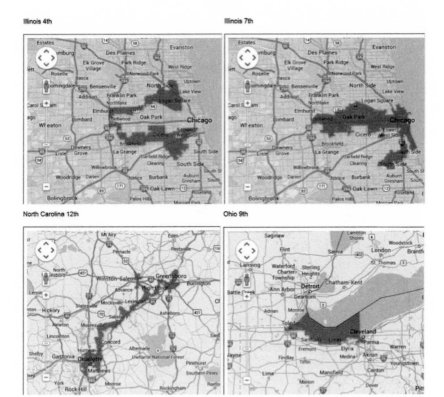

We rest our case.

6

MONEYBALL

By Martin Frost and Rich Cohen

The single most important key to understanding what has happened to
the American political process in recent years involves the evolution of campaign finance laws as passed by Congress and interpreted by the federal
courts. Bringing some order out of this chaotic situation is also the biggest
challenge for people who want to see democracy work.25

This chapter is divided into three parts: (1) a discussion of the current
state of the law and how it is currently playing out in our elections; (2) a
history of legislative and judicial developments in campaign finance during
the 40 years since the post-Watergate passage of the first modern piece of
comprehensive legislation dealing with how federal campaigns are financed;
and (3) some suggestions for remedying the situation, which will be
described in more detail in the final chapter of this book.

To get a complete picture of outside group spending in our elections, we
need to look at a range of groups and what portion of their spending is
reported to the Federal Election Commission (FEC) or to the Internal Revenue Service (IRS), and in what detail. These groups include the following:

1. Super PACs that report all their spending to the FEC and report the
names of their donors and amounts contributed. These super PACs fall into

several categories as detailed below. They may accept unlimited contributions from individuals, corporations, and unions.

2. A variety of entities such as non-profit 501(c)(4) and 501(c)(6) organizations, corporations, unions, issue-based organizations, and business associations that report certain types of their spending (but not their donors) to the FEC. These groups report only their spending on express advocacy independent expenditures (ads saying "vote for" or "vote against" a certain candidate) and, in the case of nonprofits, also expenditures on "electioneering communications" (less specific than express advocacy) within 60 days of a general election or 30 days of a primary. Individuals may also make express advocacy expenditures which are reported to the FEC. The entities may accept unlimited contributions from individuals, corporations, and unions. Some of these entities such as corporations and unions also contribute to super PACs.[26]

3. Nonprofit 501(c)(4) and 501(c)(6) organizations that do not spend all their money on express advocacy or on electioneering communications within 60 days of a general election or 30 days of a primary do make general reports to the IRS but do not publicly disclose donors. These groups do not report this portion of their spending to the FEC. They may accept unlimited contributions from individuals, corporations, and unions. Nonprofits established by the secretive Koch brothers, for example, report "express advocacy" expenses to the FEC but not the remainder of their expenses, which may go to grassroots organizing and other types of ads outside the 60-/30-day window. It is believed that during the 2011-12 cycle, Koch brothers nonprofits reported only about 10% of their expenditures to the FEC ($33.5 million spent by Americans for Prosperity on express advocacy out of about $400 million raised by all of their entities).

In a significant development, the Koch brothers empire confirmed on June 16, 2014, that it was establishing its own super PAC – Freedom Partners Action Fund – that would register with the FEC and finance express advocacy ads during the 2014 election cycle. This PAC, unlike other Koch brothers entities, would disclose all its donors to the FEC. It appeared that the bulk of Koch activities would continue to be done through nonprofit corporations that do not disclose their donors to either the FEC or the IRS. The initial budget for the Koch super PAC was $15 million, with total Koch brothers political spending in 2014 projected to be $290 million, according to *Politico.*[27]

Let's start with super PACs, which really first came into their own in the 2012 election cycle and operated full bore during the 2014 congressional elections.

A super PAC is a political action committee that may only make independent expenditures, meaning it cannot make direct contributions to candidates or parties but can engage in unlimited political spending independently of a campaign as long as it doesn't coordinate its activities with a candidate or party committee.

It would be unusual, though not impossible, for a super PAC to receive both labor and corporate contributions, as those groups are usually on opposite sides of issues and campaigns. The normal situation is for a super PAC to receive contributions either from corporations and individuals or from labor unions and individuals. Interestingly, wealthy individuals give much more to super PACs than do corporations, as many publicly-traded companies shy away from publicity about their political activities using corporate funds. Corporations, however, do give significant amounts to 501(c)(4) nonprofits, which don't have to disclose their donors.

There are many different types of super PACs. Some are set up to help a party's House or Senate candidates (like the Democrats' House Majority PAC). Others broadly advance a party's electoral agenda (like Karl Rove's American Crossroads). Still others support a particular presidential or congressional candidate, like the ones that supported Newt Gingrich (Winning Our Future, funded mostly by Sheldon Adelson), Barack Obama (Priorities USA Action), and Mitt Romney (Restore our Future) during the 2012 election. And some support candidates favoring a particular policy like environmental issues (the NextGen Climate Action PAC, set up by Tom Steyer) or gun control (Independence USA PAC, set up by Michael Bloomberg).

Donors who don't want their names disclosed can turn to the groups organized under Sections 501(c)(4) or 501(c)(6) of the Internal Revenue Code. These are the entities generally described as "dark money." Section 501(c)(4) entities operate under rules that require that they have a "primary purpose" of promoting social welfare so that, at most, 49% of the money they raise can be devoted to politics. This is a viable option for publicity-shy donors, but it doesn't provide as much bang for the buck as giving to a super PAC or directly to a candidate. Section 501(c)(6) entities promote a particular business interest.

Organizers of super PACs offer funding through nonprofits as an alternative for donors who want their names kept out of the newspaper. Karl Rove's super PAC, American Crossroads, which reported $104 million in independent expenditures to the FEC for the 2012 cycle, had a sister 501(c)(4) group called Crossroads GPS, which reported almost $70 million in independent expenditures to the FEC for that cycle.[28] Under current law, names of the donors to American Crossroads had to be reported to the FEC and names of contributors to Crossroads GPS did not. Rove and others offer one-stop shopping.

So how did this all play out in the 2012 elections?

The FEC, in an April 19, 2013, press release, reported that independent expenditures on express advocacy during the 2012 election cycle totaled $1.250 billion.[29] Of this total, $666.7 million was for congressional races, and $583.8 million was spent on the presidential campaign. A full $606.8 million was made by "soft-money" super PACs that had to disclose donors to the FEC; $300.4 million came from corporations, unions, and groups like nonprofit 501(c)(4)s that must disclose expenditures but not donors to the FEC; and $252 million was made by party political committees that rely on "hard money" contributions (made in accordance with strict federal contribution limits) that are fully disclosed to the FEC.[30] This, of course, does not include the hundreds of millions of soft-money contributions to nonprofits not required to make disclosures to the FEC when they engage in campaign activities not classified as "express advocacy."

In addition to reporting independent expenditures to the FEC, all 501(c)(4) groups are required to report their total contributions and total expenditures to the IRS but are not required to publicly disclose individual donors' names and amounts given. (This information is reported to the IRS on a separate Schedule B, which is not made public.) And as was previously mentioned, it is difficult to track the total amount of money spent by nonprofits because they only disclose to the FEC that portion of their expenditures going to "express advocacy."

The significance of all this is that candidates and political parties have now largely lost control of the message in campaigns. In many cases, the funding for a federal campaign is now one-third from the candidate, one-third from the candidate's political party (which includes both hard-money independent expenditures and soft-money expenditures from party-related super PACs), and one-third from outside voices like non-party super PACs and 501(c)(4)s. In some cases, money spent by non-party super PACs and 501(c)(4)s is much greater than one-third of the total money spent in the campaign. While politicians and the public continue to debate the efficacy of money in politics, a new regimen has haphazardly taken effect.

Under current law, candidates must raise money in relatively small amounts (election-cycle maximums of $5,200 from individuals and $10,000 from federal multi-candidate PACs). Political parties, too, must raise money in relatively small amounts ($32,400 from individuals and $15,000 from multi-candidate federal PACs). But super PACs and nonprofits can raise money in unlimited amounts from individuals, corporations, and labor unions.

As previously mentioned, publicly-traded corporations are publicity-shy and don't want their names connected with individual candidates, who may take strong stands on controversial issues like gay rights or abortion. Their contributions are more likely to be made through 501(c)(4)s, which currently face no public disclosure requirements, rather than disclosed though super PAC contributions.

Basketball star Michael Jordan, a spokesman for NIKE, Inc., summed this up very succinctly when asked why he was not supporting a fellow black North Carolinian, Democratic Senate candidate Harvey Gantt, in 1990. He said, "Republicans buy sneakers too."[31] In 2011, Target was picketed when it contributed $150,000 to an organization supporting a candidate opposed to gay marriage.

That brings us to the question of how all this came about in the first place.

Prior to 1971, relatively few laws regulated campaign finances, and those laws' chief focus had been to prevent corruption and bribery by special interests. These claims were often difficult to prove in court, let alone in election campaigns.

The Democrat-controlled Congress, with broad bipartisan support, crafted the Federal Election Campaign Act of 1974 in the midst of its investigation of the Watergate scandal and subsequent impeachment of President Nixon, which included charges based on his 1972 reelection campaign's financial abuses. The House passed the bill on August 8, 1974, a few hours before Nixon announced that he would resign at noon the next day.32

Many lawmakers were initially reluctant to support the new restrictions on both contributions and spending. But the growing clamor for Nixon's impeachment cast unfavorable light on how money was spent in his 1972 campaign; insurance tycoon W. Clement Stone, for example, contributed more than $2 million. That spurred the far-reaching legislative action, which superseded a more limited statute that had been written in 1971.

The more sweeping Senate-passed version included public financing for congressional as well as presidential elections. When the bill moved to the House, many members strongly objected that public financing of their campaigns would boost challengers; the Senate eventually backed down.

The ultimate $70,000 ceiling on House elections (and a separate $70,000 for primaries) had the beneficial effect for many incumbents of limiting their opponents' campaign activities, while the officeholders enjoyed their growing office perquisites. The ceiling for Senate elections was 12 cents per voter or $150,000, whichever was greater, plus 8 cents per voter or $100,000 in Senate primaries. Even without the subsequent inflation, those campaign limits – if they had been upheld by the Supreme Court – would have paled in comparison to the several-million-dollar expenditures that have become common practice in House elections and the spending in the double-digit millions for Senate elections.

The public financing of presidential elections was accompanied by initial spending ceilings of $20 million in the general election and $10 million for all primaries. The inflation-adjusted amount for the fall campaigns eventually reached $74 million in 2004. But Barack Obama's 2008 rejection of public financing has likely ended those presidential campaign subsidies.

Other features of the 1974 law required disclosure of campaign receipts and expenditures and created an independent Federal Election Commission to audit and publicize the reports from the candidates and PACs.

Nixon had opposed the bill. His successor, Gerald Ford, expressed some reservations but signed the final version two months after taking office with the politically apt comment, "The times demand this legislation."

The law created a whole new world in terms of how money could be raised. It provided that individuals could contribute $1,000 to a candidate's primary campaign and $1,000 to a candidate's general election. It also established multi-candidate PACs (formed with voluntary contributions from labor union members; employees of corporations; members of trade associations, such as the realtors or homebuilders; or members of interest groups, such as environmental organizations). These PACs could contribute up to $5,000 for a primary and $5,000 for a general election.

Further, there was an aggregate limit on how much an individual could contribute directly to federal candidates during every two-year election cycle and on contributions to all national party committees during that cycle. There was no aggregate limit on how much multi-candidate PACs could contribute to all federal candidates. Congress also set a separate $1,000 ceiling for individual expenditures on behalf of a candidate.

Some of these amounts (for individual contributions, and the aggregate limits) were adjusted by later legislation and by an inflation factor. By the start of the 2014 cycle, an individual could give to a federal candidate $2,600 for the primary and $2,600 for the general election. The $5,000 amount that a multi-candidate PAC could give to a federal candidate for the primary or the general election has never been changed. The aggregate limits were increased also, but the U.S. Supreme Court ruled in 2014 that those limits were an unconstitutional violation of the First Amendment's free speech guarantee.[33]

When the Supreme Court subsequently overturned the sharp spending limits in congressional campaigns, the real impact of the new law was significantly reduced. That Supreme Court case, *Buckley v. Valeo*, had some unusual features.[34] The plaintiff was James Buckley, the first-term, conservative senator from New York (and the brother of better-known political commentator William Buckley). He was joined by multiple political advocacy groups – on both the left and right – who objected to restraints on their political activities. The defendant was Francis Valeo, the obscure secretary of the Senate who had the responsibility to collect Senate campaign reports. Essentially, the suit by a junior senator – who was defeated for reelection in 1976 – against a Senate staffer, with crews of lawyers on both sides, resulted in a Supreme Court decision that virtually rewrote the Federal Election Campaign Act.

In contrast to later campaign-finance cases, the *Buckley* decision did not reveal partisan patterns, either in coalitions among the justices or in their substantive ruling. All eight justices who heard the case agreed to at least part of the opinion; and each finding was broadly, though not unanimously, supported. Five of the justices issued widely varying individual statements that dissented from parts of the ruling. The ninth justice, John Paul Stevens, had joined the Supreme Court after the case had been argued.

Relying on the First Amendment free speech guarantees, the majority held that campaign spending is entitled to those protections. With its expenditure limits, the Campaign Act impermissibly reduced expression "by restricting the number of issues discussed, the depth of the explanation, and the size of the audience reached." The Court added, "Every means of communicating ideas in today's mass society requires the expenditure of money." The justices ruled that individuals could make unlimited independent expenditures for other candidates so long as the money was not a direct contribution. However, the Court left in place the contribution limits to individual federal candidates and committees.

The primacy of the First Amendment trumped the reformers' goal of setting campaign expenditure limits. Although the justices were seeking to protect the interests of all candidates, the reality – then and now – is that incumbents generally have far more access to funds than do challengers. Consequently, most lawmakers in both parties suffered little heartburn as a result of this decision. For those who objected, their only alternative to change the law would have been to ratify a constitutional amendment. But until recently, relatively few members of Congress have supported such a step.

In practical terms, the Court-drawn Federal Election Campaign Act – including its contribution limits and disclosure requirements – became widely accepted as the law of the land. Both parties and their supporters engaged in some experimentation and pushing of limits, including the development of "leadership PACs" to give senior members of Congress

more opportunity to contribute to candidates. And the parties found creative ways to support their candidates, especially those who lacked access to
large funding.

Also, under what survived after *Buckley*, there were no limits on "soft-
money" contributions to political parties – unlimited contributions from
individuals, corporations using treasury funds, and unions using dues
money. Over a period of time, parties found ways to use this source of
money for get-out-the-vote organizing campaigns and for issue ads that did
not specifically advocate the election or defeat of a particular candidate. Use
of the latter was perfected by the Democratic National Committee and
President Clinton during Clinton's re-election campaign in 1996. Donor
names and amounts of soft-money contributions had to be fully reported by
the parties.

But the reform groups outside of Congress – most of which were political liberals – were dissatisfied, especially with the growing role of party
funds. "Soft money" became a pejorative term referring to unregulated and
usually large contributions. The news media depicted soft money as "special-interest" funds that distorted the system. And the reformers developed
proposals to restrict its use.

Eventually, bipartisan supporters pushed their plan in Congress: Senator
John McCain and Congressman Chris Shays were Republicans, and Senator Russ Feingold and Congressman Marty Meehan were Democrats. All
were mavericks in some ways. McCain in particular had gained iconic status
– especially with many political reporters – in his 2000 bid for the Republican presidential nomination, which he labeled the "Straight Talk Express."

In the face of this "good government" appeal, which had strong backing
from editorial voices and prominent celebrities, proponents of the status
quo were hard-pressed to defend soft-money contributions. Some party-
building activities seemed entirely warranted and even necessary at that
time, and this feeling continues today. Still, Tom and Martin saw the ambiv-
alence from our respective party leadership positions from 1999 to 2002.
The leaders of both parties did little to prevent the Republican-controlled
House's passage of the proposal in both 1998 and 1999. At the time, they
were confident that the Republican-controlled Senate would pigeonhole
the bill.

Those dynamics changed after the 2000 election because of McCain's prominence and the 50-50 partisan tie in the Senate following that year's election. The Senate took up the bill in early 2001 without committee review and passed it after lengthy debate that was frequently a free-for-all. In particular, Senator Paul Wellstone, a Minnesota Democrat, won approval of his amendment to restrict eve-of-election issue advertising by nonprofit organizations. Critics called his proposal constitutionally suspect under the First Amendment. But it was approved narrowly, including by some Republicans who hoped that it would eventually scuttle the entire measure. All but three Democrats voted for final passage, as did 12 Republicans.[35]

In the House, many members in both parties had reservations about the Senate-passed bill. But the reformers increased the pressure by urging members to sign a discharge petition, an unusual House procedure that forces a bill to the House floor if a majority of members join the effort.

Many Republicans faced increasing pressure from their hometown newspapers to sign the discharge petition. The *New York Times, Los Angeles Times, Washington Post,* and other large urban newspapers wrote frequent editorials calling for reforms and listing the names of obstinate representatives of their readerships who refused to sign on.

For many representatives, the only times they would crack the news or editorial pages in Chicago or New York or Philadelphia – where over a dozen members of Congress represented each readership area – was when they received either an "attaboy" or a raspberry on the editorial page. So after a few negative editorials, the path of least resistance for these members was to sign the discharge petition. A look at the final vote indicates that most of the Republicans who voted yes were from metropolitan areas, where their newspapers of record were strongly committed to the legislation.

The effort was placed on hold following the 9/11 terrorist attacks. But it was revived early in 2002 when the discharge petition gained 218 signatures. That sent to the House floor a companion to the Senate-passed bill, with a few modest changes. It passed the House 240 to 189, with 41 Republicans and all but 12 Democrats voting in favor.[36] President George W. Bush, who had taken little interest in the measure, signed into law the Bipartisan Campaign Reform Act (BCRA) despite voicing some reservations.

BCRA made several significant changes in existing law. Firstly, it banned all soft-money contributions to political parties. Secondly, it included a 30-day/60-day blackout period for ads placed by nonprofit organizations like 501(c)(4)s prior to a primary or a general election if the ads mentioned a federal candidate by name. Thirdly, it increased from $1,000 to $2,000 the amount an individual could donate to a federal candidate per primary and general election. The latter change was supported by House Democratic Leader Dick Gephardt, who was preparing for another presidential run in 2004 and would benefit from the doubling of what individuals could give to his presidential effort.

Tom and Martin were outspoken critics of the McCain-Feingold legislation as it worked its way through Congress. Both took the position that the legislation would seriously weaken the role of national party committees, which have long been a centering force in American politics, and that it would force money into outside groups on the left and the right that would then control the public dialogue. Unfortunately for the country, this is exactly what has happened.

At the height of congressional consideration, Martin had the following exchange with a major proponent of the law (a rough paraphrase):

Martin: "Taking soft money away from the political parties will weaken the party system and push money to outside groups, who will then call the shots in campaigns."

Reformer: "We have a solution for that. We will ban television and radio advertising by outside groups in the weeks before a primary and the weeks before a general election."

Martin: "What if the courts reject that provision?"

Reformer: "Our lawyers tell us we will be okay."

The specific provision mentioned by this reformer banned broadcast "electioneering communications" that name a federal candidate and are paid for by 501(c)(4) social welfare groups within 30 days of a primary and 60 days of a general election. These groups could accept unlimited individual, corporate, and union funds.

That led to the inevitable court challenges. Political activists brought a series of cases. Initially, the Supreme Court upheld the law in a 5-4 decision. 37 But several internal factors were instrumental in creating change. After

William Rehnquist died in 2005, John Roberts replaced him as chief justice. Each was a skeptic about campaign-finance reform, but Roberts appeared to have a deeper interest. In 2006, when Samuel Alito replaced Sandra Day O'Connor, who had retired, it produced an outright reversal of views and the potential for a landmark 5-4 ruling by a new Court majority. The focus turned to Anthony Kennedy, the Court's swing justice, who had been a First Amendment stalwart on campaign finance issues.

In the case of *Federal Election Commission vs. Wisconsin Right to Life, Inc.*, the Supreme Court did in June 2007 exactly what Martin had feared.[38] The case was brought by a 501(c)(4) social welfare organization – Wisconsin Right to Life, Inc. (WRTL) – that sought to run ads asking voters to urge their senators to oppose filibusters of judicial nominees during the 30- and 60-day blackout periods. WRTL was covered by this provision since it received some corporate funds.

The Supreme Court, in this case, ruled that the ads could be aired. It arrived at this conclusion by drawing a distinction between two types of ads that mention federal candidates – issue ads discussing an issue before Congress, and express advocacy ads urging the election or defeat of a named candidate. These ads fell into the former category and were permissible even though partially paid for by corporate funds.

Three years later, the Supreme Court decision in *Citizens United vs. FEC*[39] drove a stake through the heart of what remained of the blackout period for ads paid partially by corporations and labor unions. In this case, also brought by a 501(c)(4) social welfare organization, the Court held that the blackout period was not valid even though the broadcast communications (ads promoting a derogatory movie about Hillary Clinton during the 2008 presidential primaries) clearly were express advocacy, something the Court had previously held was banned by McCain-Feingold. The "electioneering communications" ban was officially dead.

Not only did this ruling end the 30-day/60-day blackouts, it was so broadly written that it allowed corporations and labor unions to be involved directly in any type of express advocacy. The Court's rationale was that corporations and unions had a First Amendment free speech right to spend money expressing their political views.

This all came full circle in 2010, when the decision of the D.C. Circuit Court in *Speechnow.org vs. FEC* and two advisory opinions issued by the FEC provided the basis for everyone (individuals, corporations, and unions) to form super PACs to engage in independent express-advocacy expenditures on behalf of federal candidates, federal committees, and federal issues agendas, with these contributions fully reported to the FEC.

Throughout all this, the Court has upheld the McCain-Feingold ban on soft-money contributions to national party committees. It's the worst of both worlds. Political parties still can't take soft money, but outside groups can take unlimited amounts. The fairy tale that was little more than a fantasy in the first place has become our national nightmare.

But the *Citizens United* case brought a strong dissent from the four justices on the Court who had been nominated by Presidents Clinton and Obama. And that, in turn, encouraged House Democrats to push for a bill that, according to its sponsors, would limit the Court ruling. The Democratic-controlled House passed the so-called "Disclose" bill to require more complete reporting of campaign activity by corporations, unions, and other outside groups – which would include super PACs; but the Senate fell one vote short of overturning a filibuster later in 2010. With the Republican takeover of the House in that November's election, the proposal was shelved – for the time being, at least. Amid little apparent public concern, the McCain-Feingold restrictions on campaign advocacy have been largely nullified, except for the soft-money ban.

The Court ruling opened the door to wide campaign finance changes. Notably, that included the creation of "super PACs." Republicans and conservative groups moved more rapidly than Democrats to create such groups in the 2010 election; Democrats jumped on board in both the presidential and congressional elections of 2012, but Republicans maintained a big advantage in total money raised.

According to 2012 post-election data analyses, the largest super PACs were Restore our Future (which was sponsored by allies of Republican presidential nominee Mitt Romney) and American Crossroads (associated with Karl Rove); each spent more than $100 million. In addition, Rove's group raised millions through its 501(c)(4), Crossroads GPS. Other large Republican tax-exempt groups were the Koch brothers' Americans for Prosperity and the U.S. Chamber of Commerce.

It is difficult to determine exactly how much Americans for Prosperity spent because it didn't start filing independent expenditures reports with the FEC until late in the election cycle, when it started running express advocacy ads calling for President Obama's defeat. Some estimates are that Americans for Prosperity and other Koch-affiliated nonprofits spent $400 million during the cycle – much of it during a time when the ads did not qualify as "express advocacy" and were not subject to FEC disclosure.

Democrats focused their outside money on super PACs: chiefly, the Obama-allied Priorities USA Action, which spent $65 million, and two congressional groups – Majority PAC and House Majority PAC – which each spent more than $30 million. Separately, the more conventional Obama campaign was the biggest overall spender, with about $738 million.

In April 2014, the Supreme Court delivered a new jolt when it ruled unconstitutional the aggregate ceilings that limited the total amounts that contributors could donate to candidates, parties, and political action committees. The decision in *McCutcheon vs. FEC* did not affect the campaign law's contribution limits to an *individual* candidate, party, or PAC. Rather, with the same 5-to-4 majority as in the *WRTL* and *Citizens United* cases, Chief Justice Roberts wrote that contributions to an unlimited number of candidates are guaranteed by the First Amendment rights of free speech and political association. To the extent that the amount of individual contributions is restricted, Roberts added, "Congress may regulate campaign contributions to protect against corruption or the appearance of corruption."

The potential impact of the *McCutcheon* decision may be chiefly for what it portends. Relatively few donors reportedly had been meeting the $123,200 combined candidate and committee contribution ceiling in a two-year cycle. So it remains to be seen how many more would increase their aggregate contributions – while still complying with the limits of $2,600 to a candidate in a primary or general election, $5,000 to a PAC, and $32,400 to a national party committee.

Perhaps more intriguingly, while the "soft money" ban on contributions to parties remained in effect, it seems possible that the current Supreme Court majority could overturn other parts of McCain-Feingold. Notably,

some officials in both parties plus their lawyers have hoped that the two parties will regain some of their lost influence relative to the outside groups.
Still, some reformers hoped to drum up public support on the purported
evils of money in politics. They worry, for example, that new tools
unleashed by the Court rulings could result in developments such as "joint
fundraising committees" in which party groups accept multi-million-dollar
individual contributions. But it's hard to see why donors in either party
would contribute to hundreds of congressional campaigns where there is no
real contest.

Other Democrats encouraged a more sweeping response. Senate Democrats stepped up their support for a proposed constitutional amendment by
Senator Tom Udall of New Mexico that would, in effect, give Congress the
authority to overturn the series of Supreme Court decisions that have relied
on the First Amendment to protect unlimited spending on campaigns.
These would include *Buckley vs. Valeo* (on spending limits) and *Citizens
United* (on unlimited spending on express advocacy by corporations and
unions). Still, any constitutional amendment faces steep barriers: two-thirds
approval in both the House and Senate, plus ratification by three-fourths of
the states.

There might be other ways to circumvent indirectly these Supreme
Court decisions. Given the Court's shifting 5-4 majorities, the inevitable
upcoming vacancies will likely yield a renewed focus on campaign finance
law and perhaps changes in current rulings. For that matter, creative advocates and their lawyers might pose new arguments to the current justices.
Nor would the recent Court decisions prevent leading political players –
including the two national parties – from collaborating on their own
informal steps, such as increased disclosure or restrictions on dealing with
outside political groups.

Some reformers believe that the only way to resolve these problems is for
a political scandal that will result in fundamental campaign finance changes.
But such expectations have been voiced for many years, with no sign of the
apocalypse. The adverse impact for policy and politics seems unlikely to be
resolved unless and until both parties in Congress resume working with
each other.

The consequences of these decisions, however, have increased partisan polarization in Congress and led to more, not less, influence by special-interest groups.

Super PACs and interest groups now often play in primary elections in safe, partisan districts, while party committees generally stay away. In a safely Republican district, for example, more ideological groups such as Heritage Action, Freedom Works, and Club for Growth can put unlimited dollars behind a primary candidate while traditionally there has been no super PAC to buoy their opponents. Their endorsements become a sought-after commodity by GOP primary candidates and, when successful, a strong force within the caucus, often at odds with party leaders.

When these groups defeat a widely-respected incumbent or front-runner in a primary (Senator Dick Lugar of Indiana or Congressman Mike Castle of Delaware, for example), they put fear in other incumbents that if they do not toe the line with these groups, they could be the next casualties.

Tom remembers one congressman agonizing about voting to reopen the federal government after its shutdown. The member's sympathies were with the leadership, but he had the practical problem of an announced Tea Party opponent with a small electoral base. The three conservative super PACs mentioned above were scoring the vote and recommending a no vote. "I cannot afford to have them target me," the member confided. So he took the path of least resistance and voted no, reasoning that the vote was going to pass anyway and his support was not required.

Unfortunately, this reasoning is oft-repeated by members of both parties, making it more difficult for party leaders to lead and rendering compromises more difficult to achieve and governing a casualty.

Concluding Note

Sometimes in politics truth is stranger than fiction.

When super PACs were just getting started in 2012, nationally-known humorist Calvin Trillin (incidentally, Martin's wife's cousin) wrote a satirical piece for the *New York Times* on the requirement that there be no coordination between a candidate and a super PAC supporting the candidacy.[40]

In the piece, Trillin discussed a mythical super PAC, "America the Super," set up by the mother of mythical candidate Jeff Gold, who was running for the Senate. Trillin interviewed the PAC chief executive (the candidate's mother) on the question of coordination.

Trillin: "Well, you do understand the assumption some have that there might be more contact than the spirit of the law intends there to be, given your closeness with Mr. Gold."

Super PAC CEO: "My closeness? What do you mean by my closeness?"

Trillin: "Because you're, well, his … "

CEO: "Because I'm his mother?"

Trillin: "Well, yes, because you're his mother, it's natural for people to assume that the two of you often talk – "

CEO: "He never calls. He never writes." (Trillin didn't need to add that this is a classic Jewish mother complaint about a son.)

And then, during the 2014 campaign, we found out that Trillin's mythical super PAC wasn't so mythical after all. *USA Today* reported on July 18, 2014, that Space PAC, a super PAC supporting the candidacy of Florida Democratic congressional candidate Gabriel Rothblatt, had raised $225,000 – all of it contributed by the candidate's parent, Martine Rothblatt.[41]

Also, the *Boston Herald* reported on August 6, 2014, that Shirley Grossman, the mother of Massachusetts Democratic candidate for governor Steve Grossman, gave $100,000 to a super PAC supporting her son's candidacy (Mass Forward PAC).[42] Mrs. Grossman, 92, told the *Herald*, "I believe in Steve. He's well-educated, honest, experienced, and all of the ideas he has are great." Candidate Grossman insisted that he'd had no prior knowledge of his mother's contribution.

And this was a bipartisan phenomenon in 2014. On July 18, 2014, the *Washington Post* reported two examples on the Republican side.[43] According to the *Post*, Mike Turner, a candidate for Congress in a Republican primary in Oklahoma, was supported by a super PAC funded by $135,000 from his mother and grandfather. Ben Sasse, a Republican candidate for the Senate in Nebraska, was supported by Ensuring a Conservative Nebraska, a super PAC funded by a $100,000 contribution from his great-uncle, Rupert Dunklau. "I'm his great-uncle, and that's the reason," Dunklau said.

As cousin Calvin found out, you can't make this stuff up.

TOM'S RESPONSE

In essence, the so-called "reforms" passed by previous Congresses have had the net effect of imposing ceilings on an individual's contributions to candidates (the 1974 post-Watergate reforms) and moving campaign dollars away from the political parties (McCain-Feingold). As I asked during the debates on Shays-Meehan (the House version of McCain-Feingold), "Where do you think this money is going to go? Do you think that by eliminating certain contributions to the parties, which have been the centering forces in American politics for 200 years, they will simply disappear?"

The answer, of course, is that the so-called soft money didn't disappear. It found its way back into the system, in other ways. Tax-exempt 527 organizations were its first manifestation, and these groups tended to favor Democrats at first. When Republicans cried foul and sought clarifying amendments, Democrats were not eager to move forward.

Then came the blockbuster *Citizens United* decision. Independent groups and super PACs sprang to the forefront, with the GOP and conservative-leaning groups leading the way. Now it was Democrats crying foul and Republicans holding fast. Many of the new entrants into the campaign discourse are entirely unregulated and their donors undisclosed. The result has been to turn campaign-finance reform efforts on their head. A subsequent discussion with Chris Shays, the House sponsor of the reforms, revealed that he regretted the way his efforts had turned out. Today, special interests have never been stronger, the parties have never been weaker, and the political process has never been so polarized.

Sometimes, the Law of Unintended Consequences makes a mockery of legislators' noblest efforts. With the elimination of soft money and movement of money away from the parties and candidates, ideological and special-interest groups have filled the vacuum and political candidates have reacted accordingly. Combine that with the now numerous single-party districts and the ideological media models, and this threesome has proved combustible for a political process once dependent on compromise and civility.

Moreover, as online contributions have replaced the old postal solicitations for campaign money, red-meat messaging has flourished and been rewarded. Where else can a congressman yell, "You lie!" during the president's State of the Union address and rake in nearly a million dollars in campaign funds online in the next week? At least those dollars were subject to federal limits and transparency rules.

And finally, the Federal Election Commission has fallen into complete disarray, as commissioners vote their partisan biases in 3-3 votes on even minimal efforts to clarify these evolving court decisions and technological advancements.

7

ALL POLITICS IS NO LONGER LOCAL

By Tom Davis

Tip O'Neill, the legendary House Speaker, devotes a chapter of his book *Man of the House* to the title, "All Politics is Local." He recalls his race for the Cambridge City Council, the only race he ever lost, after which his father noted that he had received a tremendous vote in other areas of the city but hadn't worked hard enough in his own backyard. His dad's advice? "All politics is local."

O'Neill goes on to note that the lesson also applies to Congress. He writes, "You can be the most important congressman in the country, but you had better not forget the people back home." Tip recalls that many good members of Congress arrived in Washington and became so focused on important national issues that they lost their connection to their own constituents, and learned this lesson the hard way.

But as the saying goes, "that was then and this is now." In the evolution of American politics over the past 30 years, the "local" aspect of winning elections, though still relevant, has taken a back seat to party affiliation and ideological orientation. Members with strong local ties to their constituencies have been displaced by voters who feel that party identity and how it relates to the national leadership and national issues are more important than simply liking their local representatives.

For example, it would be hard to find members of Congress more in tune with their constituencies than Democrat Gene Taylor from Mississippi's Gulf Coast. Elected in a special election in 1989 after the GOP incumbent died in a plane crash, Taylor held the seat for 20 years by large electoral margins.

In 2008, while Obama received 32% of the vote (his lowest percentage in the state) at the top of the ticket in the 4th congressional district, Gene Taylor received 74.5% of the vote for his reelection. Taylor had received less than 60% of the vote only once, in 1996, but had recovered and had been polling over 70% consistently since that time.

Hurricane Katrina struck a devastating blow to his district and to Taylor himself. His own house, more than 100 years old, was washed away, along with his neighborhood. He personally rebuilt his home and led the fight against the insurance industry, which claimed that flooding, not wind, was responsible for the damage to thousands of homes along the coast. That experience deepened his personal connection with his constituents.

But his popularity and connection to his constituency just weren't enough in 2010, in an off-year election when reaction to Obama's health care bill was at its zenith. Taylor was washed out of his seat by a Republican tide even though he'd voted against Obamacare, the Dodd-Frank banking bill, and other Democratic initiatives. He had long been the most conservative Democrat in the House, had voted to impeach President Clinton, was endorsed by the NRA, and had a solid pro-life voting record.

But after 20 years, Taylor had gotten careless. In 2007, he was a rare Democrat who voted against Nancy Pelosi for Speaker, sensing – correctly – that his constituents along the Mississippi coast would not find her San Francisco-brand leadership palatable. But in 2009, in order to preserve his subcommittee chairmanship on the Armed Services Committee, he had voted for her to be Speaker. In the volatile 2010 election, that was all Taylor's opponent, a state legislator named Steve Palazzo, needed.

The vote count in Palazzo's win over Taylor was 105,613 to 95,243, securing the future of the district for the GOP. Taylor was taken out in an *off-year* election. He had survived Republican tsunamis in presidential election years. His party's presidential vote and his own percentages are shown in the chart below:

Taylor and Presidential Election Margins[44]

Year	Democratic Presidential %	Republican Presidential %	Taylor %
1992	32	54	60
1996	35	56	58
2000	32	66	79
2004	31	68	64
2008	32	67	74

In 2014, Taylor attempted a comeback as a Republican, running against Palazzo for the Republican nomination. He understood that party identity and national politics now trumped local politics in congressional races. He showed that he retained an impressive connection to the district, even when running for a new party. But Palazzo won a bare majority of the votes and avoided a runoff, while Taylor got 43% and other candidates split the remainder.

What happened to Gene Taylor? How could an incumbent with prior electoral vote totals in the 70%-plus range suddenly plummet in an off-year election?

First, his vote for Pelosi in 2009 made him part of the Democratic "problem" in the eyes of GOP voters in his district. He had not supported her in the past, and he had also refused to support Dick Gephardt, her predecessor. But now he could be labeled an enabler of putting liberal Democrats in power, even though on individual issues he often opposed the Democratic leadership.

Secondly, national Republicans, through their campaign arm (the NRCC), decided to put some money into the race to more fully define Taylor as a national Democrat. Although Taylor still maintained a spending advantage, the Republicans were able to put more muscle into their message that Taylor had "gone national," voting with national Democrats.

And finally, the mood of the general public, and particularly of the Republican base, was one of anger toward Obama. They wanted to send the president a strong message and this was their only opportunity to do so.

Gene Taylor's career as a Democratic congressman was over, as was the case for many other Democrats across the country who had previously demonstrated personal gravitas in Republican districts. The net 63-seat gain for Republicans was their largest off-year gain in 62 years!

And as so often happens in electoral sweeps, the nationalization of the election also caused some Republican casualties in dark blue areas where Republicans had heretofore survived. Charles Djou of Hawaii and Joseph Cao of Louisiana, both GOP incumbents in heavily Democratic districts, were defeated. Bob Ehrlich, Maryland's popular Republican former governor, was trounced in his comeback attempt in the dark blue Free State. In California, two female hi-tech leaders, Carly Fiorina and Meg Whitman, were clobbered in their spirited, high-spending attempts to win as Republicans in a state that was no longer considering Republicans.

Also taken out in "the wave" were many longstanding entrenched Democrats in districts the Democrats are unlikely to regain for decades. Chet Edwards in Texas; Ike Skelton, the chairman of the Armed Services Committee, in Missouri; John Spratt, the Budget Committee chair, in South Carolina; and Rick Boucher in Virginia were all swept out of office, finding that voters angry at Washington were willing to put aside personal and local considerations to send the message.

Rick Boucher had represented his southwest Virginia area for 28 years and Republicans had been unable to touch him. Although the district was voting Republican nationally (McCain had bested Obama 59% to 40%, even as he lost the state), Boucher had not polled at less than 60% in decades. He was unopposed in 2008 and in 2006 had defeated Bill Carrico, a member of the Virginia House of Delegates (now a state senator), better than two to one.

Obama's health care bill, plus his environmental policies, backfired in a district with counties dependent on coal for jobs. The president was very unpopular in this Appalachian district, and though Boucher had taken great pains to distance himself from the president, Republicans sensed a real opportunity to win.

Their efforts to recruit A-list Republicans State Senator William Wampler (son of the incumbent Boucher had beaten in 1982) and State Delegate Terry Kilgore failed. However, the State House majority leader, Morgan

Griffith, was recruited to make the run. The problem with Griffith, an articulate, able campaigner, was that he did not live in the district. A small part of
his state district was in the 9th congressional district, but his home was a few
hundred feet outside of the district boundary.

If this had been a suburban district, where shopping center faded into
shopping center and one freeway section away was two congressional districts away, residence probably never would have been an issue. However,
the 9th district, shoehorned in the state's southwest corner, had undergone
the least amount of change of any district in Virginia. The population, outside of a couple of university towns (Blacksburg and Radford), was contracting as its young people exited the region in search of jobs elsewhere.

Boucher jumped on the fact that he was a longtime resident of the district and Griffith was outside of it. Griffith responded using a tape measure
to show how far outside the district his home was – "about a foot," he said,
with slight understatement. Regardless, the voters didn't seem to care.

In an increasingly nationalized environment, Griffith, although outspent,
raised enough money to get out his message and won the election 95,726 to
86,746. Griffith's home was put into the 9th district in the 2012 redistricting
and he went on to win a landslide reelection in what promises to be a long
and successful congressional career.

The Boucher-Griffith dynamic is also a further demonstration that all
politics is no longer local, but is national, when it comes to congressional
elections. The advent of party branding, better targeting by the national parties and super PACs, and increased mobility of the population have made
formerly safe districts like Boucher's into more party-oriented constituencies.

The country had seen these kinds of landslides before in off-year elections: in 1958, 1974, and 1994. But 2010 was different in several ways. For
one, Democrats didn't rebound two years later in many of these areas; the
realignments became national and permanent. Secondly, in 2012, many of
the 2010 GOP gains were strengthened in the redrawing of the congressional district boundaries during the decennial redistricting. This was
buoyed by the 2010 state legislative elections, which resulted in Republican
majorities who were then responsible for redrawing the district boundaries.
This in turn reduced Democratic opportunities to win back most of the

seats that were lost in 2010. Moreover, the congressional vote patterns were now congruent with presidential voting patterns. Incumbency was helpful, but presidential vote preferences, with few exceptions, were dispositive.

But 2010 didn't occur in a vacuum. Already, many districts were discarding locally popular members of the minority party and voting nationally. I recall a conversation with Connie Morella, a very popular and media-savvy Republican congresswoman from heavily Democratic Montgomery County, Maryland, after the 2000 election.

Morella was easily the most liberal Republican in the House. She refused to vote for Gingrich for Speaker in 1997, though she voted for Hastert in 1999. She had the support of many liberal groups, including NARAL (the abortion rights group) and the Human Rights Campaign Fund, as well as endorsements from the *Washington Post*. She had faced vigorous opposition in 1998 but triumphed with 60% of the electoral vote.

In 2000, Morella was held to 52% of the vote and lost her home precinct. She was devastated when she came to me as campaign chair and asked for my take on the outcome of her election. I said, "Connie, these voters just want a Democrat." And in 2002, with some help from the Democratic legislature's redistricting of the congressional district boundaries, she was defeated, even as our polling showed her at a 70% approval rating on Election Day.

In Morella's case, the changing demographics and boundaries were major contributors to her defeat. Among voters who had lived there longer than 10 years, she was still winning, albeit by reduced margins. But among newcomers, she was getting clobbered.

I saw the same trend in my own polls. Newcomers voted nationally, not locally, and I did not have enough time to personalize the district for these newcomers. But even among many longstanding supporters, I was slipping.

I had one voter stop me on Election Day in 2006 to tell me how I'd helped his family on a disability issue and how proud he was of my service, but he said he couldn't vote for me. He had to send a message to President Bush and I was the best conduit for doing that. I replied that he could vote for me and I would personally deliver his letter to the White House. However, he would not be appeased. Politics for him was no longer a local affair, it was national. And though I survived the 2006 election, running well ahead of my running mate, Senator George Allen, it was clear that politics was changing – not just for 2006, but forever.

Today, ticket-splitting is the exception, not the rule. This is a result of several forces that have combined over the past decade.

These forces are (1) the ideological sorting of the parties; (2) residential sorting, where people tend to live in enclaves of like-minded people; (3) political gerrymandering of districts; (4) better targeting of vulnerable districts by both national parties and interest groups; and (5) increased mobility of voters and workers, resulting in less community identification.

Ironically, as discussed in our chapter on the new normals, state laws today tend to exclude straight party-voting levers on voting machines, actually making it harder, on balance, for a voter to vote a straight ticket. Nevertheless, straight-ticket – nearly parliamentary – voting patterns have persisted.

The propensity of voters to vote for the same party for Congress and the presidency is at a 100-year high. Part of this is because so many districts are out of reach of the other party because of the way they are constituted. Districts drawn to constitute solid majorities for one party do not, in today's world, elect a member from the other party to represent it, except in rare instances.

That has not always been the case, as we witnessed with Connie Morella and Gene Taylor. They were but two of dozens of other members who not only survived, but thrived, in "enemy" territory.

In 2014, only five congressional districts where Obama received more than 52% of the vote were represented by Republicans. Conversely, only five districts where Romney received more than 52% of the vote were represented by Democrats.[45]

Split-Ticket Districts

Democrats in Romney over 52% Districts		Republicans in Obama over 52% Districts	
Congressman	% Voting for Romney in 2012	Congressman	% Voting for Obama in 2012
Matheson (D-UT-4)	68	Miller (R-CA-31)	57
Rahall (D-WV-3)	65	Valadao (R-CA-21)	55
McIntyre (D-NC-7)	59	LoBiondo (R-NJ-2)	54
Barrow (D-GA-12)	55	Ros-Lehtinen (R-FL-27)	53
Peterson (D-MN-7)	54	Runyan (R-NJ-3)	52

When Democrats Matheson and McIntyre announced their retirements in 2014, it was already anticipated that their districts would turn Republican. Similarly, when Miller and Runyan declared they would retire, it was expected that Miller's district would become Democratic and Runyan's would become a tossup.

Compare this to 1988, when four Democrats were elected in districts that gave Bush over 70% of the vote, as shown below:

1988 Democrats Elected in 70% Bush Districts

District	Bush %	Incumbent Name	Incumbent %
FL 1	73	Hutto	67
FL 11	70	Nelson	61
GA 7	70	Darden	65
GA 9	71	Jenkins	63

A more recent comparison is the 2000 election, when Al Gore edged out George W. Bush in the popular vote but Bush won a narrow Electoral College majority. In that year, 29 Democrats won in districts where Bush received over 52% of the vote, while nine Republicans won in districts where Gore was over 52%.

Note that in 2000, Independent Ralph Nader was siphoning off 2.7% of the national vote that would have gravitated toward Gore, making the nine GOP victories in these districts even more remarkable. Nine incumbents (eight Democrats and one Republican) won in districts in which the opposition presidential candidate received over 60% of the vote. How times have changed!

Four years later, in 2004, 28 Democratic members won in districts where Bush received over 52% of the vote, while 10 Republicans won in districts where John Kerry won at least 52%. Although ticket-splitting for congressional races was on the decline, 8% of all House seats were claimed from the other party's presidential turf (defined as a 52% district for the presidential winner).

In 2008, 18 Republicans survived in districts President Obama carried by 52% or more. In all, 38 Republicans won in districts carried by Obama. Plus, 32 Democrats won in districts carried by McCain by 52% or better, with 40 Democrats in all surviving in a McCain district. Note that 23 of these 32 Democratic districts with 52% or better McCain numbers were in the South.

But the coalition Obama had assembled, coupled with the initiatives he and the Democratic Congress pushed, quickly sorted out members who held seats in hostile territory. In the South, Democrats who tried to localize their races saw angry voters wanting to submit a protest vote against Obama's party. Many Democrats chose to retire and many others were defeated in their campaigns for reelection.

The electorate, behaving as though we were a parliamentary democracy, began to vote even more solidly along party lines. Many Democrats who had survived 2008 but found themselves in Republican-behaving districts saw stronger opponents and more resources poured against them than in the past. The 2010 midterm turnout turned ugly for members with the Democratic label in the GOP-leaning districts.

Much has been written about the blown opportunities by Senate Republicans running exotic candidates in Nevada, Colorado, and Delaware. But none of these states was solidly Republican. They all had Democratic legislatures going into the midterms. Stronger candidates would have made the difference in these purple states, where candidates still mattered. But the GOP was finding that the party label, absent major gaffes, was enough to carry them in nearly all red and many purple states in 2010.

The 2010 election decimated the "Blue Dog" Democratic ranks. The Blue Dogs were a group of the House's most fiscally conservative Democrats, many from Republican or swing districts where fiscal conservatism often served as a complement to strong local ties in holding the seats. All three Blue Dog co-chairs were defeated for reelection.

Of the Blue Dogs' 51 members, 23 were defeated outright and 12 others chose not to run for reelection over the next two cycles. These results solidified the solid liberal control of the Democratic caucus and, with the help of the Tea Party, a more solidly conservative Republican conference emerged. The Democrats' movement to the left and the GOP's to the right had been brewing for years, and the results of the 2010 elections made the transformation complete.

As the following *National Journal* congressional vote analysis demonstrates, Democrats were now exclusively liberal and Republicans exclusively conservative. For three straight Congresses, the Senate Democrats' most conservative member was more liberal than the most liberal Senate Republican, and the same was becoming true in the House.

The Incredible Shrinking Middle[46]

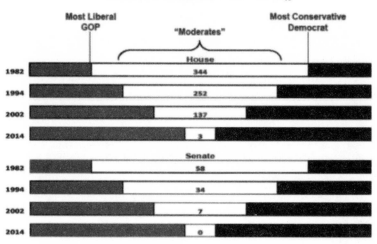

The parties are now, as political scientists like to say, "ideologically sorted." Unlike in past years, there are no longer any liberal Republicans or conservative Democrats. Parties now fit into tightly-wrapped packages, with interest groups and super PACs playing a large role in defining the parameters of their respective constituencies.

There are fewer and fewer pro-life Democrats or pro-choice Republicans in office. The nomination process itself makes it difficult for such candidates to be nominated. Take the case of Pennsylvania's Tim Holden. Elected in 1992 from a Republican-trending district, Holden was a pro-life, pro-gun, pro-labor Democrat who fit his conservative-leaning district in south-central Pennsylvania. He sided with the GOP on some fiscal issues and on tort reform, but he had solid labor credentials and a party unity support in the House of over 90%.

Holden was moderate enough to win reelection in a 2002 Republican-gerrymandered district against another incumbent, Republican George Gekas, largely on the strength of his support in Schuylkill County. However, responding to his Republican district, which carried for McCain in 2008 even as the state went 53% to 46% for Obama, he voted against Pelosi for Speaker in 2011 and against the Affordable Care Act (Obamacare).

When, during redistricting in 2012, the Republicans redrew the boundaries of the 17th congressional district, they figured they couldn't defeat Holden. So they moved Holden's Schuylkill base into a Democratic district, packing Scranton and Wilkes-Barre, both heavily Democratic cities. Much of the district was new to Holden and, though he carried his home county handily, Democrats in the newer parts of the district, realizing that it was now a Democratic seat and that they could have a "real" Democrat representing them, rejected Holden 57% to 43% in his Democratic primary against an able and more liberal Democrat, Matt Cartwright. Cartwright was assisted by a super PAC, the League of Conservation Voters, and the trial lawyers, staples of the national Democratic coalition.

This is but one example of how the party base voters want consistency with the party line and will not tolerate, except in extraordinary circumstances, members who show any level of independence. Holden had been a pretty solid labor vote, but the AFL-CIO is only a part of the Democratic coalition. Trial lawyers and environmentalists that make up the Democratic primary voters want reliable Democrats for their issues as well.

As long as Holden ran in a GOP-leaning district, his pro-tort-reform and pro-coal votes helped brand him as an acceptable general election choice. Democrats understood that he was better than a Republican, so he was generally left alone in party primaries. But when the district was reengineered as safely Democratic, liberal interest groups claimed it for themselves.

The same can certainly be said of Republican primary voters, only with an exclamation point! This will be discussed in some detail in our chapter on base voters, but such stark disparities between the parties on issues ranging from abortion to the environment to labor issues clearly make party identity shorthand for voters who are otherwise unschooled. This furthers party-line voters who know exactly what they are getting when they pull the party lever.

Until the mid-1970s, there was little ideological consistency between the parties. Liberal Republicans abounded in the Northeast. Conservative Democrats emerged with regularity from the South. Party loyalties going back to the Civil War had liberals competing against conservatives in one-party states, within the dominant party's primary.

But the Voting Rights Act, the emergence of the dominance of social issues, the polarizing media models, and ideological super PACs all changed that. Party branding now dominates political considerations by voters in general elections.

Ironically, the largest group of American voters is not Republicans or Democrats, but independents. While not all independents are moderates or even swing voters, they do not generally participate in party primaries. In fact, many states bar their participation in the nomination process, leaving them only the choices presented by the major parties on Election Day. Moreover, as was explained earlier, in these one-party districts, most general elections are little more than constitutional formalities. The partisan makeup of the legislative district is predetermined by the way it is drawn in redistricting or, in the Senate, by the residential sorting process. The only question is which member of the dominant party will go to Washington.

Contributing to this straight-ticket phenomenon is the fact that with fewer swing districts, members who do manage to survive in hostile districts are heavily targeted. A decade ago, many such members escaped serious opposition, assuring their reelection and rewarding more independent or bipartisan voting behavior.

Today, if a member of Congress represents a district in which the other party is strong, that member can rely on a heavy barrage of negative "defining" ads to polarize the electorate. For instance, many Democrats who voted against Obamacare or were not in Congress at the time of the vote have been hit with ads saying they supported it because they did not favor outright repeal.

Democrats, in turn, have taken relatively moderate Republicans in swing districts and tied them to the Tea Party. Often it has worked. Politicians who could personalize their constituencies were rare. As House district demographics change, with new people moving in, in today's world, the party label trumps local issues the vast majority of the time.

It is not difficult to find a few votes (such as in the elections for Speaker) where even the most independent-minded members voted their party lines. In those cases, a well-funded media campaign highlighting those votes can portray an independent-minded candidate as a bitter partisan.

Today's social mobility can change the demographics of a political constituency literally overnight. We have discussed the fast-paced changes in urban areas and around employment centers. As Americans and immigrants relocate for various reasons (e.g., jobs, retirement, education), the political complexions of various areas change. Sixty-two percent of New Hampshire's residents were born in another state! This is a far cry from the Grover's Corner of 1930 in Thornton Wilder's *Our Town*.

Mobility within the United States and immigration from outside the United States are at record levels, which means we're trading in continuity and familiarity in many areas for a far less localized political structure. There are still areas – vast swaths of rural America – that are not attracting newcomers and where roots still matter. However, when one views the American political landscape in total, the only constant is change.

In towns and cities across the country, relative newcomers who have little familiarity with the constituencies they wish to represent are elected to office at all levels. Take New Jersey's delegation. For every member like Rodney Frelinghuysen (the fifth generation in the Frelinghuysen family to represent New Jersey in Congress), there are several members like Rush Holt (son of a West Virginia senator), Albio Sires (born in Cuba), and Jon Runyan (who came to southern New Jersey when he played football for the Philadelphia Eagles).

Typical is George H.W. Bush, who eschewed his family heritage in Connecticut, where his father was a senator; Senator Jon Kyl of Arizona, whose father was a congressman from Iowa; or California's Nancy Pelosi, whose father was a congressman and then mayor of Baltimore. Kathleen Sebelius, Kansas's former governor, is the daughter of John Gilligan, who was the governor of Ohio.

That is not to say that local roots don't matter, particularly in primary elections, where issues often become blurred and all candidates take similar stands, consistent with their party platforms. In those cases, strong local showings often make a difference. However, in general elections, local roots are making less of a difference than party identification, ethnic brandings, or cultural positions.

Localizing one's political identification is still good political positioning, when it can be achieved. But it is getting harder to do so in the current environment and, more often than not, that takes a back seat to the party-line voting habits of most voters, whose ties to their local community are not as strong as they were a generation ago.

Senate seats, though not gerrymandered, are also often determined by party identification, as statewide constituencies are much too large and subject to too much in-migration over a six-year term to personalize to any great degree.

Personalization can still be done, and in a few districts still works. But in a political world where issues and ideology tend to motivate most voters (and particularly primary voters), the "all politics is local" strategy of a decade ago proves less and less relevant.

The following chart, compiled by our friend Rhodes Cook, illustrates the demise of ticket-splitting in House districts:

The Demise of Split-Ticket Districts[47]

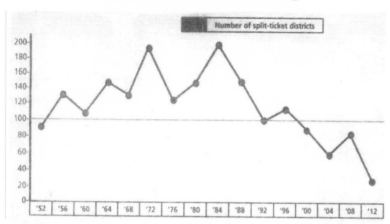

THE ERIC CANTOR SAGA

On June 10, 2014, one of the biggest upsets in congressional history occurred in the Republican primary in Virginia's 7th congressional district. The Republican incumbent, a seven-termer and House majority leader, was defeated for re-nomination by a little-known college professor named David Brat. Eric Cantor had a 50-to-1 spending advantage and the endorsement of nearly every Republican officeholder in the district. Pre-election surveys (there were few, as no one thought the race was competitive) by the Cantor campaign showed a lead of 30 points for the majority leader.

The next day, pundits were scurrying to explain this surprising upset, which, incidentally, wasn't even close; it was 56% to 44% Brat (36,110 to 28,898). The explanations for the outcome were all over the map. "Eric didn't spend enough time in his district." "Too many Democrats crossed over and voted in the Republican primary" (which was open to all voters). "The Republican base was upset that Cantor had voted to raise the debt ceiling and he was for immigration reform." "Cantor spent too much time picking intraparty fights." "He ran a bad campaign, attacking an unknown opponent with little money and giving him oxygen he would otherwise not have had." "Redistricting brought in too many Tea Party voters."

All of these explanations have some relevance to the end result, but in the final analysis one element was missing: all politics was, in fact, *not* local.

What beat Eric Cantor was his inability to explain how his national leadership role would help his constituents locally. Here you had the second most powerful Republican in Congress unable to explain why his role was an advantage to his primary voters.

In effect, Cantor's Republican base had elected him to stand up to President Obama. His constituents wanted a congressman who would channel their anger at the president. And this is what Cantor did during the first four years of the Obama administration. When Speaker John Boehner was viewed as working with the president on a budget deal, Cantor was seen as undermining the efforts, leading a GOP caucus in revolt to any agreement that smacked of tax hikes (or, as we politicians like to describe them, "revenue enhancements"). Cantor was a leader who stood behind the government shutdown. He also brought up several dozen efforts to repeal Obamacare.

However, as Cantor matured as a party leader and saw the shutdown kill any chances for his party to elect a governor in his home state of Virginia in 2013, and as he maneuvered the disparate interest groups in the Republican coalition on the immigration issue (the Chamber of Commerce demanding reform, the Tea Party demanding no amnesty), many hard-core conservatives started to view him as a collaborator with the president, not the fighter against him that they wanted.

Leaders have a responsibility to the country to produce a legislative work product; and that is what Cantor, as majority leader, started to do. But many of his constituents were not interested in legislative outcomes or solutions that involved palpable compromises. They wanted it their way or no way.

A national Pew poll, released contemporaneously with the primary, showed that "a logical point of compromise for most Americans is splitting things down the middle. But a significant minority – and a substantial share of the active and engaged electorate – see things differently, saying their side should get more of what it wants in political negotiations." The survey of 10,000 homes noted that consistent conservatives (who make up the bulk of primary voters) want their leaders to stick to their positions, as opposed to making compromises, by a 63% to 32% margin. Even "mostly conservative" voters split evenly on the question.

Tom chairing a D.C. Subcommittee hearing. On his left are Counsel Howard Denis
and Bob Dix.

Tom with Representative Patrick Kennedy (left), Senators Mitch McConnell (center left) and
Robert Torricelli (center right) on "Meet the Press" with Tim Russert (right), September 2, 2000.

Tom meets with actress Jane Seymour, who testified before his committee.

Tom meets with Governor Arnold Schwarzenegger. Congressman Dana Rohrabacher (R-CA)
is in the background.

Tom and Muhammad Ali.

Tom, with wife Jeannemarie (middle) and Speaker of the House Nancy Pelosi (D-CA) (left),
being sworn in for his seventh term.

Tom and Senator John McCain (R-AZ).

Tom with Congressman David Dreier (R-CA) at D.C.'s "Buddy March", September 2000.

Tom with President Ronald Reagan.

Tom and wife Jeannemarie with Prime Minister of the United Kingdom Tony
Blair and Mrs. Blair.

Tom and Representative Henry Waxman (D-CA) on "Meet the Press," March 13, 2005.

Tom and Major League Baseball Commissioner Bud Selig before congressional baseball game. Tom is wearing the uniform of the Prince William Cannons, a Carolina League team located in his district. This was after the steroid hearings.

Tom on the campaign trail.

Tom with Representative Carrie Meek (D-FL) and singer Stevie Wonder. Photo taken in Jerusalem.

Tom on left, with Representative Alcee Hastings (D-FL), Speaker of the House Newt Gingrich, and Representative Tom Latham (R-IA) at the 1995 bipartisan retreat.

Tom (with arms on chair) in the Oval Office with President George W. Bush at a bill signing. From left, Representatives Wittman (R-VA), Garrett (R-NJ), and Boucher (D-VA), Senator John Warner (R-VA), Tom, Representative Goodlatte (R-VA), and Virginia governor Tim Kaine.

Tom and wife Jeannemarie eradicating cocoa plants in the Andes Mountains in Colombia with Congressman Frank Wolf (R-VA).

Tom, as the Fairfax Board chair, meeting with Mike Mohler (the president of the local fire-fighters' union) and Glenn Gaines (the Fairfax fire chief).

Tom greets King Abdullah II of Jordan, with Majority Leader Dick Armey (R-TX).

Tom with New York Yankee pitching great Roger Clemens, before his testimony on steroids.

Tom and fellow page Carey Epps carrying the electoral ballots from the Senate to the House, to be counted, December 1964. In background is Senator Carl Hayden (D-AZ), President Pro Tempore of the Senate, and Senator Tom Kuchel (R-CA).

Tom with Senator Everett Dirksen and President Dwight D. Eisenhower, 1964.

Tom with members of Virginia's congressional delegation, 1999.
Front row, left to right, Senator Warner, Governor Gilmore, Senator Robb, Congressman Bateman.
Back row, left to right, Congressmen Pickett, Goodlatte, Davis, Moran, Scott, Sisisky.

Tom, behind President Clinton at signing of D.C. Control Board Bill. From left, D.C. delegate
Eleanor Holmes Norton, Chairman Bill Clinger, President Clinton, Tom, Congresswoman Connie
Morella, and Office of Management and Budget Director Alice Rivlin.

Tom meets with President Richard Nixon and young voters. Left to right, Tricia Nixon, Tom,
Ken Smith, Angella Harrison, Ken Reitz, President Nixon, unknown, George Gorton, Angela
Miller, Ed Cox.

Tom talks with President Clinton and Speaker Gingrich on D.C. Control Board.

Martin with Dallas mayor Ron Kirk, who later served as U.S. Trade Representative.

Martin with folk singer Peter Yarrow of Peter, Paul and Mary. Yarrow appeared at several fundraising events for Martin.

Martin, lower row center, at a House Rules Committee meeting early in his career.

A very young Martin throwing out the first pitch at the Texas Rangers home opener in 1979. The Rangers' ballpark was in Martin's district.

Texas Democratic congressional delegation in its glory days, Spring 1989.

Martin with one of his mentors, former DNC chairman Bob Strauss of Texas,
and Bob's wife Helen.

Martin and South African president Nelson Mandela. One of Martin's motivations to run for Congress was a deep commitment to civil rights.

President George W. Bush speaking to a House Democratic Caucus retreat in early 2001 when Martin was caucus chair.

Martin and his wife JoEllen with Michelle and Barack Obama at a White House holiday reception.

A photo from Martin's 1978 successful Democratic primary race with his oldest daughter, Alanna. This appeared in an endorsement pamphlet sent out by the local National Education Associations affiliate.

Martin, left rear, rides to Texas with President Jimmy Carter on Air Force One. Pictured front is Martin's good friend, Texas congressman Charlie Wilson.

A very young Martin Frost visits with Speaker Tip O'Neill early in Martin's career. O'Neill appointed Martin to the Rules Committee in Martin's first term.

Martin, third from left, chats with Speaker Jim Wright, Congresswoman Barbara Kennelly, and DNC chair Chuck Manatt at the annual Speaker's Club golf tournament.

Martin lights a candle at the annual U.S. Capital Holocaust Memorial Service. Martin was the only Jewish congressman elected from Texas in the 20th century.

Martin and Asleep at the Wheel lead singer Ray Benson. The group headlined several
fundraisers for Martin.

Martin and Czech Republic president Vaclav Havel when he came to Washington to address a
joint session of Congress.

Martin visits with President Jimmy Carter. Martin was north Texas chair of the Carter-Mondale campaign in 1976.

Bill Clinton and Al Gore appear with Martin in Corsicana, Texas, on their post convention bus tour in 1992.

Martin and his good friend Texas governor Ann Richards at one of Martin's country western fundraisers in Texas.

Martin and Russian president Mikhail Gorbachev on his visit to the U.S. Capitol.

A meeting of the House Democratic leadership with President Clinton. Left to right, Martin, President Clinton, Minority Leader Dick Gephardt and Minority Whip Dave Bonior.

Martin and Shirley Temple Black, U.S. Ambassador to Czechoslovakia. Martin chaired a special
U.S. House Task Force to help the parliaments of Eastern and Central Europe from 1990-95.

Martin and Israeli prime minister Benjamin Netanyahu. Martin has photos with six Israeli
prime ministers.

Martin was part of the first congressional delegation to Berlin following the opening of the
Berlin Wall in 1989.

Martin joins Bill and Hillary Clinton at a White House Christmas party.

Martin and Congressman John Lewis tour a defense plant in Martin's district.

ALL POLITICS IS NO LONGER LOCAL

Thus, when national leaders do make compromises (which are necessary to govern in divided government), their base constituencies view them as caving in or selling out. These are not "politics is local" dynamics. These are "politics is national" dynamics.

Ironically, Cantor had led the fight against earmarks as a party leader. In the past, earmarks – which allowed members of Congress to arrange appropriations for things like highway projects or park acquisitions – allowed members to localize their races and show their constituents they were producing for them. And a party leader could produce significant earmarks for his district. But as earmarks disappeared, it restricted a member's ability to show clout in Washington. It also made appropriation bills harder to pass, but that is another story in another chapter.

In Cantor's case, it made it harder to argue that his "clout" was helping the district. For many ideological voters, who control primaries, it appeared he had abandoned his constituents (read, primary voters, because the 7th district is a staunchly GOP seat), and they wanted to send him a message.

Thus, at the core, it was indeed national issues that defeated Eric Cantor. Certainly, spending more time in his district could have given him more opportunity to explain his positions. However, his having assumed a national party leadership post necessarily nationalized his race. Cantor's brand became part of Congress's brand and particularly the House GOP's brand. With such a national profile, he was a fixture on the Sunday talk show circuits. His fundraising prowess made him a highly-demanded presence both in his colleagues' congressional districts and in such wealth-laden areas as Silicon Valley, New York City, and Los Angeles.

One could argue that Cantor's absence from his district laid the seeds for his demise. However, he'd experienced no problems in previous primaries, such as in 2012, when faced with a challenge from the right. It was the changing dynamics of leadership decisions that separated him from his Republican primary voters.

Today, with congressional approval often hovering in the low teens, few leaders are popular back home. Senators Harry Reid and Mitch McConnell both have had high negatives in their home states, and Cantor's prior reelection percentages were far from impressive in such a safe GOP seat. Still, few thought his problems would be in a primary. Widely ostracized in the liberal media, Cantor was anathema to the liberal media and Democratic base. But caught between the Scylla of a very conservative primary electorate and the Charybdis of moderate voters critical to party success who wanted legislative compromise, Cantor had a difficult balancing act to maintain. In the end, as is the case in most single-party districts, it was the primary voters who held the keys to winning. Other voters were irrelevant.

Ray Allen, the Cantor campaign guru, blamed Cantor's loss on Democrats doing mischief by crossing over into the Republican primary and voting for Brat. Brian Umana, a former Democratic campaign operative, claimed that many Democrats engaged in the primary in an "anyone but Cantor" wave. He noted that the campaign manager for Cantor's 2010 opponent, Green Party nominee Floyd Bayne, became Brat's coordinator for Chesterfield County.

Also supportive of that conclusion is the turnout model. In 2012, the total primary vote for Congress was 47,037. That race was held in a backdrop of a Senate primary. The turnout in Cantor's losing 2014 primary effort was 65,008 voters, an increase of nearly 38%. The 2012 presidential primary, held separately (in March rather than June), also yielded a smaller turnout than the Cantor-Brat primary, which is an oddity in current Virginia politics. In every county except Spotsylvania, which Cantor carried, the 2014 turnout exceeded that in the presidential year.

2014 Congressional Primary vs. 2012 Presidential Primary: Turnout Differentials

Local Jurisdiction	2012	2014
Chesterfield County	12,495	13,150
Culpeper County	1,760	2,899
Goochland County	1,426	2,733
Hanover County	5,205	12,884
Henrico County	11,836	20,239
Louisa County	1,170	2,363
New Kent County	986	2,036
Orange County	1,277	2,004
City of Richmond	4,199	3,121*
Spotsylvania County	3,680	3,579
Total	44,034	65,008

*Only a small portion of the city is in the 7th district.

While conceding that some crossover voting inevitably occurs in these races, I dispute the assertions that Democrats made a difference in the outcome. Such an explanation can be exculpatory for Cantor's pollster, who missed the mark badly. And the young Democratic operative who voted for Brat can be explained by the fact that "victory has a thousand fathers." A closer look at the analysis of the vote totals reveals that the 2012 presidential primary was held after the race was largely decided and had only Mitt Romney and Ron Paul on the ballot. Also, the 2012 congressional primary vote exceeded the 2012 presidential primary totals, though the races were held three months apart.

The Hanover, Henrico, Goochland, etc. numbers represent counties with strong Republican areas where there simply are not many resident Democrats to participate. Chesterfield County, which was cited as an example of liberal participation, showed a smaller increase.

That Cantor ran a poor campaign is an understatement! His spending more money on steak dinners than Brat spent on his campaign in total is but one example of an incumbent who "didn't see it coming." In addition to the money spent from Cantor's campaign coffers, there were several large independent expenditures on his behalf, such as the $300,000 invested by the American Chemistry Council. Moreover, there is widespread agreement that Cantor's negative ads against Brat were not credible and only provided needed name identification for the challenger. In fact, Cantor's best counties (Orange, Culpepper, and Spotsylvania) were outside the media market where Cantor attacked Brat.

Campaigns are usually subject to multiple factors that affect the outcome. However, it is our considered opinion that Cantor was defeated because he was viewed as too soft on Obama, too willing to compromise, and too eager to abandon conservative principles by a constituency (particularly the primary voting universe) that wanted the opposite. Had Cantor been traveling in his district more, it may have helped him pick up on the signals indicating he was in trouble. But ultimately, it was national politics, not local politics, that led to the defeat of one of the GOP's most promising stars.

MARTIN'S RESPONSE

What happened to Eric Cantor reminds me of an incident in my own congressional district in January of 2001. I had just been reelected to my second term as House Democratic Caucus chair – the third-highest leadership position for House Democrats.

President Bill Clinton, during the last few days before he left office, invited some other House Democrats and me to spend the weekend at Camp David, the presidential retreat. That was the same weekend as a big parade through downtown Ft. Worth celebrating the Martin Luther King, Jr., holiday. I opted to go to my district to march in that parade rather than spend the weekend at Camp David.

My late wife, Kathy, who was at that time Adjutant General of the Army, was – to put it mildly – upset that I had passed on the chance for the two of us to go to Camp David. I explained that it was more important that I be with the constituents that weekend than with President Clinton.

It doesn't make any difference how big a shot you may be in D.C. if you forget the people who sent you there in the first place. Somehow, Eric Cantor, a very able politician, forgot that lesson during the time leading up to his primary defeat. That certainly wasn't the only reason he lost, but it clearly didn't help.

8

DO INDEPENDENTS MATTER?, AND THE COLLAPSE OF THE MIDDLE

By Tom Davis

In a polarized society, within a polarized political process, the reasonable question that arises is whether independent voters matter at all. In a gerry-mandered Congress, where over three-fourths of the House districts are pre-drawn to elect a specific party, what role can an independent play? Do independents matter?

The answer is simple: it depends.

It depends on whether they are allowed to participate in party primaries. It depends on what the electoral composition of the constituency is made up of. It also depends on ballot access laws, electoral roles, and registration requirements. The irony is that over the last two decades, the two major political parties have been losing market share, while independents are the most quickly-growing group by registration. Yet at the same time, politics has become more partisan and more polarized.

As more Americans have become disillusioned by the two major political parties, politics has not shifted toward the middle, but has yo-yoed between the extremes of the two parties. This chart, taken from political scientists L.

Sandy Maisel and Mark D. Brewer's book, *Parties and Elections in America*, illustrates the trend toward independence:

Americans' Party Identification, 1952-2008

Identification	'52	'56	'60	'64	'68	'72	'76	'80	'84	'88
Strong D	22	21	20	27	20	15	18	17	17	17
Weak D	25	23	25	25	25	26	25	23	20	18
Ind. D	10	6	6	9	10	11	12	11	11	12
Ind. Ind.	6	9	10	8	11	13	15	13	11	11
Ind. R	7	8	7	6	9	10	10	10	12	13
Weak R	14	14	14	14	15	13	14	14	15	14
Strong R	14	15	16	11	10	10	9	9	12	14
Apolitical	3	4	2	1	1	1	1	2	2	2

Identification	'92	'96	'98	'00	'02	'04	'08
Strong D	18	18	19	19	16	16	19
Weak D	18	19	18	15	17	16	15
Ind. D	14	14	14	15	15	17	15
Ind. Ind.	12	9	11	12	8	10	14
Ind. R	12	12	11	13	13	12	10
Weak R	14	15	16	12	16	12	12
Strong R	11	12	10	12	14	16	13
Apolitical	1	1	2	1	1	0	0

This irony is readily understandable because, as the Pew Research Center has noted in its massive research project entitled "Political Polarization in the American Public," "political participation is strongly related to ideology and partisan antipathy. Those who hold consistently liberal or conservative views and who hold strongly negative views of the other political party are far more likely to participate in the political process than the rest of the nation."

This results, graphically, in a consistent U-shaped pattern, with higher levels of engagement on the right and left of the ideological spectrum and lower levels in the center.

One can conclude from the study that those who participate the most and are most active tend to dominate the political process. So as more voters abandon the two major parties and opt for independence, they leave the partisan nomination process to those who are the most ideologically inclined, the most activist-minded, and the least likely to compromise. The result is that the nomination process, usually a primary but sometimes a convention (as in Utah and Virginia), is left to the most ideological and passionate voters. This makes it more difficult for moderates to win a contested nomination procedure. For incumbents from safe partisan districts (which are the most numerous), the way to survive is to stay with the activists and not to compromise, which leads to more polarized political behavior.

Many states forbid independents from participating in party primaries, restricting the electorate to more ideological participants. Other states allow independents to vote in party primaries, and some states have no restrictions on who can participate in party nominations because they have no party registration.

In my state of Virginia, registration is not by party so that, in theory, anyone can vote in a primary. The political parties, though, have the discretion to nominate by convention, a system that is often used to restrict the involvement of outsiders. In both the 2013 and 2014 elections, the state GOP decided to nominate its candidates running for statewide office by conventions held in Richmond and Roanoke, respectively.

The 2013 convention was open to anyone. To be a delegate to the convention, all one had to do was pre-file a form. Nearly everyone who filed was allowed to come and participate. There were no uniform rules. Some counties had pre-file rules that were known by insiders. Many counties had formal caucuses to elect their delegations, but as a practical matter, everyone who wanted to come to Richmond on a Saturday and spend their time in the convention center could vote.

The votes were apportioned by jurisdiction, so that in rural Grayson County, 30 votes were apportioned among two delegates, each casting 15 votes. In populous Richmond, where the convention was held, each individual delegate's vote was worth less than one vote. It was proportional. Such rules tended to hurt the urban, more moderate areas, where participation was higher, while in more distant, rural enclaves, delegates were voting up to 18 votes per person.

However, in a four-ballot convention, the delegates who stay the longest see their proportionate votes go up as delegates who are less committed go home after their candidates are dropped or they find they cannot stay a full Saturday. Most active duty military are precluded from participating since they are away and cannot attend. Only people who can afford the time and expense to drive to the convention and stay for the day attend. This "privilege" is generally exercised by only the most ideological voters. As the old saying goes, "liberals and conservatives have passion, moderates and independents have lives." Thus, the conventions have been dominated by strongly-committed conservatives.

When I speak to business groups about the polarization and lack of compromise in today's Washington, I inform them that they think they have performed their civic duty when they walk out of the polling place in November with an "I Voted" sticker on their lapels. As we wrote earlier, little do they realize that in the majority of districts around the country, the election was decided in the primary, while most of them sat on the sidelines.

One-party districts are dominated by those who show up for the primary. For most of America, because of ballot laws or inertia on the part of many citizens, that group is a restricted group of people with a narrower view of the political process than most of us. Elections belong to those who are engaged and active in the process, not the skeptics and non-participants. "Politics," as University of Virginia professor Larry Sabato likes to say, "is not a spectator sport."

Yet most independents are indeed spectators and are not involved in the nomination process. And not all self-professed independents behave independently. There is a substantial body of evidence to show that many self-declared independents are, in fact, hidden partisans. Political scientist William G. Mayer, in his classic book, *The Swing Voter in American Politics*, notes that these hidden partisans "embrace the independent label and the resonances of civic virtue associated with it, but [their] actual attitudes and voting behavior are every bit as partisan as those who embrace party labels more openly."

The following chart illustrates how independents register in large numbers in strongly partisan states with party registration:

Independent Registration in Heavily Partisan States

State	Independent Registration	Presidential Performance
Massachusetts	52%	Solidly D
Connecticut	43%	Solidly D
New York	26%	Solidly D
New Jersey	47%	Solidly D
Colorado	34%	Swing
California	27%	Solidly D
New Hampshire	42%	Swing
Maine	40%	Solidly D
Kansas	30%	Solidly R
Alaska	58%	Solidly R

So who are the real independent voters and how do they differ from party voters? One dominant feature of undecided voters is not their registration, their demographic profile, or their political ideology. It is their tendency toward electoral aloofness. They tend to be less interested, less involved, and less connected to the political process; and they are much less likely to vote. In close races, they tend to break for the winners. Thus, in the bulk of races with party primaries and one-party constituencies, independent voters are irrelevant.

In these races, which the authors see constituting close to three-quarters of House and Senate races, independents do not participate in primaries and do not matter in general elections. In most major cities, an independent voter is a person without a voice. Nearly all races in these major cities are decided in Democratic primaries. Some cities have circumvented this by choosing to elect their mayors in nonpartisan elections. Cities such as Chicago, Los Angeles, Houston, Dallas, Phoenix, and San Diego allow everyone to vote in the mayor's race, with runoffs among the top two candidates. Other cities – such as New York, D.C., Philadelphia, Baltimore, Indianapolis, and St. Louis – hold partisan elections.

But it is in the congressional elections where the drawing of lines predetermines the partisan outcomes, marginalizing independents. And in one-party states, from Republican Utah to Democratic Rhode Island, independents are routinely excluded from mattering in most elections.

However, even in these partisan strongholds, competitive races occur – particularly in gubernatorial contests – when the dominant party makes mistakes.

Although Utah has elected only one Democrat to the Senate since 1950 and last voted for a Democrat for president in 1964, it will, upon occasion, elect a Democratic governor. Similarly, heavily Democratic states like Massachusetts, Rhode Island, Maryland, and Hawaii will elect Republicans for governor, but revert to the GOP in Senate races only in rare circumstances. In these races, independents can be aroused and play an important role in shaping the outcome.

A few fundamentals are important in understanding exactly who independent voters tend to be:

1. They are less partisan by nature in refusing to pick a party upon enrolling to their electoral behavior. This is a large and statistically significant difference between partisans and independents. That is not to say that many independents do not behave as partisans, but on balance, they are less inclined to do so.

2. They are more moderate than party voters. Survey after survey on topics from guns to abortion to taxes puts independent voters in between the self-described Republicans and self-described Democrats. That is not to ignore the fact that there are many independents who are so registered and identified because they believe the Republicans and Democrats are not ideological enough. Senator Bernie Sanders of Vermont, an Independent, certainly fits that mold on the left. But on balance, as the following chart indicates, independents tend to be less ideological and more moderate:

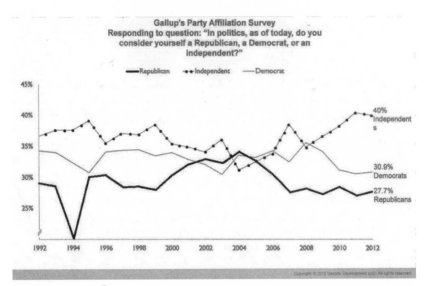

Gallup's Party Affiliation Survey
Responding to question: "In politics, as of today, do you
consider yourself a Republican, a Democrat, or an
independent?"

——Republican   -•-Independent   ——Democrat

3. Independent voters tend to be less interested in and less informed about politics. They are consistently less interested in day-to-day politics, but they do follow campaigns and, because they have less attachment to a given political party, are more likely to be persuaded by campaign advertising.

4. Independent voters are not demographically different from other voters. Despite claims from Rush Limbaugh and others about the multitude of "low-information voters" who voted in the presidential year of 2012, those voters bore a striking resemblance to Democratic base voters (e.g., young, single women and people of color). Independents come in all shapes and sizes and vary from those who are cross-pressured on issues (e.g., socially liberal, economically conservative) to those who do not engage in politics unless their status or livelihood is threatened. Independents are a very diverse group.

5. Independent voters are more likely to split their tickets. Owing no affinity or allegiance to either party, these voters are more likely to vote for the person rather than the party. However, when, as the late political scientist V.O. Key observed, "the shoe is pinching," independents will often throw out the old and buy a new pair. Reactive voting can often be reflected in straight-ticket voting by independents, if they are angry enough.

We often do not discern between base voters and independent voters. For example, conventional wisdom provides that Republicans perform better in off years (when the older, more affluent voters tend to dominate), while Democrats do better in presidential years (when more minority and low-income voters show up at the polls).

Yet the biggest Democratic year in a generation was arguably 2006, an off year, when Democrats won the House (with a 30-seat gain) and Senate and captured many governorships. In 2004, by contrast, George W. Bush was the first presidential candidate who posted a majority since 1988! The Bush race saw a massive turnout effort among voters who often didn't participate in elections. Buying voter lists from gun clubs, religious groups, etc., the campaign incentivized passive voters, including many independents, to vote Republican in Ohio and other swing states.

But 2006, an off year, turned out to be a phenomenal year for Democrats, though turnout was greatly reduced from 2004. Although larger turnouts often favor Democrats because of greater participation by poorer and minority voters (groups that traditionally vote more Democratic), the question one should be asking is, "Who turned out?" A large turnout can benefit Republicans if their base is angry and if independent voters share in that anger and are motivated to direct their anger at Democrats.

With the political parties so sharply divided, it is independents who *can* make the difference in many races – but only if they participate. And with district lines often drawn to elect only one party's candidates, the bat is literally taken out of their hands in general elections. In a majority of states, independents can participate in primaries. However, as a rule, because of the aforementioned reasons, they don't.

The previously cited Pew survey measured levels of political activism and engagement along the ideological spectrum. The results noted that political engagement takes many forms, from volunteering to contributing to attending campaign events to voting. The analysis concluded that "on every measure of engagement, political participation is strongly related to ideology and partisan antipathy: those who hold consistently liberal or con- servative views, and who hold strongly negative views of the other political party, are far more likely to participate in the political process than the rest of the nation."

DO INDEPENDENTS MATTER?, AND THE COLLAPSE...   155

The survey went on to show that 78% of those who are consistent conservatives say they always vote, compared to 58% of consistent liberals and only 39% of those who hold a mix of liberal and conservative values.

The donation rates are even more pronounced, with 31% of consistent liberals and 26% of consistent conservatives contributing, but only 8% of those with mixed ideological views having donated to a campaign in the two years covered by the survey.

Although "mixed" voters outnumber both conservatives and liberals, their participation rates marginalize their effectiveness. And the Pew survey did not distinguish between participation in primaries versus general elections, though given the ideological partisan preferences of conservatives as Republicans and liberals as Democrats, we believe it is safe to assume even greater disparities in primary participation between the ideologically committed and those who tend to be less so.

The overall efficacy of a mixed or independent voter in one-party districts appears to be limited under current participation levels. Politicians, sensing these turnout models, tend to gear their campaigns to voters who are most likely to vote, volunteer, and contribute, and this has the significant effect of pushing candidates to the polar ends of each party. So while independents in many states are given the same participatory opportunities as their more partisan and ideological neighbors, they do not avail themselves of them.

Unless and until the participation rates rise among independents and moderates, the political landscape will be dominated by those who are the most philosophically and ideologically committed. The elected leaders, taking their cue from those voters who bother to show up, will govern accordingly.

In the political jurisdictions that are purple and competitive, independents can certainly make the difference. However, many political consultants in these competitive districts often opt to double down on their party base, seeking to enhance their turnout and therefore dominate the electoral demographic on Election Day. Their belief is that it is easier to find and persuade a party stalwart to get out and vote than to convince a more disconnected independent.

Liberal Democrat Terry McAuliffe employed such a strategy in his 2013 Virginia gubernatorial race against archconservative Republican Ken Cuccinelli. Many political observers believed that Cuccinelli's performance in office had been too far out of the mainstream to attract independent-minded voters. Cuccinelli had denied global warming, defended personhood legislation, and ruled against domestic partners' insurance coverage at state universities. Observers felt this would make him vulnerable to attacks among upscale, libertarian-minded voters in many suburban and urban areas of the state.

However, the McAuliffe team saw something else in the state's evolving electoral alignment. For two straight presidential elections, President Obama had won by substantial margins, persuading hundreds of thousands of minority voters and college town inhabitants to vote Democratic. He hadn't achieved this with a subdued, moderate approach to cultural issues. He'd run as a liberal and encouraged new voters to participate in the process.

McAuliffe, recognizing the propensity of Virginia voters to cast a gubernatorial vote against the president's party (this had occurred in nine straight gubernatorial elections) and realizing the president's standing in the Commonwealth was declining, decided to double down on turnout. He supported gay marriage, the EPA regulations on coal, Medicaid expansion, and Obamacare; and by doing so, he tapped into the Democratic base voters in the African American community and in northern Virginia.

McAuliffe lost independents by six points on Election Day, but the 2013 turnout model closely resembled the 2012 presidential turnout model in its composition. In both cases, 20% of those who voted were African American. Huge margins in northern Virginia and college towns were recorded. The turnout drop from 2012 was significant, but the declines were equally distributed.

In 2009, when Republican Bob McDonnell was swept to victory, the electorate was decidedly Republican in its composition. Feeding that was Democrat Creigh Deeds's positioning himself as a more moderate Democrat. The result was that Republicans angry with Obama showed up disproportionately compared to base Democrats, who stayed asleep. In both races, independents opted to cast a net protest vote against Obama, but the emboldened Democratic voter turnout base made the difference for McAuliffe in 2013, while that same base stayed home for the more centrist Deeds's race in 2009.

McAuliffe didn't write off the independent vote, and he had a robust organization – Republicans for McAuliffe – that included Virginia Beach's Republican mayor and numerous former GOP legislators and contributors. But the Democratic candidate made few concessions to the middle in his policy positions, except to state that he would not interfere with the state's right-to-work law and would be a job creator. He continued to hammer his opponent for being out of the mainstream; and his explosive ads in northern Virginia, in which he attacked Cuccinelli on social issues, minimized the anti-Obama feeling among moderates.

Although most commentators expressed surprise that Cuccinelli lost by only three percentage points, the real story was that he lost at all. Anti-Obama sentiment was running high (the president's favorable/unfavorable ratio was worse than it had been in 2009, when the Republicans had swept all three statewide offices). In nine straight previous elections, Virginia had used the gubernatorial contest to send a message to the president by electing the opposition party to the post. And Terry McAuliffe had entered the race with the weakest résumé of any Democratic candidate in a couple of generations.

Mark Warner, Virginia's incumbent Democratic senator running in 2014, pursued a different path, running exceptionally well with independents, who had shown a propensity to support him in the past. So no one-size-fits-all strategy should be employed.

In conclusion, we would note that all voters are important in swing states and districts, but independents play a *de minimis* role in one-party constituencies, both because they are outnumbered and because they generally do not participate in great numbers in the primaries. Thus, they are substantially ignored by a majority of the members of the House and Senate. In presidential elections, where nearly everyone shows up, independents can become the deciding factor in purple states. However, because independents behave, well, independently, they seldom resemble a bloc.

Independents are not all moderate swing voters. Many are more ideologically intense ideologically than their partisan counterparts. Still, in presidential races, they become relevant and can hold the balance of power.

Independents can become more of a force in American politics when their participation levels improve in both primary and general elections. Until that happens, they will continue to resemble spectators, rather than actual players.

9

RELYING ON BASE VOTERS MAKES COMPROMISE MUCH HARDER

By Martin Frost

This is a subject we have mentioned in various chapters in this book already, but it is worth putting everything together in one place because of its significance on the current partisan division in Congress and the difficulty it presents for compromise.

Partisan gerrymandering of House districts has made the bulk of the chamber's 435 seats safe for either Republicans or Democrats. In 2012, only 17 of the 234 Republican House members were elected from districts carried by Barack Obama, and a mere nine of the 201 Democratic House members were elected from districts carried by Mitt Romney. This means that the old days when voters split their tickets, voting for a presidential candidate of one party and a congressman of another party, are long gone. As recently as the 2008 election, 38 of the 178 Republican House members were elected from districts carried by the Democratic presidential nominee and 40 of the 257 Democrats were elected from districts carried by the Republican presidential nominee.

Some ticket-splitting still occurs in Senate races, but not nearly to the degree that it once did. Entering the 2014 elections, a total of 12 Democratic senators represented red states carried by Romney and nine Republican senators represented states carried by Obama.

Part of the historic ticket-splitting phenomenon can be attributed to the fact that Democrats hung on in the South for years after most southern states started voting consistently for the Republican candidate for president. Conversely, some Republicans hung on in the Northeast and parts of the Midwest for years after states in these regions started consistently voting Democratic for president.

Democratic congressional strength in the South could be attributed to several factors: (1) a continuing antipathy toward the Republican Party as a result of the post-Civil War treatment of southern states by the radical Republicans in Congress during Reconstruction, and (2) the seniority system for selecting committee chairs that gave southern Democrats in both the House and the Senate an unusual amount of power when Democrats controlled one or both chambers of Congress.

The South had started to flirt with Republicans as early as 1928, when the Democrats nominated New York governor Al Smith for president. Smith was a Catholic and a "wet," meaning he favored repealing Prohibition. As a result, the "Outer South" states, members of the old Confederacy that had lower percentages of black populations, voted for Republican Herbert Hoover. These states included Virginia, North Carolina, Florida, Tennessee, and Texas. Arkansas, the only other Outer South state, stayed loyal to the Democrats, probably because of the presence of Joe Robinson, Arkansas's senior senator, who was Smith's vice presidential running mate.

In 1952, Dwight Eisenhower won those same southern states, with the help of the southern mountain regions (which were traditionally anti-slavery and had been less supportive of secession) and in-migration from the North. At the time of the 1964 Civil Rights Act, southern Republican presence in the House came from districts that were Mountain Valley districts (in states such as North Carolina, Virginia, and Tennessee) and northern migration districts (Charlotte, Dallas, St. Petersburg, and northern Virginia). The bulk of southern districts stayed true to their Democratic antecedents, bound to the Democrats on the race issue.

But racial issues were tearing up the Democratic Party. As blacks moved away from southern farms to the employment centers in the North, they were greeted by the Democratic big-city machines in New York, Chicago, Detroit, Baltimore, Philadelphia, and other cities. They were recruited to the Democratic Party, made more palatable by FDR and Truman, and became largely but not overwhelmingly a part of the Democratic base in key states. Not surprisingly, northern Democrats, whether out of conviction or due to the new constituencies' politics, began demanding equal treatment for all races in the South.

Once the Democrats dropped in 1940 the requirement for a two-thirds vote to nominate a presidential candidate, the South's near veto of the national ticket ended and national Democrats set about supporting civil rights legislation, over the objections of their southern wing.

In 1964, President Lyndon Johnson, joined by most Republicans and northern Democrats, passed the landmark Civil Rights Act. A year later, passage of the Voting Rights Act ensured black participation in southern voting; and over the course of the next two decades, many southern conservative whites moved to the GOP, while blacks became a dominant force in southern Democratic primaries. Johnson has been famously quoted as saying, "There goes the South," when he signed the Voting Rights Act, which substantially increased the political power of blacks in the South.

It took a while before this change took effect. Respected senior white southern Democrats – like House Appropriations chairman Jamie Whitten of Mississippi and Senate Armed Services chairman Sam Nunn of Georgia – were able to stay in office long after political change started in the South; but once they retired, their seats starting going Republican.

Also, the Republicans successfully used the Voting Rights Act against House Democrats by utilizing it as a justification for packing as many blacks as possible into a relatively few new districts while bleaching the surrounding districts by removing black voters who were vital to the reelection of a number of moderate white southern congressmen (see Chapter 5).

The *Washington Post*'s Wonkblog, in a May 16, 2014, study of the most gerrymandered districts (using a compactness standard) in the country, drove this point home: "Contrary to one popular misconception about the practice, the point of gerrymandering isn't to draw yourself a collection of overwhelmingly safe seats. Rather, it's to give your opponents a small number of safe seats, while drawing yourself a larger number of seats that are not quite as safe, but that you can expect to win comfortably." Of the six most gerrymandered districts in the country identified by the *Post*, four were minority districts from North Carolina, Florida, and Texas – southern states where Republicans controlled the redistricting process in the 2011 round of line-drawing.48

After the 2012 elections, 98 members of the House Republican Conference were from the South, and additional GOP members were from the Border States of Kentucky, Missouri, and West Virginia. But as recently as 1982, the GOP only had 34 seats in the 11 states of the Confederacy. The locus of power in the GOP clearly has shifted southward.

Congressional Republican political power in the Northeast and parts of the Midwest, where the party was able to elect moderate members willing to work across party lines, also started to diminish at about the same time Republican fortunes began to rise in the South. For years, some moderate Republicans in the Northeast and Midwest were able to continue to receive support from organized labor, particularly the building trades. However, after the Democrats lost the House in 1994, there was significant pressure on organized labor to abandon support for these Republicans because their seats were essential to the Democratic Party's efforts to retake the House.

Also at about the same time, longtime moderate Republican senators from the Northeast and Midwest began to leave office, either for personal/ health reasons or because of electoral defeats. These included people like Jacob Javits of New York, Clifford Case of New Jersey, Hugh Scott of Pennsylvania, and Ed Brooke of Massachusetts.

The most dramatic effect was in the House. Newly-elected southern Republicans tended to be social conservatives on issues such as abortion, guns, and school prayer. And they were much less inclined to compromise than were the moderate and conservative Democrats they replaced. Their views became the clear majority position in the Republican conference and pushed the House GOP farther to the right. This was exacerbated by the rise of the Tea Party movement, which sent to Congress a new group of Republicans who were willing to risk the credit rating of the United States in showdowns on issues like the continuation of Obamacare.

A somewhat comparable situation was also occurring on the Democratic side in the House. Successful GOP efforts to drive out of office moderate and conservative Democrats from the South and Border States meant that the Democratic Caucus moved further to the left. Congresswoman Nancy Pelosi came from the more liberal wing of the party when she was elected Democratic leader and later became Speaker. Pelosi, a tireless fundraiser, actually had to be a moderating force in her caucus from time to time when liberal members wanted to push the caucus too far to the left.

The Senate became very competitive. As moderate Republicans from the Northeast and Midwest were replaced by Democrats and moderate Democrats from the South were replaced by Republicans, it became harder for either party to put together a significant majority. The few southern Democrats who had survived all this change – Mary Landrieu of Louisiana, Mark Pryor of Arkansas, and Kay Hagan of North Carolina – were pressed hard by Republican challengers in 2014. And Tea Party Republicans like Ted Cruz of Texas, Rand Paul of Kentucky, and Mike Lee of Utah made compromise between the two parties more difficult.

The upshot of all this is that many House members in both parties worried about primary challenges from more extreme individuals in their own parties, and this made it even harder for them to consider political compromise with the other side. As a result, some Republican House members who wanted to move to the center from time to time were frozen in place by the conservatives of their own party and had to play to the base in order to survive a potential primary challenge. Primaries can be particularly tricky because they tend to be low-turnout elections, and a well-organized faction within a member's own party can cause real problems for an incumbent. Thus, for most members, the primaries became the focus of their reelection efforts.

In both 2010 and 2012, Tea Party candidates for the Senate won Republican primaries or party conventions but then lost the general election because they were too conservative. This lesson was not lost on other Republican incumbents like Pat Roberts of Kansas and Orrin Hatch of Utah, who, in their next reelection campaigns, had to vote the straight, very conservative line in the Senate to prevent a successful challenge for re-nomination. Once again, this served to make compromise across party lines more difficult. The old-line business establishment in the GOP worked hard in 2014 to defeat Tea Party candidates in some states, realizing that such candidates made it harder for business-friendly Republicans to hold the House and retake the Senate.

I personally know several thoughtful Republican members of the House from my home state of Texas who clearly would like to move to the center on some issues but live in mortal fear of a conservative primary challenge. To head this off, they vote in lockstep with the rightward members of their party even though their personal views are in another direction.

Democrats also must look over their shoulders at potential primary challengers, though this is normally not as great a factor in my party. A classic example of a damaging challenge from the left occurred in Arkansas senator Blanche Lincoln's reelection campaign in 2010. Senator Lincoln had to withstand a withering attack from her left in the Democratic primary. She won, but the effort so drained her financially that she was easily defeated by a Republican that fall.

Another factor that compels candidates of both parties to play to their respective bases is increasing party polarization in recent elections. It used to be conventional wisdom that the candidate who won the independents would win the election. The aforementioned 2013 election of Terry McAuliffe as governor of Virginia demonstrated that this is not always the case today.

McAuliffe lost independents by 6% but still won the elections by 3%. Party identification in Virginia, now a classic swing state, had changed so much that 40% of the population identified as Democratic and 34% of the population identified as Republican. McAuliffe, in a brilliantly-executed campaign, won nearly unanimously among Democrats and the Republican candidate won Republicans by a similar margin. The Democratic share of the vote was so much larger than the Republican share that McAuliffe could lose independents and still win the election. Had he played too much to the middle (as 2009 Democratic gubernatorial candidate Creigh Deeds did), he may not have been able to motivate his minority and northern Virginia base to turn out in the numbers they did.

Republicans may now face a comparable situation nationwide. The Republican Party has become the majority party of white voters; however, as described in Chapter 4, the white share of the total electorate has dropped significantly in the last 20 years, falling from 87% in 1992 to 72% in 2012. And Democrats still get close to 40% of the white vote. As the minority share of the electorate grows and as Republicans are badly beaten among minority voters, it will become increasingly difficult for them to win national elections unless they can change the equation. This is particularly true if the GOP cannot figure out how to win a greater percentage of the Hispanic and youth vote, the most quickly-growing parts of the electorate. The Republican base, still very important in the nominating process, is shrinking while the Democratic base is growing.

Successful Republican candidates must play to the base to win nominations, and successful Democratic candidates must play to the base to win general elections. That is a classic recipe for gridlock.

There is considerable irony in all this. Appealing to the base social conservative and Tea Party vote is critical to the success of many Republicans in a party primary. Appeals to the minority and single woman base of the Democratic Party are now critical to the success of many Democrats in general elections campaigns. Thus appeals to base voters operate differently in each party. To the extent that the GOP base controls primaries and the Democratic base is vital to general election victories, compromise becomes more difficult after an election.

A classic example of the strength of Democratic base voters on formulation of public policy after an election is the environmental movement. Key members of the environmental community had been early supporters of Obama in 2008 and were important to his reelection in 2012. The environmental community was dead set against approval of the Keystone Pipeline to transport hard-to-refine, dirtier oil from Canada to the United States. Environmentalists had provided early financial support to Obama in 2008 and had been important in his efforts to carry states like Colorado in both 2008 and 2012. Because of their opposition to Keystone, Obama delayed a final decision on the pipeline for several years.

Another example is the power of the gay community, which had rallied to Obama in both 2008 and 2012. Obama was uneasy about the issue of gay marriage, but he eventually announced that he was in favor of it. Certainly the fact that public opinion and court decisions were moving in the direction of gay marriage was significant, but the loyalty of these base voters also had to have entered into Obama's thinking at some point.

Another example of the power of base voters on political compromise is the hardcore conservative base of the Republican Party, so important to winning party primaries and to the party's presidential nomination fight. A number of thoughtful Republicans nationwide have understood how important arriving at a compromise on immigration reform is to the party's ability to attract Hispanic support in the future. However, the hardcore GOP base has been opposed to anything approaching amnesty for long-term Hispanic residents, and this has hampered the party's working for political compromise on this issue.

The importance of working the base vote in a general election was driven home to me in 1994. My district at that time had a Democratic performance index (DPI) of 52.7% based on how the average statewide Democratic candidate performed in my district. Since I normally enjoyed some Republican support as well, my election percentage was usually much higher than that figure.

However, it became clear in the course of the campaign that it was going to be a dicey year for Democrats. In fact, that fall we lost control of the House for the first time in 40 years. Many of my Democratic colleagues never saw this coming and didn't work the Democratic base hard enough to win reelection. I did early polling and understood that this election would be tough.

As a result, I devised a campaign strategy that included strong attention to the minority base in my district with the assumption that I wouldn't get very many crossover Republican votes and might even lose some conservative Democrats that year. My district was about 20% black (with most of that population concentrated in the southeast Ft. Worth section of my district). My campaign plan was predicated on the black community voting its strength. This meant that the black share of the total votes cast that year needed to be as close to 20% as possible. In some years, black turnout had lagged and not approached that amount.

The mathematical calculation for a win was very straightforward: I needed 95% of the projected 20% black turnout, 40% of the projected 75% white turnout (anchored by my support among labor union members who worked at defense and auto plants in the cities between Dallas and Ft. Worth), and a majority of the projected 5% Hispanic turnout.

My campaign consultant, Jim Duffy, was a veteran of many Democratic races in the South and totally agreed with the strategy. Basically, Duffy told me to "live in southeast Ft. Worth" the last 30 days of the campaign. While we worked the rest of the district mostly with direct mail and broadcast media, I spent almost all of my personal time attending events in southeast Ft. Worth. In addition to attending black church services on Sundays, I was at every church banquet, every meeting of black sororities and fraternities, every function held by the NAACP or other black civic organizations, and even some black funerals. My car knew by itself the way to that part of my district.

Additionally, my campaign ran a highly-organized absentee and early vote program in the black precincts. Under Texas law, senior citizens could vote by mail and anyone could vote early in person during an early vote period that extended for several weeks, including one weekend. Remarkably, almost half of the votes cast in my black precincts were from mail-in absentees and in-person early voting.

On Election Day, I survived with 52.8% of the vote districtwide (almost the exact DPI for the district). Black turnout as a percentage of total votes cast was almost exactly 20%.

The hardcore base had saved me.

How did I respond to this narrow escape? Did I change my voting record to reflect the black turnout that had saved my career? The answer was that I didn't need to alter my voting record because I normally had a 100 score on the NAACP voting studies and had, from the start, committed myself to the cause of civil rights. However, I did look for opportunities to shore up my support in the white community, particularly in the two rural counties to the south of Dallas County that had been added to my district in 1992. I concentrated some of my time on agricultural issues and looked to the advice of my Texas colleague Charlie Stenholm, a senior member of the House Agriculture Committee, on how to vote on matters important to that part of my district.

There are other examples in recent years of how the Democratic base saved Democratic candidates in general elections.

During my second term as chair of the DCCC (1998 election cycle), there were still a number of districts in the South and Border States with black populations between 20% and 35% – prior to when the Republicans successfully used the Voting Rights Act as a club to pack black voters into a relatively small number of districts.

Recognizing an opportunity for the DCCC, I set up a special task force headed by veteran black congressman Charlie Rangel of New York and accomplished political operative Donna Brazile to maximize black turnout in these potentially swing districts. They put together a very effective plan, and its success was a major contributor to the Democrats' picking up five seats. That was the only time in the 20th century that the party of the president gained seats in the sixth year of a president's eight years in office.

President Obama, in both his 2008 and 2012 campaigns, won the presidency by maximizing turnout among Democratic base voters – blacks, Hispanics, young voters, gays, and single suburban women. The question remains as to whether future white Democratic nominees can replicate what Obama did in 2008 and 2012.

TOM'S RESPONSE

I had a similar problem with my party base in 2006. Polling in my district in early January showed that I was beating my strongest potential Democratic opponent, but I was only polling at 51% (my opponent was polling in the high 20s). In prior years I had usually been near 60% at that point in a campaign. Moreover, I had just come off my best legislative session ever. Something was different, and my pollster told me that President Bush was very unpopular and voters were taking out their displeasure with the president on me.

I made two major adjustments to my usual campaign plan. One was that through major media, I emphasized my differences from the Bush administration and the GOP leadership in Congress, especially on social issues. President Bush was polling a favorable rating only in the high 20s, and doubling down with the White House would further alienate me from swing voters who were mad at the president.

Also, I nailed down what Democratic support I had previously held: the Professional Firefighters, the Letter Carriers, and a handful of other unions.

Though I had sponsored right-to-work legislation and voted to repeal Davis-Bacon wage legislation, my committee chairmanship enabled me to work closely with several unions, including several federal employee unions. Together, we put forth a coalition to stop an AFL-CIO endorsement of my opponent, which was normally an automatic for a Democratic candidate in Virginia.

I did not want, nor could I have gotten, the endorsement for myself, as my labor record was not strong. But the AFL-CIO required a two-thirds vote to endorse. My opposition research revealed that my opponent's law firm had done legal work decertifying unions from the workplace and had even advertised that work in order to draw potential clients. It was a large firm and labor law was not his niche, but he was a partner and shared in the spoils of that work. In the end, we were able to neutralize the AFL-CIO and stop the endorsement.

I also spent many hours engaging in ethnic outreach. We sent mail in Korean to Korean American households, set up phone banks contacting Korean households, and ran ads on Korean-language TV and radio. We worked the mosques and had a targeted Vietnamese get-out-the-vote/advocacy plan. I drew the support of key tech and Hispanic leaders, particularly from the Salvadorian community. (I had visited El Salvador earlier that year and publicized it through Hispanic media.)

Unlike Martin, I did not double down on my base vote (in the exurbs of western Prince William County). I worked it, but there were two helpful factors that allowed me to invest my efforts in swing voters elsewhere. The first was that I had Senator George Allen running for reelection. He played hard to the base as being against gay marriage, pro-life, and for tax cuts. He drove the base's turnout. Additionally, once my opponent and the Democrats started attacking me for being too conservative (as they always did), the base would come home. Also, the state had a ballot measure outlawing gay marriage, which turned out the churches. Although I was not affiliated with the ballot measure, I was the beneficiary in Prince William County.

That is exactly what happened. Although the GOP lost 30 seats on Election Day, I was reelected with 56% of the two-party vote. George Allen lost a squeaker, losing my congressional district 56% to 44%. I had run 12 points ahead of the top of the ticket. Recognizing that "the base" was not enough to win, I had identified the weak links in the Democratic coalition and gone after them.

All told, of the 198 seats GOP candidates won on Election Day 2006, only seven had higher Democratic performance metrics than mine. I had contravened the "base vote" strategy by going after the get-able independents and Democrats. Fortunately for me, my Democratic opponent, seeing Bush's numbers in the tank, made no effort for the Republican vote. He conceded it to me, allowing me to go after his voters.

10

THE NEW MEDIA: POLARIZED AND SEGMENTED

By Martin Frost

Few things have evolved more rapidly in the time since Tom and I left Congress (in 2008 and 2004 , respectively) than the role of new media in American politics.

I will take a run at this subject because of my background in journalism and my role as both DCCC chair and Democratic Caucus chair, which brought me into daily contact with national and local media.

I started off wanting to be a reporter covering politics. My background includes being editor of my high school and college newspapers and earning a degree in journalism from the University of Missouri's School of Journalism. While in college, I was a summer intern for three years at the *Ft. Worth Press* in Texas.

Following graduation from Missouri in 1964, I covered county government for the *Wilmington News-Journal* (Delaware) for a year and then spent two years covering Congress for *Congressional Quarterly Weekly Report* in Washington, D.C. Prior to entering law practice in Texas, I was an on-the-air staff member for Dallas's KERA-TV's *Newsroom* program, which Jim Lehrer moderated before going to Washington to co-anchor the *McNeil-Lehrer Report* for PBS.

My congressional career paralleled some major developments in political media. The C-SPAN cameras providing live coverage of the House of Representatives were turned on in March of 1979 (my first year in office). CNN started providing 24-hour cable news coverage in June of 1980 (my second year). The Internet came about sometime during the early 1990s (midway in my congressional career). What a difference all three of these developments made.

Live C-SPAN broadcast of "special orders" at the end of each congressional session, when members could take the floor and talk at length on any subject, was key to Newt Gingrich's rise to prominence. He understood that there was an audience out there watching and that it didn't make any difference whether or not anyone else was on the floor while he was speaking. In fact, some of his attacks on Democrats so outraged then-Speaker Tip O'Neill that O'Neill ordered the C-SPAN cameras to pan the chamber to show that Gingrich was speaking to an empty room. And one day, O'Neill went into the well of the House to answer Gingrich in such a manner that House Minority Whip Trent Lott had the Speaker's words "taken down." That meant that the Speaker had violated the rules of the House by the nature of his attack on Gingrich and thus couldn't speak on the floor for the remainder of that day. This brought national attention to Gingrich and embarrassed O'Neill.

Gingrich and his allies also used special orders to criticize the subsequent House Speaker, Jim Wright, who ultimately resigned as Speaker due to ethics issues raised by Republicans. It can be argued that C-SPAN helped create Gingrich, who understood this new technological development in ways that Democrats were slow to grasp.

Of course, someone who lives by the sword also dies by the sword. Gingrich's successes against O'Neill and Wright made him overconfident. His over-the-top use of media when he insisted on calling for the impeachment of President Bill Clinton against the advice of some in his own party helped trigger his downfall.

The role of 24-hour cable news ultimately proved to be much greater than that of C-SPAN. CNN first came to national attention during the assassination attempt on President Ronald Reagan in March of 1981. That network was the only outlet really covering the story when it first developed. The commercial networks were all playing catch-up. CNN probably hit its high-water mark with Operation Desert Storm in 1991, when everyone (including officials at the Pentagon) was keeping up with the bombardment of Baghdad by watching CNN.

And then a brilliant political broadcaster named Roger Ailes figured out that there was significant money to be made by starting a conservative alternative to CNN, and Fox News was born. His invention turned out to be a major moneymaker and has had a dramatic influence on politics in the United States. A large number of people across the country who felt disenfranchised by the major networks and CNN suddenly had a place to get their news.

This was driven home to me dramatically when I left Congress following my defeat in 2004 and Brit Hume hired me as one of the Democratic voices on Fox. (I had consistently urged my Democratic colleagues to appear on Fox when I was caucus chairman so that its audience was at least exposed to an alternative point of view.) I had family in South Carolina who always saw me when I was on Fox. In fact, they would also tell their friends whenever I appeared. It seemed like every white resident of South Carolina watched that one channel, particularly in the small towns where I had relatives. They mostly didn't agree with my politics, but they were proud of my notoriety.

Ultimately, NBC realized that there was another audience of liberals who would watch a cable channel that catered to their views and put significant resources into its new venture, MSNBC, which like Fox passed CNN in viewers.

And so the cable wars were born. CNN, which often provided the most objective and comprehensive news coverage, fell behind both Fox and MSNBC because CNN did not have a brand and did not have enough loyal viewers who wanted coverage that really was "fair and balanced" (to quote Fox's slogan). And what you got on both Fox and MSNBC – particularly in the primetime evening hours – was often hot rhetoric that further polarized the country. Both MSNBC and Fox had some outstanding objective journalists like Andrea Mitchell and Chuck Todd (MSNBC) and Chris Wallace (Fox). And MSNBC's "Morning Joe" is a real effort to present a bipartisan view of American politics. CNN has continued to put excellent journalists like Wolf Blitzer and Jake Tapper in key timeslots, but their ratings have not recovered. We sometimes forget that television is first and foremost in the business of making money. What sells is what gets shown.

After four years, Fox and I ended my exclusive arrangement by mutual agreement. I really did want the opportunity to appear on other outlets, such as MSNBC and CNN. And just as my family in South Carolina had seen me on Fox, my Democratic friends now started seeing me whenever I was on MSNBC.

Talk radio has also been a major player in politics for some years now, mostly on the right. Rush Limbaugh figured out that someone could be both ideological and entertaining, and attract a large following in so being. Democrats have been slow to develop talk radio hosts that are as entertaining as Rush, even though he is often outrageous and simply wrongheaded in his politics. When I was driving between engagements in my districts, I would often tune in to Rush Limbaugh because I wanted to know what the opposition was saying and because I admired how clever he could be, even when I disagreed with him.

And then there is social media – Facebook, Twitter, YouTube, etc. So many people these days, particularly young people, use the Internet as their primary source of information. I personally love the breadth of material available on the Internet. But it's important to realize there is no editor for much of what appears, and the Internet is full of inaccuracies of both liberal and conservative biases.

This is not to say that the Internet hasn't been a boon for politics. It has made fundraising much easier – so much so that President Obama rejected federal funding for his presidential campaigns in both 2008 and 2012 because he could raise significantly more money through direct appeals online than the federal government could provide him for the general election. For many candidates, it has become common practice to raise campaign money in small sums through solicitations via the Internet. This has far less overhead than old-fashioned telephone or mail appeals to donors. The Internet has also made it much easier for challengers to raise money and for new candidates – such as Senators Elizabeth Warren and Ted Cruz – to raise campaign funds from these true believers.

Any discussion of the Internet and social media generally must recognize the dramatic effect both have had on substantive politics around the world and here at home. Many observers have pointed out the role that Facebook, Twitter, and YouTube played in the Kiev Maidan protests that led to the 2014 overthrow of Ukrainian president Victor Yanukovych and in the pro-tests at Cairo's Tahrir Square that forced Egyptian president Hosni Mubarak to step down. The role of social media is particularly important in countries where the government controls the broadcast free media and often does not permit dissenting voices to be heard.

It has been argued that Facebook and Twitter didn't cause these revolu-tions but did speed up the process by providing organizational tools. Sascha Meinrath, the director of the New America Foundation's Open Technology Initiative, made an interesting observation: "Social Media have become the pamphlets of the 21st century, a way that people who are frustrated with the status quo can organize themselves and coordinate protest." Thus they have supplanted the pamphlets that spread the word among colonies in the months and years leading up to the American Revolution. It's also worth pointing out that many autocratic nations, such as China, routinely try to block access to social media sites like Facebook.

There certainly are examples of how such sites have affected events in current-day America – in ways that politicians of my generation never anticipated. The Tea Party movement successfully used social media as an effective tool in turning out large numbers of people to protest Obamacare at town hall meetings in the summer of 2009. While these protests didn't derail the legislation, it can be argued that they laid the groundwork for the Republicans to regain control of the House in 2010.

New York congressman Anthony Weiner's highly-publicized fall from grace was driven by his posting of inappropriate pictures of himself on Twitter.

And both President Obama (in 2008) and Mitt Romney (in 2012) suf-fered significant embarrassment when comments they made went viral. When people in small towns lose their jobs, Obama said during his primary, "it's not surprising then they get bitter, they cling to guns or religion...." For his part, Romney told a Florida fundraising audience, "There are 47% who are with [President Barack Obama], who are dependent upon government, who believe that they are victims, who believe the government has a respon-sibility to care for them." Both of these comments were made in what both candidates thought were private sessions with contributors, but which were recorded and sent across the country via social media.

My colleague Bobby Etheridge from North Carolina was defeated for reelection in 2010 following a rude shoving match encounter he had with someone who claimed to be a student working on a project but would not further identify himself. It didn't make any difference that the "student" and his cameraman may have been trackers sent by the Republicans. All that counted was what people saw on the screen when the encounter was posted on YouTube and appeared on the late Andrew Breitbart's right-wing *Big Government* website.

It is interesting to examine how candidates like President Obama and incumbent members of the House and Senate have used new media in a positive way to promote their campaigns and to communicate with constituents.

The Project for Excellence in Journalism at the Pew Research Center takes a look every four years at how presidential candidates use the web and social media in their campaigns.

In its study covering the period from June 4-17 during the 2012 campaign[49], Pew noted in its overview,

"A new study of how the campaigns are using digital tools to talk directly with voters – bypassing the filter to traditional media – finds that the Obama campaign posted nearly four times as much content as the Romney campaign and was active on nearly twice as many platforms. Obama's digital content also engendered twice the number of shares, views and comments of his posts."

The study showed a dramatic difference in the use of Facebook, Twitter, and YouTube by the two campaigns. It revealed that during the period studied, Obama had 1,124,175 Facebook likes and Romney had 633,597. Further, it showed Obama had 150,106 Twitter retweets, compared to Romney's 8,061. Also, it indicated that Obama had 839,933 YouTube comments/likes/views and that Romney had 399,225.

The study then posed a question: "How important is digital campaigning: does more digital activity really translate into more votes?" It answered, "While there may be no simple answer, throughout modern campaign history successful candidates have tended to outpace their competitors in understanding changing communications." It cited FDR's use of radio, John F. Kennedy's use of television, and Ronald Reagan's "recognition of the potential for arranging the look and feel of campaign events in the use of satellites and video tape."

It then concluded, "Candidates quicker to grasp the power of new technology have used that to convey a sense that they represented a new generation of leadership more in touch with where the country was heading."

To get a view on how a typical member of Congress uses social media to communicate with constituents and the press, I visited the office of Texas congressman Marc Veasey, who represents the 33rd district (Dallas-Ft. Worth area). Veasey turned 43 in January of 2014; his political career spans both the period before social media became a major factor and the current era, when any members of Congress who ignore it do so at their own peril.

The first thing I learned was how his office uses social media to communicate with the press. His primary outreach is through Twitter; his office tweets reporters about upcoming public appearances rather than relying on email (reporters receive so many emails each day that they often don't read all of them) or text messaging, which are reserved for special occasions. Also, Veasey will often publish a tweet as he travels to a particular event. As of May 2014, his Twitter handle – @repveasey – had over 3,000 followers. At that time his Facebook page had nearly 5,500 followers and included links to videos and photos.

At events Veasey attends, congressional staffers take pictures to post on his congressional website or Facebook. Also, district staffers who attend events with Veasey are responsible for letting the D.C. staff know which reporters are in attendance so they can check tweets and other online entries reporters post about what happened at the event. I have personally noticed that Bud Kennedy, a columnist for the *Fort Worth Star-Telegram*, is particularly good about tweeting something almost any time I show up at a public event in either Ft. Worth or Dallas even though I've been out of Congress for 10 years.

Veasey also has his own YouTube channel and posts floor statements he delivers (downloaded from C-SPAN by staff), videos of appearances on national and local media, and remarks filmed in a studio in the Longworth

House Office Building maintained for members of Congress. These videos also are often posted on his official website.

On his official website, Veasey posts his voting record as well as his district schedule for events that are open to the public and an electronic newsletter.

Just maintaining this web page and links to various social media requires attention by two staffers.

When I was a member of Congress, we made many of these same efforts to connect, but they were not all done electronically and certainly not done in real time. It made me tired just learning about everything Veasey and his staff manage on a daily basis to communicate with constituents. But that is something that every congressman and senator must take seriously.

All of this has led to polarized public opinion and made political compromise much more difficult. I come from a tradition that believes in free media – I would not want to see government try to intervene in the marketplace and attempt to censor even extreme views. However, we must all realize that this freedom of expression guaranteed by our Constitution comes with a price that makes bipartisan government that much more difficult.

Maybe there is a way to get the public to accept more rational, less partisan discussion of public issues. We need to all keep trying to make this happen.

Tom's Response

I agree with much of what Martin says about the new media, particularly the quote from the Pew Center study indicating that candidates grasping the new technology convey a sense of leadership that is more in touch with where the country is heading and are therefore able to dominate communication of a message. This has been an area where Republicans have been slower to develop and innovate, ceding much of this territory to the Democrats.

In particular, Democrats' dominance of younger voters comes in part by their better online communications infrastructure, particularly the utilization of handheld devices. But political history has shown that over time the other side catches up, and Republicans are beginning to close the gap.

The Republican National Committee (RNC) is sinking far more resources into the effort than its cash-strapped Democratic counterpart (the DNC). However, working off the excellent base of Obama for America (OFA), the administration's organizing arm still remains dominant.

As media and political communications have evolved from radio to television to cable to the Internet, political campaigns have adjusted accordingly. When I started out at the local level, candidates' media campaigns were all about spinning their narratives to print reporters and having them printed in the newspaper. If a story was good enough, they could reproduce it and redistribute it as a neutral validation of their message. If they had the money, radio and television ads would supplement (or sometimes supplant) their earned media. But today it is vastly different, and politics has been changed forever.

The importance of Fox News to Republican primary voters cannot be overstated. When the federal government was shut down in 2013, one GOP member, feeling the heat from his civilian Department of Defense employees, told a reporter he would vote to reopen the government. This statement played well with the vast majority of his constituents. However, Fox decided to portray him and 17 other Republicans as backing down from Democrats, and he was labeled on the tube as a traitor to the conservative cause.

All of a sudden his political base exploded with nasty emails. His phone rang off the hook with calls from "former" supporters, and his local Republican leaders erupted. The congressman, ever wary of a contested primary, walked his statement back and the deluge subsided. When the House voted to reopen government, this member voted no. The media had stopped reporting the news and was now influencing outcomes.

Another Republican member went to the floor of the House to denounce Grover Norquist, the chief guru in the fight against tax increases. The speech did not receive much response until it was featured on Fox News, at which point angry conservatives from all over the country lit up the congressman's switchboard like a Christmas tree.

The fact is that conservatives tend to watch Fox News because it has commentators and hosts that reflect their values. Psychologists call this cognitive dissonance, in which viewers tune in to have their own opinions validated.

Much of the same can be said for MSNBC in the evenings as well. Ed Shultz, Al Sharpton, Chris Matthews, and Rachel Maddow offer liberal perspectives and usually invite liberal guests to discuss the news of the day. One Democratic member told me he watches it at night to get his "fix," his reinforcement for the next day's partisan battles.

An alien watching Fox and MSNBC on the same evening might think it was observing two different planets. The two networks feature speakers that dutifully recite their parties' talking points. Often, the two channels disagree on basic facts! It makes one ponder – if the two sides cannot even agree on the facts, how could they ever come together on a solution?

I remember one conversation in the Republican cloakroom, in the middle of an immigration debate. "What is amnesty for the undocumented?" asked one member. Another member answered, in a moment of off-camera candor, "It's whatever Fox and the talk radio commentators say it is." These comments apply to both the left and the right, but they demonstrate the growth of new media in influencing outcomes and the limitations of political leaders in trying to explain them.

The Internet, as Martin noted, adds to the polarization. One former Obama cabinet member confided that the "crap-to-content ratio" of the Internet was excruciatingly high. How can one explain basic facts to people who don't want to hear them? Or, as one GOP leader put it, "How do you argue with stupid?"

Political leaders feel stymied by new media, in which the communications are ubiquitous, the content is not vetted, and there are no rules of engagement. Anything goes. Private conversations are not respected. Any action or misstatement can be blown up, edited, and distributed on You-Tube in a nanosecond. These new "law of the jungle" rules do not bring out the most candid political behavior. Rather, they tend to keep politicians safely in their own party boxes, wary of compromise and reluctant to take a lead on anything controversial.

It should be noted that much of what passes for raw news is actually nothing more than a business model that thrives on giving people what they want to hear. In an age where many get their news or political impressions through a tweet or news brief, it is no wonder that political gridlock continues.

11

HOUSE ELECTIONS: A SCIENCE UNTO THEMSELVES

By Tom Davis

The House of Representatives and the Senate are very different animals of the same species. Although both are products of our democratic system, they were designed to operate separately and represent different constituencies. They were the result of a great compromise at the founding of our Republic, intertwining the New Jersey Plan, which gave each state equal representation, with the Virginia Plan, which apportioned our national legislature, or Congress, by population.

In short, the founders wanted the Senate to represent the states and the House to represent the people. That may, to some, be a distinction without a difference, but in practice and in law, the differences are real.

Originally, the "people" had little to say about who their senators were, for it was the state legislators who elected senators for six-year terms. The "people" directly elected their House members for two-year terms. Thus, if the public became angry, it could vent its frustration every two years and turn out the House of Representatives, but only one-third of the Senate could turn over in that same time period. This preserved some stability in the system (the Senate) while allowing the public to express displeasure in more frequent intervals (the House).

We all remember, from history, the Lincoln-Douglas debates during the 1858 campaign for Illinois's Senate seat. What many historians fail to note is that although Lincoln lost to Douglas, he outpolled Douglas by 4,085 votes. However, because of a gerrymander in the Illinois legislature, Douglas was elected 54-46 when the legislature convened on January 5.

The Constitution was changed in 1912, via the 17th Amendment, to allow the public to directly elect senators. The amendment allowed each state to decide how to fill vacancies in the event of a senator's death or resignation, underscoring the fact that even with direct elections, senators still represent the states. In 36 states, the governor appoints a successor, who typically fills the seat until the next regularly scheduled general election. In a few of those cases, the legislature places limitations on the governor's selection – for example, by setting scheduling rules or requiring that the successor come from the same party as the previous senator. In the other 14 states, according to a compilation by the National Conference of State Legislatures, a special election must be held to fill the vacancy; some of those states permit a short-term appointee in the interim, but a few do not.

House members, always popularly elected, have their vacancies filled only by special election, maintaining that close tie to the people they represent. The only leeway given to the state in House special elections is the date of the election, and most states give the governor a great degree of discretion with that timing.

Many argue that senators, representing statewide constituencies, represent broader-based electorates than House members. In general that is true, but seven states have only one House member, meaning that the House and Senate members share the same constituencies. When I was in Congress, I also liked to note that my House district in northern Virginia contained more people than the entire states of Wyoming, Alaska, and North Dakota did.

Representing smaller constituencies allows House members, as a general rule, to personally get to know a larger percentage of their voters than senators do, and it necessarily makes a campaign for the House a much different undertaking than one for the Senate. This will be addressed later in this book.

Also note that senators must live in the states they represent, but House members do not have to live in the districts they represent. As a rule, it is better to live in the political jurisdiction you represent. You get to vote for yourself. You live in proximity to your voters and can carve out a local identity much more easily. But while living in your district might be smart politics, it is not required to run for a House seat.

For years, Ron Paul lived in the heart of Tom DeLay's 22nd district (Texas). He had represented Fort Bend and Brazoria Counties until he left the House to run for the Senate in 1984, when DeLay was elected to succeed him. When Paul later returned to the House after his first run for president, his new 14th district included large portions of the former 22nd district as well. A population boom had doubled the size of the southern Houston suburbs; and Paul, with a national fundraising base and goodwill among many 14th district voters he had previously represented, made a comeback in 1996, defeating Congressman Greg Laughlin in a Republican primary. Laughlin had previously been elected as a Democrat and had switched parties after the Republicans had taken the House in 1994.

There is an abundance of examples of politicians picking a district they think they can win and running without the benefit of a local residence. With social mobility so high and districts that are created in such odd shapes that they share no community of interest, voters do not put a candidate's residency high on their list of issue priorities. Residency can still be an issue, demonstrating connection or lack thereof to the voter base, but only if it is linked to other facets of non-connection to the district.

For example, members who no longer maintain a home in their districts (having moved their family to Washington) are attacked routinely, but only as part of a narrative showing that such members have lost touch with the voters. The attacks are usually supplemented with a recitation of unpopular votes, foreign trips, etc. demonstrating that members have lost interest in the voters they represent. This is, of course, not unique to the House. Senators Richard Lugar of Indiana and Tom Daschle of South Dakota were lambasted for not having homes in their respective states after they were elected. But the cost of having two homes, one of them in the expensive D.C. market, is too much for some members to afford.

Some House members sleep in their offices during the weeks Congress is in session and skedaddle back to their homes when the last vote of the week is gaveled down. This leaves scant time to legislate, attend hearings, or get to know other members (particularly those from the other party), but voters seem less concerned about those points and prefer to see their members back at home. Better to be attacked for poor legislative outcomes (for which there is a shared responsibility that crosses party lines) than for becoming out of touch or "going Washington."

Financing House Campaigns

House campaigns can be expensive. In the 2012 election cycle, the average competitive race saw each candidate spending over two million dollars. This confirms the adage that in today's politics it costs a lot of money just to lose. The two-million-dollar figure, however, is often just the beginning. In a two-party competitive race, political committees associated with the parties (National Republican Campaign Committee, or NRCC, and Democratic Congressional Campaign Committee, or DCCC) will often add hundreds of thousands of dollars in independent expenditures on top of that. Moreover, super PACs, which abound, can bring in additional money often totaling hundreds of thousands of dollars.

I always advised candidates to raise early money and show a large "cash on hand" in their campaign accounts as the filing deadline neared. Having a large campaign kitty can deter many would-be challengers who are awed by how much they will need to raise just to get started. In fact, many congressional races are won at the filing deadline for this very reason.

In 1994, my Democratic incumbent had less than $100,000 cash on hand as I was preparing to make my decision whether to challenge or not. I knew I could raise that amount in my kickoff, so I proceeded undeterred. Had she had triple that amount, I probably would have backed off.

Today, many incumbents carry over large amounts from previous campaigns as a message to would-be challengers of what they face financially if they should choose to run. It is an often effective tool in deterring strong opposition.

The antidote, of course, is for potential challengers to either be self-funders or sell themselves to super PACs who can make up the difference.

The special election in March 2014 to fill the Florida seat (St. Petersburg) that had been held by deceased congressman Bill Young is a case in
point. Democrat Alex Sink raised and spent $3.1 million on her own behalf,
and the DCCC kicked in with additional contributions of $2.2 million. The
Republican nominee, Dave Jolly, although facing a competitive primary,
raised a mere $1.4 million; but the NRCC came in with $2.2 million to supplement the effort. The Center for Responsible Politics noted outside
interest groups and super PACs spent $4.5 million on the race, of which
$2.8 million was for Jolly.

That alone is astounding! What is even more telling is that of the total
campaign outlays, only one-third was spent by the candidates. Party committees spent another third, and super PACs and other groups combined
for the final third of the total amount spent.

This district is hardly an anomaly; although, to put it in context, some
unique factors influenced the participation of all concerned. For one thing,
the St. Petersburg area had long been held by the Republican Party. Since
1954, when Bill Cramer had claimed the seat for the GOP, only two people
had represented the district – Cramer and Young. When Cramer ran for an
open Senate seat in 1970, his former aide, then-State Senator Bill Young,
easily held the seat for the Republicans.

St. Petersburg had been a haven for midwestern WASP retirees for decades, so the area's political behavior was more like that of a midwestern
Republican district than that of a southern district. So when the district was
created in 1952, young Cramer – a 30-year-old Harvard Law-educated state
legislator who had overseen the GOP's win of a majority of county offices in
1950 – ran, with Eisenhower at the top of the ticket. Cramer lost narrowly,
winning Pinellas County (St. Petersburg) but losing the rest of the district,
including smaller Hillsborough County (Tampa).

But in 1954, Cramer was back for another try against Courtney Campbell, the Democrat who had narrowly defeated him in 1952 by a margin of
50.7% to 49.3%. This time, Cramer triumphed by a similar margin and set
himself up for relatively easy reelections until he decided to vacate the seat
and run for Senate in 1970.

Though Cramer ultimately lost his Senate race, he carried St. Petersburg
handily; and Bill Young triumphed decisively in his House race.

Over time, demographic patterns changed and St. Petersburg became more Democratic and thus more competitive. Al Gore won Pinellas County by 16,000 votes in 2000 (Nader had 10,000 votes), and 2004 saw the Bush-Kerry race dead even. This district had become one of the nation's relatively few truly competitive House districts.

Nonetheless, Young was continuing to win, with redistricting assistance from the Republican state legislature, which took downtown St. Pete out of his district and moved it into a district with Tampa. Moreover, Young had ascended into the chairmanship of the House Appropriations Committee, where he was able to bring jobs back to the region. Young remained personally popular, but the Democratic trend of his district had the eye of the DCCC strategists, who waited for years for Young's retirement to make their move on the district.

In 2012, the GOP-led state legislature tried to fortify the 13th district for Young, but he faced a spirited challenge from a young attorney named Jessica Ehrlich. Though underfunded and not on any target lists, Ehrlich held Young to 57.6% of the vote as Obama once again won the district (in the 2008 presidential campaign, he had beaten McCain by a margin of 52% to 48%). That was Young's closest reelection in 20 years; and as Young was by then 82 years old, the Democrats took a keener interest in the district.

Upon Young's death in October 2013, the swing seat became a "must-win" district for both sides. For Republicans, the seat – which they had held for 60 years – was a symbol of Republicanism. For Democrats, this was an Obama district that they had to have to get any chance to win back the House.

Democrats won round one when they scored a recruiting coup, convincing Alex Sink, the former elected chief financial officer of the state, to run. She had lost a 2010 race for governor by one percentage point, but had carried this district handily. Republicans tried to recruit the mayor of St. Petersburg and a sitting state senator but were rebuffed by both. They ended up nominating David Jolly, a former aide to Bill Young and a lobbyist, after a contested primary that featured dueling endorsements from Young's widow (for Jolly) and Young's son (for another candidate).

National Republicans were initially not optimistic about their chances. Out-raised, out-recruited, and having drained Jolly's campaign coffers in the primary, they were not off to a good start. However, losing a Republican-held seat in a special election was not the signal the NRCC wanted to send going into the midterm elections. So it doubled down, spending hundreds of thousands of dollars on a race the Republicans were losing.

Historically, however, midterm elections generally trend against the party of the president, though each race is different. I remember the Republicans losing Denny Hastert's seat after he resigned as minority leader in 2008. That same year, the GOP lost two other seats – in Louisiana and Mississippi – in special elections. In all three districts, the Republicans had divisive primaries and the Democrats used the election as a protest against President Bush, whose numbers were sinking. Those races portended a 20-seat gain for Democrats that November.

In the case of the special election for Young's Florida seat, the cavalry was called in. Special-interest super PACs from each side inundated the airwaves, Internet, and streets, advocating for their preferred candidates. All things being equal, this should have been a Democratic pickup; but, as always, all things were not equal. The race was turned into a referendum on President Obama and Obamacare, and the GOP scored a narrow but decisive victory, with 89,099 votes for Jolly and 85,642 votes for Sink.

Sink, sensing the lay of the land going into the midterm cycle, declined to run in the November general election and, after some faux steps, the Democrats failed to file a candidate, leaving Jolly unopposed for reelection. This placed the seat safely in GOP hands for another election cycle.

The third-party independent expenditures in this race were undoubtedly the beginning of a trend in targeted races. The candidates raise as much as they can, but they can be smothered with expenditures from interest groups and super PACs, which are not subject to the same fundraising limitations as candidates or parties. However, with fewer and fewer House seats in the competitive range, we can expect to see more outside money poured in to influence the results.

Prospective competitive House candidates must be expected to raise or personally contribute hundreds of thousands of dollars to be competitive today. There were a handful of House races in 2012 where the winners spent under a half million dollars, but eight of those ten seats had incumbents with little or no opposition.

One exception was Gloria Negrete McLeod (California's 35th district), who spent only $344,428 on her own race in a newly-carved, safely Democratic district. However, she was aided by a $3 million independent expenditure from New York City mayor Michael Bloomberg's Mayors Against Illegal Guns, which targeted her chief opponent, Representative Joe Baca, who had represented a part of the district before the redraw of the district boundaries. The two Democrats were competing for a redistricted seat after having been the top two candidates who led the field in California's new jungle primary.

In competitive seats, party leaders look for candidates who can attract money. Self-funders are often preferred because it means the party can deploy its resources elsewhere. As the NRCC chair in 2002, I flew out to Colorado to meet a banker named Bob Beauprez because he had the financial gravitas to make the newly-created 6th district competitive. Beauprez didn't live in the district, but he had plenty of connections there. And since it was a brand-new district given to Colorado after the 2000 census, we figured he had the best chance of winning. We helped him through a tough primary and he went on to win three terms before running statewide.

In elections in safe or relatively safe party districts, the national parties generally stay out of the primary unless an exotic candidate could put the seat in jeopardy. This "hands-off" primaries attitude has given some ideological groups a carte blanche to get into party primaries and elect an advocate. The result is a more ideological caucus, but since the winner is nonetheless one of the party, leaders feel it is in their interest to stay out and put resources elsewhere, where they can win a seat that could otherwise go to the other party.

The result is that ideological and special interest groups are now empowered in a way few could have imagined when campaign finance reform was passed in 2002. For roughly 80% of House races, the primary is, for all practical purposes, the election. If the party leaders continue to choose to deploy their resources only in the marginal districts, the more ideological groups will dominate the nomination process. This has given rise to more ideological candidates having more resources and, therefore, producing more successful primary outcomes.

It is, therefore, not surprising that the House caucuses of both parties have become more ideologically polarized. The rules have been rigged to advantage the wing and special-interest groups. Prospective candidates for the House now pay their respects to these groups before entering the race, hoping for their support or, at a minimum, their neutrality. It also means that party leaders have little control over the outcomes in these safe districts. By focusing their attention on the 20% of districts that determine which party will control the majority, they ignore a majority of the races that will determine who controls the party caucus. Only a handful of incumbents in either party lose in these primaries. But they increasingly tailor their messages for the ideological wings to avoid challenges. Consequently, the ideological groups have gained a large influence.

In 2014, Republicans controlled the House by a comfortable, though not insurmountable, margin. But the center of the House GOP conference is considerably different from the center of the nation. This makes it more difficult for the GOP brand to win a national election or be competitive in many states. The sum makeup of House districts is not representative of the makeup of the country's total electorate. Nor is the center of the Democratic caucus close to the nation's center. Traditionally, the House has been the more ideological legislative body.

HOUSE DISTRICTS

The key thing to understand in analyzing House races is that no two districts are alike. Observing a district's partisan vote patterns tells you little about the constituencies of those districts. Race, ethnicity, geographical location, income, age, and education level all have their own variables, and the particular balance in each district is different.

In 2012, the poorest district in the country was Jose Serrano's district in the south Bronx, with a median income of $23,894. It gave Obama 97% of the vote that year. The second poorest district in the country was Hal Rogers's district in southeastern Kentucky, with a median household income of $29,627. It gave Obama 23% of the vote. Serrano's district was urban, 66% Hispanic, and 33% black. Rogers's district was rural and 97% white.

In 2014, six of the ten wealthiest districts in the country (by median household income) were Democratic and four were Republican. Nine of the ten most educated districts were Democratic, while nine of the ten least educated were also Democratic. Eight of the ten districts with the highest median age were Republican; and a ninth, held by Democrat Patrick Murphy of Florida, was carried by Romney. Nine of the top ten Hispanic districts were Democratic (the one Republican district was substantially Cuban but carried by Obama), while all majority-black districts were heavily Democratic.

Generalizations are easy to make, but every district has its own demographic, its own context, and its unique electoral oleo. We have discussed the dynamics of safe party seats, but the 20% of districts that are potentially swing are the ones that make the difference in which party controls the House. And unlike the Senate, the House runs strictly on majority control. The late Speaker Nick Longworth once stated, "The role of the minority party is to help make up the quorum and collect their salary."

The House majority party decides which bills come to the floor, what amendments are offered, and how much time is allotted for consideration. The majority controls committee ratios, staff allocations, and the overall schedule for the chamber. There is little opportunity, absent a discharge petition, for a separate majority of the House to work its will absent permission from the majority party's leadership. This is why parties allocate their resources to the districts that are most likely to determine which party is in the majority.

Unlike with safe party districts, party leadership pays lots of attention to those seats that are considered marginal. Incumbents are assisted with fundraising and given key bills and amendments to offer, or are put in the spotlight for media appearances. Candidates are carefully recruited to ensure the party is running first-tier challengers for those incumbents in shaky districts or more marginal open seats.

As the NRCC chairman, I would often travel to key districts and meet with potential candidates. Often I was recruiting not just the potential candidate, but the spouse as well. The decision to run for Congress is ultimately a family decision and is particularly tough in a marginal or competitive district.

The constant commuting to and from Washington keeps members away from their families and is particularly challenging when younger children are involved. Weekdays, while members are in Washington, the spouses are home taking care of the kids. When members return home, often exhausted from the week's legislative business in D.C. and a long plane ride, constituents demand to meet them. They are expected to attend community events in the evenings and all weekend long and then fly back to Washington. Depending on where the members live, the often weekly trip home can take up to six hours one way. That leaves precious little family time.

In a campaign year, members must put up with trackers, surprise YouTube confrontations, and negative personal attacks. Without spousal support of this effort, it is difficult for a marriage to survive, so it is imperative the couples understand what is involved.

All that being said, the opportunity to serve in Congress and to make a difference for the country can be an alluring inducement to run.

When initial meetings with candidates were promising, I would buy them and their spouses plane tickets to D.C. and have them meet the party leaders (the Speaker, perhaps the president, and other well-known figures). I would invite the prospective candidates to a Republican Conference meeting, introduce them and let them speak, and then ensure we had another dinner – after an extensive tour of the Capitol and a day of meeting prospective supporting PAC directors – to seal the deal.

In 2000, our polling showed that only one Republican candidate could win an open House seat in Rhode Island. This was ordinarily not GOP territory, but as the party's leader, I was constantly probing to find opportunities others may have dismissed. The prospective candidate was Jeff Pine, the state's attorney general, and our polling surveys showed him beating all Democratic comers by ten points. No other Republican was even close.

We brought Pine to Washington. I even took him on a trip to the baseball All-Star Game at Fenway Park. But in the end, he opted not to run, citing his family time and a lucrative career in the practice of law. I couldn't blame him, but it was further evidence that Congress is not such an alluring vocation for everyone. Good candidates need to have their hearts, their heads, and their families committed to the effort to be successful; and sometimes the ablest, the best, and the brightest have other attractive options.

Winning control of Congress is a serious business with serious consequence. And just like every business, it is a competition for talent.

I would further note that the skills needed to win elections – such as
glad-handing, raising money, and speaking publicly – are not always congruent to those needed to legislate – like crafting legislation, cajoling members, and making the needed compromises to get the legislation through
committee and passed into law. But if one doesn't get elected in the first
place, those legislative skills won't matter.

I remember talking to one pollster about her candidate for a high-profile
office and asked, "But what kind of governor will he be?" She replied,
"That's not my problem. My job is to get him elected." (She did.)

In a way, the question of governance is one for voters to ask. Yes, the candidate may be a good parent. Or the candidate may be a person of faith. Or
perhaps the candidate has a background or ethnic profile voters identify
with. But can the candidate govern?

That is probably not on the voters' minds when they go into the booth.
In today's polarized political atmosphere, winning is everything. Governing
is often an afterthought.

TARGETING DISTRICTS

Which districts do political parties target? As with so many of the topics
we've been discussing, the answer is both simple and complex.

On one level, districts are targeted based on their degree of competition.
Districts with a generally Republican or swing makeup were put high on my
priority list right after elections. Where had we come close? What incumbents had underperformed, revealing some level of vulnerability for the next
cycle? What incumbents had made mistakes during the cycle with a bad
vote, a vocal gaffe, or a scandal? What open seats gave our party a chance?
And, with what seats were we on defense?

That is "Targeting 101."

Though the initial list can be as high as 80 seats, it gets whittled down
depending on a number of factors. First and foremost is the ability to attract
a quality candidate to run. A quality candidate can raise campaign funds,
holds some level of esteem within the community, or has a compelling
resume that will be marketable to the general electorate.

However, some candidates who are interested in running for public office not only have none of the above, they also carry baggage. Baggage isn't just found in voting records. It could be controversial business practices. It could be a criminal record or personal foible, such as a tax lien or bankruptcy, or perhaps an ugly divorce. All of these elements enter into a campaign today; and with opposition research growing more sophisticated, there is very little that is out of bounds in a campaign.

Sometimes, the most highly-recruited general election candidate cannot get through the nomination fight. Often, in such instances, the seat drops off the radar screen. At the end of the day, party committees and super PACs don't like to waste resources, so the initial target lists usually shrink.

Races are routinely added or subtracted from the target list based on changing circumstances. In 2010, as it appeared that a huge GOP wave was forming, many seats were added to the GOP target list in the closing weeks as polling showed that additional resources in some districts could bring more seats into competition. In wave years like 2006 and 2010, many candidates who in a normal year would have been consigned to also-ran status emerged with congressional seats. The sophisticated polling by the parties and super PACs allows few opportunities to go unnoticed.

The number of non-targeted candidates who have won seats in Congress in recent history can be counted on one hand. Parties have no philosophical litmus test for engagement and are driven only by the determination to win seats and be in the majority. For the leadership of both parties in the House of Representatives, as the legendary former Green Bay Packers coach Vince Lombardi used to say, "Winning isn't everything. It's the only thing."

MARTIN'S RESPONSE

Even though Tom's chapter is written from his perspective as chair of the NRCC, it is also generally applicable to what I experienced in my time as chair of the DCCC. His description of recruiting prospective candidates is dead on.

Another classic example of recruitment involved Mark Udall and an open seat in Colorado in 1998. Another candidate – someone who had previously run unsuccessfully for state office in Colorado – visited me to discuss the race. He told me that he was going to be "pure" and not accept any contributions from PACs. Well, campaigning had become so expensive that Democratic candidates who wouldn't accept money from labor and pro-environmental PACs in a state like Colorado started the campaign with at least one hand tied behind their back. As soon as that candidate left my office, I called in my executive director, Matt Angle, and asked, "Who else do we have for this race?" The answer was Mark Udall. He served five terms before winning a race for Senate in 2008.

One of my favorite stories involves the recruitment of Dennis Moore for an open seat in the Kansas suburbs of Kansas City. When the moderate Republican incumbent who had held the seat for many years retired, she was replaced by a far-right-wing Republican, Vince Snowbarger, who won a contested Republican primary against a more moderate candidate and subsequently won the general election. I was minding my own business listening to testimony in the House Rules Committee one day when this newly-minted congressman came before us to testify on a noncontroversial bill. He was such a space cadet that I walked out of the committee room and called Matt Angle. My question again was, "Who do we have for this race? We can beat this guy." The answer proved to be Dennis Moore, a former prosecuting attorney, who won that election and served for six terms until he retired for health reasons.

But my absolute favorite story has to be the 1998 election of Rush Holt to a previously GOP district in New Jersey. Rush had been valiantly campaigning in a tough district for months, and no one gave him much of a chance of winning. It just so happened that Rush's cousin, Alan Mollohan, was a member of Congress from West Virginia, and every time I saw him on the floor of the House he would ask, "What are you doing for my cousin Rush?" The answer had always been that Rush's district had not been targeted by the DCCC.

Then lightning struck. The Republican incumbent, Mike Pappas, took to the floor of the House during special orders at the end of the session one day and sang a ditty about the Whitewater special prosecutor, Ken Starr, to the tune of "Twinkle, Twinkle, Little Star." The problem was that Congressman Pappas sang badly off-key. In fact, he couldn't carry a tune in a wheelbarrow. The message also was politically off-tune for this moderate New Jersey district. Rush's campaign took the audio tape of this ditty and put it – with the tag line to his commercial ad, "Out of Tune, Out of Touch" – on drive-time radio in Pappas's district. It set the race on fire. The DCCC took one look at new poll numbers and purchased one day of New York City media market television time, featuring the off-key congressman. Rush won that race and served eight terms until he retired in 2014.

On another subject, one of the biggest challenges facing incumbents running for reelection to the House is the changing nature of their constituencies over a period a years due to demography. Sometimes these can be for the good; other times they are harmful. The successful politicians keep their eyes open and their ears to the ground.

A classic example of this occurred in my own congressional district in north Texas. Following the 1980 census, three suburbs south of Dallas – Duncanville, DeSoto, and Cedar Hill – were added to my district. At that time, these three areas were heavily white and hardcore Republican. In the 1984 presidential election, the Democratic nominee, Walter Mondale, received less than 20% of the vote in these three suburbs.

However, everything changed during the next 20 years as a result of middle-class blacks and Hispanics moving from the inner city into close-in suburban communities. I first started to notice the political change in the Republican sweep of 1994. My Republican opponent, Ed Harrison, underperformed in these three suburbs – a factor that helped me hold my seat in a very tough year. The full extent of this demographic change was driven home when Duncanville High School won state in both football and basketball in the 1998-99 school year, relying heavily on black players. Further evidence of this change was made clear in a survey showing that DeSoto High School had had, since 1997, numerous players who'd been drafted in high rounds by teams in the National Football League.[50]

By the time I left Congress at the end of 2004, all three of these suburbs were Democratic.

Politics is a tough business. As we like to say, "it isn't beanbag." But for political junkies like Tom and me, serving as chairs of our respective parties' House campaign committees was actually a lot of fun.

12

SENATE ELECTIONS: VOTERS STILL MATTER

By Martin Frost and Tom Davis

As was explained in the previous chapter, the Senate was designed by our government's framers to be different from the House of Representatives. Senators were to represent states and representatives were to represent people. Thus, in the early days of the Republic (actually, for the first 124 years), senators were elected by state legislatures.

When the Seventeenth Amendment establishing direct election of senators by popular vote was ratified, the role of senators began to change as well. The democratization of the Senate changed the body from an elite group of power brokers to an assembly of more mundane "politicians." Instead of responding to the pressures of state legislators, who controlled a senator's political destiny, the members of the "upper body" (as they like to call themselves) had to respond to the people, the voters at large. This ushered in an era where the whole system of incentives began to change.

Running for the Senate is very different from running for the House. It is somewhat like running for president in that it is winner-take-all within a state, rather than just from a portion of a state where the politics may be very different from statewide trends.

Let's start with the basics.

1. A Senate candidate has to be at least 30 years old by the time he will be sworn into office, as opposed to 25 for a House candidate.

2. The full term for a senator is six years, with a third of the Senate seats up for election every two years. A full House term is two years, with the entire House up for election biennially.

3. Due to the fact that under the Constitution, senators represent states and the House represents people, it is possible to be appointed to the Senate when a senator dies in office or resigns. No one can ever be appointed to the House; a special election must be held to fill a vacancy. Normally, a Senate appointment only lasts until a special election can be held. Often – but not always – the governor of the state appoints someone who agrees to be a caretaker and who will not be a candidate in the next election, special or regular.

In 2014, Montana's governor appointed John Walsh to the Senate when Max Baucus resigned to become ambassador to China, and Walsh was nominated to run in the next regular election in November. Unfortunately for Democrats, Walsh dropped out of the contest in August following plagiarism charges involving his education in the military. Under Montana law, there was no requirement for a special election to fill out the remaining year of Baucus's term, though many states do require special elections to be held, no matter how little time remains in a senator's term.

4. It certainly helps to be personally wealthy in case you need to help finance your own campaign, though of course this is not required. However, proportionately, there are far more millionaires in the Senate than in the House.

5. There are still a number of purple states where a candidate of either party can be elected; however, in an era of increasing straight-ticket voting, there are fewer and fewer Democrats elected from red states or Republicans elected from blue states. By the luck of the draw, Democrats in 2014 had to defend seven Democratic Senate seats in red states (Alaska, Montana, South Dakota, West Virginia, North Carolina, Arkansas, and Louisiana). Due to creative gerrymandering, there are fewer purple congressional districts remaining in the House. As the nation increasingly sorts itself by regions, the number of states with one senator from each party has been

steadily declining. In 2014, there were 17 divided states in the Senate, of which eight were among the Midwest's 12 states.

6. Senate candidates are normally chosen in statewide primaries; however, political parties in a few states (like Virginia and Utah) can use conventions to choose their nominees.

We both considered running for Senate at different points in our career, but neither of us wound up making the race.

In Tom's case, he considered running for an open seat in 2008 but was denied the opportunity when conservatives who dominated the state GOP – fearing he might win a statewide primary – opted for nomination by convention, where the conservative wing of the party controlled the process. Tom then chose not to run again for his House seat that fall, opting to retire, as he likes to say, "undefeated and unindicted." This was a decision he has never regretted.

In Martin's case, he asked to be considered for appointment in 1993 when Senator Lloyd Bentsen resigned his seat to take a cabinet position in the Clinton administration. Had he been appointed, he would have run for the unexpired term in a special election. But Governor Ann Richards appointed someone else, who turned out to be a lackluster candidate and then lost the special election to a Republican, Kay Bailey Hutchinson. Martin might well have lost the special election if he had been appointed since the state was in the process of turning Republican, and his congressional career would have been cut short by 11 years.

Running for the Senate is by no means easy.

Senate candidates are often unknown statewide unless they have previously held statewide office. Members of the House, well-known in their own districts, often don't realize how unknown they are outside of their own media markets. It comes as a shock. And senators who have been in office for several terms and have not recently faced significant opposition often have to reintroduce themselves to voters through costly media campaigns.

Also, circumstances must be right. Martin's Rules Committee colleague Alan Wheat, a black member of Congress from Kansas City, Missouri, decided to run for the Senate in 1994. Even though Wheat was an extremely competent member, Missouri was not yet ready to embrace a black candidate statewide, at least not in the very Republican year of 1994. Ron Kirk, a highly respected mayor of Martin's hometown, Dallas, ran for the Senate from Texas in 2002. Like Wheat, Kirk was a terrific candidate; but like Missouri, Texas was unready to embrace a black candidate statewide. Democrat Barack Obama did not have the same problem in Illinois when he was elected to the Senate in 2004, nor did Deval Patrick when he was elected governor of Massachusetts in 2006. Illinois and Massachusetts were ready to embrace such change but Texas and Missouri – admittedly tougher states for Democrats – were not. Neither did Republican Tim Scott have trouble winning his election in South Carolina. Although African American, his conservative views prevailed over any concerns about his race.

Interestingly, timing has been right for many women to win Senate seats. Entering the 2014 elections, there were 20 women (16 Democrats and four Republicans) serving in the Senate, which represented a significant increase from prior years. When Martin joined the House in 1979, only one woman served in the Senate; no Democratic woman served until Barbara Mikulski (Maryland) was elected in 1986, although Democrats Hattie Caraway (Arkansas) and Maurine Neuberger (Oregon) had served previously in seats to which their husbands had been elected before passing on while in office. Since then, women have been elected from both parties and from various regions of the country.

Additionally, the right candidate must make it through the primary process in order to be elected in the fall. The Republicans kicked away as many as five potential Senate seats in 2010 and 2012 by nominating exotic candidates who were unacceptable statewide in states where the GOP should have had a real chance at victory. These included Nevada, Missouri, Delaware, Indiana, and Colorado. The business wing of the GOP made a concerted effort in 2014 to help more mainstream candidates win Senate primaries so that the party would not make the same mistakes again.

And then there is the situation with new media. Bad news travels so fast these days that a campaign can be completely turned around based on something that has little relevance to a candidate's ability to serve. This also may well prevent good people from running. It certainly will have an effect on their families. Our experience is that spouses take negative campaigning even harder than the candidates do. This too may prevent some capable people from entering races.

And certainly continued gridlock in Washington will have an effect on potential candidates' interest in serving. It's hard enough to convince people to go through the grueling process of running for office if they don't believe much can be accomplished once they're there.

Trying to move from the House to the Senate has its own unique set of issues. Since you can't run for both the House and Senate in the same election, an incumbent House member has to make a calculated decision. Is it worth giving up what typically is a safe House seat in order to take a chance on being elected to the Senate? The six-year term and increased national visibility are tempting for many House members, but some have later regretted running after giving up a promising House career only to lose a bid for Senate. (The only exception to this situation is running in a special election caused by the death or resignation of a sitting senator, when you don't lose your House seat if you unsuccessfully run for the Senate.)

Normally, senators who are "in cycle" and want to run for president have to make a choice if their parties end up nominating them, as they can't appear in two separate places on the ballot. Some states have made an exception to this rule. For instance, Texas changed its election rules in 1960 so that Senator Lyndon Johnson could run for both vice president and reelection to the Senate simultaneously. Johnson was elected to both the vice presidency and the Senate in November of that year and then resigned his Senate seat prior to being sworn in as vice president. This led to Republican John Tower's winning the ensuing special election even though he had lost to Johnson in the Senate race months before. Delaware law similarly allowed Joe Biden to be simultaneously elected vice president and senator in 2008.

Despite the risks involved in making the effort, the transition from the House to the Senate happens frequently. In 2014, the top three Democratic senators – Majority Leader Harry Reid, Majority Whip Dick Durbin, and Democratic Policy Committee Chair Chuck Schumer – were all former House members. Neither of the top GOP Senate leaders – Minority Leader Mitch McConnell and Minority Whip John Cornyn – had served in the House. But former Senate GOP leaders Bob Dole and Trent Lott started their careers in the House. At times, close to 50 senators in Congress have had House experience. It is interesting to note that some of the more confrontational junior Republican senators – such as Ted Cruz, Mike Lee, and Rand Paul – did not have a House background. Perhaps having no experience in a legislative body, where teamwork is essential to results, emboldened them to strike a more independent course in the Senate.

Cruz was elected to an open seat in Texas in 2012 by defeating an establishment candidate in the Republican Primary – Lieutenant Governor David Dewhurst. Cruz was able to ride the Tea Party wave by running as an outsider at a time when distrust in government was high. However, he was not a political novice. He had served as Texas's solicitor general (an appointed position) and reportedly had been planning a political career since his days at Harvard Law School. He was articulate and captured the sentiment of a Republican Party in Texas that was rapidly moving to the right, just 12 years after George W. Bush concluded his governorship as a "compassionate conservative."

Among the full committee chairs in the Senate in 2014, a number were previous House members. Senate Republicans had a comparable share of former House members in top committee posts.

Some senators, such as Ben Cardin (Maryland) and Ed Markey (Massachusetts), waited patiently for years before finally making a Senate run. In Cardin's case, he was able to run for an open seat. Markey ran in a special election after John Kerry resigned to be Secretary of State. However, things don't always work out so well. Democratic congresswoman Shelley Berkley from Nevada gave up her House seat to run for the Senate in 2012 and was defeated. That same year, Republican Rick Berg gave up his House seat to run for an open North Dakota Senate seat after just one term. He lost in the general election to Heidi Heitkamp. Three House Republican members ran for an open Senate seat in Georgia in 2014; all lost, finding it hard to be an "outsider" if you run as a congressman.

Berg's 2012 loss to Heitkamp was a classic example that in Senate elections, candidates and campaigns still do make a difference, even in a state that normally votes overwhelmingly for the other party for president. Heitkamp defeated Berg in a deep red state. She had previously held statewide office in North Dakota and was very knowledgeable about energy issues – something very important to her state because of the recent shale oil boom in the Bakken field. Also, Berg may have suffered from a sense among voters that he was trying to move up too fast.

Moreover, as a sitting freshman in the House, Berg attracted all the negativity of being part of an unpopular Congress, but had none of the benefits of holding office, having only served two years. This was not enough time for him to familiarize himself with voters or gain much in the way of tangible accomplishment.

Martin met Senator Heitkamp shortly after her election, and his impression was that she was a female version of a "good ole boy." She fit that state like a glove: conservative on some basic issues and clearly a good retail politician in a small state where that still mattered.

We would also note that North Dakota had a history of voting Republican at the presidential level but sending Democrats to Congress. From 1986 to 2010, no Republican represented the state in Washington, D.C. Its delegation during that period consisted of two Democratic senators and one Democratic House member. In fact, to find a time when North Dakota's congressional delegation was entirely Republican, you would have to go back over 50 years.

Heitkamp's success shows that despite the growing influence of Washington-based party and advocacy groups in managing and financing Senate races across the nation, voters should not be taken for granted. That's especially true in states with small populations, where campaigns often involve more personal contact. Even the little states get two senators, just like the mega-states that have far more constituents and more costly advertising rates. The smaller electorates provide for individual candidates to personalize their electoral appeals through face-to-face contact in a way that candidates in most states cannot.

Yet even with their occasionally more independent bases, these small-state senators feel considerable pressure to be party loyalists once they arrive in Washington. An advantage of serving a small state is that the constituency can be more manageable on both the local issues and politics. That helps to explain why Democratic Party leaders in the Senate have, over the past decades, come from Montana, West Virginia, Maine, South Dakota, and Nevada. Still, as American politics has evolved into a more parliamentary behavior, the ability of senators to vote contrarily to their states' partisan index is becoming more difficult.

Another enormous challenge facing high-profile senate candidates today is the amount of scrutiny they face because of the new media, as discussed in Chapter 10. Due to the closely contested nature of the Senate as a whole, everyone knows which Senate races could make the difference in one party or the other controlling that body. Candidates running in those particular states receive both national and regional media coverage and must constantly be on their toes. One bad miscue that ends up on YouTube and a campaign can be dramatically changed. The pressure to perform and not make a major mistake is constant. This has had the effect of scripting senators and keeping them insulated from voters in more spontaneous environments.

In 2014, everyone knew that southern Senate seats held by three incumbent Democrats might determine the balance of power in the new Senate. Thus, Mark Pryor (Arkansas), Mary Landrieu (Louisiana), and Kay Hagan (North Carolina) became household names, and the national media watched their races constantly. Super PACs and out-of-state money poured into these races over a year before the election. Voters were informed that the election was not about who would represent them, but about which party would control the Senate. Millions were spent by red challengers in red states trying to nationalize the races, while the incumbent blues spent millions trying to localize them.

An occupational hazard of being in the Senate is that many senators look in the mirror each morning and see a future president staring back at them. A total of 16 presidents once served in the Senate, though only three have been elected to the White House directly from the Senate. Thus, quite a few senators spend time considering how to get nominated.

Why have so few senators in modern times actually been elected president? Governors who have executive experience seem to have a leg up as far as the public is concerned. Also, career legislators have difficulty constructing a vision of where they want to take the country and tend to communicate in "legispeak." An example was when Bob Dole, the Senate majority leader, was asked a question in a presidential debate and remarked, "We could hold hearings on it." Not exactly inspiring leadership!

Of course, exceptions to that rule include John F. Kennedy in 1960 and Barack Obama in 2008. Several more senators – such as Harry Truman and Lyndon B. Johnson – have been elected vice president and then have become president when the president died while in office. Other senators have won their parties' nominations and then lost the general election. These include Robert Dole, John McCain, and John Kerry.

Compare the failures of those veteran senators to the successes of Kennedy or Obama, neither of whom the authors would describe as a first-tier senator. Both were young and generationally transformative figures who were unencumbered by Senate traditions. They were far from prodigious legislators, but their oratory was visionary, compelling, and moving. Their speeches were classic campaign poetry.

The third senator to be directly elected president, Senator Warren G. Harding, was the product of convention horse-trading and predated the modern telegenic media campaigns, although his good looks offered an attractive presentation to voters. Again, his Senate record was devoid of significant legislative accomplishment.

Another disincentive for individuals considering a Senate run is that congressional dysfunction is not just limited to the House. The 60-vote rule to cut off a filibuster against legislation has led to deadlock on major issues. Also, a sharp partisan divide, exacerbated by partisan media, has made compromise very difficult even though that used to be a hallmark of the Senate.

Some observers believe that in recent years the election to the Senate of many House members who came to age during the Gingrich revolution has made the Senate much more like the highly partisan House. Others, such as the authors, believe the outsiders' approach has been even more debilitating on Senate productivity.

This subject was explored by Sean Theriault, a professor at the University of Texas, and David Rohde, a professor at Duke University, in the October 2011 issue of the *Journal of Politics* in an article entitled "The Gingrich Senators and Party Polarization in the U.S. Senate".[51] Theriault later wrote a book on the subject, *The Gingrich Senators*, published by Oxford Press in 2013.

Theriault and Rohde did a statistical analysis showing that Republican senators who had served in the House during Gingrich's 20 years in office were less likely to act in a bipartisan manner than Republican senators who had never served in the House with Gingrich.

Don Wolfensberger, the former Republican staff director of the House Rules Committee and a resident scholar with the Bipartisan Policy Center, discussed this situation in an article for the Congress Project of the Woodrow Wilson Center.₅₂ He noted that while Theriault and Rohde "argue that the more the Senate is populated by former House Members who cut their political teeth during the Republican revolution ... the more the Senate is taking on the coloration of its more populous counterpart ... I maintain that the partisan turn in [the House] began in the late 1960s with the Democrats' reform revolution that culminated in the 1970s by replacing the old order of committee government with party governance. It simply accelerated under the Republicans."

Whatever the reason, many House members have brought some partisan baggage with them when they moved to the Senate. In fact, the Senate today looks more and more like the House, with its polarization and emphasis on political messaging – something the Founding Fathers tried to avoid by giving senators six-year terms and giving the Senate authorities not vested in the House, such as ratifying treaties and confirming high-level presidential appointments to the judiciary and executive branches.

Still, important contrasts remain between the two chambers and their members. With its smaller size and more freewheeling rules, the Senate provides more opportunities for freelancers. Senators are accorded much more public exposure than House members; senators of both parties are regular guests on the Sunday morning television shows. Their demonstrated success in appealing to larger constituencies also means many of them are more public relations-savvy. Many House members resent the additional national television exposure accorded senators, and this sometimes makes it more difficult for the two bodies to work together.

The Senate's confirmation authority over presidential appointments to federal agencies (including the Cabinet) and the judiciary makes the Senate a much more relevant body for presidents. The ability to confirm key appointees necessitates an ongoing relationship between the commander in chief and individual senators, given the state of current Senate rules and the ability of even one senator to hold up a confirmation for a period of time.

House members are irrelevant to the confirmation process, and as a result are rarely consulted on nominations.

And then there is the issue of money. Senate campaigns have almost always been more expensive than campaigns for individual House seats; however, the money being spent by candidates and outside groups in individual Senate races has dramatically increased in recent years, a result of both increased campaign costs and changes in the law implemented by the U.S. Supreme Court relating to independent expenditures by individuals, corporations, and unions. The total amount spent in the 2012 Senate race in Massachusetts, when Elizabeth Warren defeated Scott Brown 53% to 47%, was more than $70 million. We anticipate spending in Senate races to continue to increase.

The fact that Senate constituencies tend to be much larger than House constituencies is certainly one reason that Senate races cost more. But even in small states where the House member is elected statewide, the Senate campaigns are exponentially more expensive. This is because in the Senate, with only 100 members, a seat is worth more than in the House, where there are 435 members.

Unless candidates are independently wealthy and willing to devote a significant portion of their personal fortunes to the race, they have to spend an extraordinary amount of time raising the money necessary to run. This is particularly challenging if the candidate is an incumbent member of the House or Senate with major legislative duties. Sometimes, senators start raising money for their next campaigns shortly after being sworn in for a six-year term.

Fundraising for a Senate campaign often involves crisscrossing the country to raise money in a variety of cities and states. Martin got a good taste of this during the four years he served as chair of the DCCC and had to be constantly raising money all over the country for the committee. During those four years, he devoted much less time to his Rules Committee duties than he did during the rest of his career in the House. Fortunately, Martin had an excellent staff; and since he had already been in the House for 16 years, he had a pretty solid handle on matters that directly affected his congressional district.

As discussed in Chapter 6, the emergence of super PACs following the Supreme Court's decision in the *Citizens United* case and the growth of non-profit 501(c)(4) organizations have also dramatically changed the landscape in Senate campaigns. These outside groups can now spend millions of dollars in Senate races opposing an incumbent, often early in the campaign. This alters the issue environment and causes Senate incumbents to spend money early to answer these attacks.

Senate incumbents of both parties normally enjoy a significant fundraising advantage. However, the aggressive presence of advertising by outside groups early in the two-year election window can quickly dissipate an incumbent's fundraising head start. We saw examples of this in Louisiana, North Carolina, and Arkansas during the 2014 elections.

Also, early money spent by outside groups bolstering a challenger helps improve the challenger's poll numbers, which in turn helps the challenger raise more money for his or her campaign. Senate campaigns increasingly have become two-year contests, and often are run like start-up businesses that increase their payroll and pace as the months go on. The chief difference from the corporate world is that most congressional campaigns shut down after the November vote, though senators as well as House members increasingly maintain a small continuing staff – especially for fundraising.

Incumbents now understand the benefits of early money and are putting the word out to friendly super PACs (the one set up to support Senate candidates of a particular party, as well as those run by groups sympathetic to a senator's positions), which in turn just ups the ante even further in terms of total spending.

Fundraising has risen to such a level in Senate campaigns that almost anyone running for the Senate today needs a national financial base. It used to be that a Senate candidate could make the circuit of major-money states such as New York, California, Texas, and Florida and significantly supplement fundraising in his home state to the degree that he was ready to take on the world. Now, not a day goes by when citizens' email inboxes aren't flooded with pleas from Senate candidates from all over the country seeking support. Many people don't read them; however, online fundraising has become an integral part of all Senate races and does yield major results for many candidates. People also receive numerous direct mail pitches, though the online messages are often more compelling because they are interestingly presented and not as long as the hard-copy letters.

Should there be any real impetus for legislating limits on campaign spending or on the activities of super PACs or non-profit (c)(4)s, it is likely to originate in the Senate, since the level of spending in Senate races has escalated so dramatically in recent years.

THAD COCHRAN'S COMEBACK

Challenges to incumbency, of course, can also be a factor in a party primary, as Republicans saw in Mississippi during 2014, when Thad Cochran barely defeated Tea Party challenger Chris McDaniel.

Nowhere in recent political history has a more dissonant, unlikely coalition come together than in the case of the Mississippi Senate Republican primary runoff in June 2014.

Seventy-six-year-old Thad Cochran, a six-term senator and former chairman of the Senate Appropriations Committee, was forced into a runoff by State Senator Chris McDaniel from Jones County. In the state where conservative Democratic Rep. Gene Taylor was ousted in 2010 because of his party ID (see Chapter 7), an old-style southern coalition emerged that crossed partisan lines – but with modern twists. For now, this contest seems the exception that proves our broader rule. But it reveals the opportunities that are available to shrewd politicians who respond to unique local circumstances.

McDaniel had narrowly led in the first primary with 155,040 votes versus 153,564 votes for Cochran, but had fallen short of 50% due to a third candidate. Per Mississippi law, a runoff election was held three weeks later. Traditionally, when southern incumbents are forced into a runoff, they lose. There are numerous examples of this, including Donald Stewart in Alabama and B. Everett Jordan in North Carolina, both in the 1970s. So political pundits were busy writing Thad Cochran's political obituary up until the date of the runoff.

Conservative groups – including the Club For Growth, the Tea Party Express, and the Senate Conservative Fund – saw blood in the water and anted up millions of dollars to the McDaniel campaign to ensure Cochran's defeat. In the aftermath of a disappointing first primary, American Crossroads (the super PAC founded by Karl Rove) withdrew its support for Senator Cochran and decided to fold its tent and deploy its assets to other races.

If this didn't look bleak enough for Cochran, two weeks prior to the runoff, the Tea Party movement got its first scalp of the primary season when Eric Cantor was surprised in Virginia. This upset set the conservatives on fire. An unprecedented number of dollars and volunteers flowed into the McDaniel campaign. Although Cochran had held a fundraising advantage in round one, round two was developing differently.

To understand what happened next, a brief primer on Mississippi politics is in order. Politically and racially, Mississippi is the most polarized state in the Union. It is 37% African American and home to the largest percentage of black voters of any state. Mississippi was ground zero for the civil rights movement in the 20th century, and the racial divisions today are expressed in the state's partisan political alignment.

In 2012, Romney received over 90% of the white vote, while Obama received over 97% of the black vote. Mississippi hosts the largest percentage of black officeholders of any state, nearly all of them Democrats. The state's House delegation includes three white Republicans and one black Democrat (Bennie Thompson). Legislative lines are subject to the Voting Rights Act, producing white Republicans and black Democrats. In the Mississippi state legislature, the 52-member Senate includes eight white and 12 black Democrats and 32 white and no black Republicans; and the 122-member House includes 21 white and 37 black Democrats and 63 white and no black Republicans. In short, partisan politics here are divided among racial lines.

The rules of engagement in Mississippi primaries are also unique. There is no party registration. All registered voters can vote in the primaries of their choosing, but since both parties' primaries are the same day, there have been few examples of crossover voters interfering in the other party's primary. A black Democrat voting in the GOP primary is considered an "act of treason." And since the legislative districts are largely one-sided affairs and many counties are decidedly black or white, there is even less incentive to cross over.

The runoff provisions are similar, with this caveat: voters who partici-pated in the Democratic primary at any level are barred from voting in the Republican runoff.₅₃ In this case, the first primary showed a total of 313,483 Republicans voting in the Senate primary and 397,822 Democrats partici-pating in the Democratic primary. (The participants in primaries tend to be the most active and engaged in both parties, as noted in Chapter 8.)

Thad Cochran had a thoroughly conservative record in the Senate, with rankings of over 85% from the American Conservative Union and under 10% from the AFL-CIO and the Americans for Democratic Action. How-ever, Cochran had a conciliatory demeanor, had worked in a bipartisan manner with Democrats in the Senate, and had delivered billions of dollars in projects for his state, arguably the poorest in the country. To members of the Tea Party, such pork-barrel log-rolling was exactly the kind of activity they had come to loathe; Cochran was a symbol of D.C.'s spending more money than it had and driving up the deficit. To others, Cochran had deliv-ered the bacon, supported the agriculture bill (and food stamps), and helped rebuild the Mississippi coast after Hurricane Katrina. McDaniel had taken the position that hurricane relief should be offset with other spending cuts and was uncertain whether he would have supported Katrina relief.

No southern senator forced into a runoff primary had won in over 30 years; the last one to do so was John McClellan in 1972, who defeated David Pryor in an Arkansas runoff. Additionally, runoff primaries generally had seen a smaller turnout than the original primaries. This was due to the fact that fewer candidates were competing and fewer races were in play across the state in both statewide and local races. Also plaguing the Cochran camp was the reality that the intensity of voters was with McDaniel. Despite protestations from the Cochran camp that his followers didn't turn out because they didn't believe he was in trouble, the reality was that he was indeed in trouble. Deep trouble.

Originally, for the Cochran camp, there was no Plan B. No one had envi-sioned a runoff, as the third candidate in the first primary – an unknown named Thomas Carey – had polled a paltry 4,854 votes. However, it was enough to deprive McDaniel of a majority of votes.

Cochran's only chance was to expand the electorate and run the primary runoff like a general election. The matter was complicated by the fact that the Democrats had nominated a credible candidate, Travis Childers, a former two-term congressman from northern Mississippi. Childers was a decided underdog against Mcdaniel and a non-starter against Cochran, but Democrats felt they had an outside chance should the incumbent lose the primary.

Expanding the electorate meant recruiting black and moderate white voters who had not voted in the first primary to vote in the runoff. The Cochran message was clear: the primary election had been the general election, for all intents and purposes, and to stop the hardline McDaniel, Cochran needed their votes.

The African American leaders who had a cordial relationship with Cochran began to mobilize. Their plan ran basically under the radar screen so as not to polarize white voters who had voted for Cochran in the first primary. The black Democratic mayor of Vicksburg urged 2,000 supporters, in an email, to vote for Cochran. Credell Calhoun, a black Democratic State House member and former state Democratic Party staffer, recorded a phone call for the senator, alleging that Cochran stood between the state and the Tea Party, which would do away with services.

Full-page ads in black newspapers lauded the senator as a champion of historically black colleges. "We're asking Democrats to cross over and vote in the Republican primary to ensure our community's interests are heard," claimed the All Citizens for Mississippi group headed by black pastor Ronnie C. Cudrup, Sr.

Wayne McDaniels, president of the Jackson branch of the NAACP, put it like this: "We know what the Tea Party is trying to do. So we weighed the field and concluded that with Cochran, we know what we've got and we like what we've got."

The strategy worked. Turnout increased in the second primary by 20% statewide. But in the 24 counties with a majority African American population, turnout increased an average of 40% over the first primary. The remaining 58 counties' turnout increased about 16%. In the end, the increased turnout in African American areas made the difference. In 70% black Hinds County (Jackson), Cochran's margin increased from 5,180 to 10,965 between the first and second primaries. This chart shows the increase in turnout in selected majority black counties:

Selected African American Counties
2014 Mississippi U.S. Senate Run-Off – Cochran Margin

County	First Primary	Second Primary
Coahoma	313	705
Bolivar	689	1,143
Sunflower	413	758
Tunica	149	242
Sharkey	231	442
Hinds	5,180	10,965
Noxubee	64	99
Claiborne	49	183
Yazoo	235	617

The Cochran camp also went after GOP votes along the Gulf Coast, reminding residents of the help the senator had provided them during Hurricane Katrina and contrasting it with McDaniel's opposition to hurricane aid.

In fact, both sides doubled down on their bases of support. McDaniel improved markedly in his home of Jones County and in Desoto County, a suburb of Memphis. In Desoto, turnout increased from 12,967 to 15,404 and McDaniel's margin increased by 767 votes.

McDaniel's team was prepared for this increase in black turnout and had poll-watchers in hundreds of heavily black precincts throughout the Mississippi Delta and other areas, to challenge voters who may have voted in the Democratic primary the first go-round. Although no records exist as to how many Democratic primary voters were challenged, it is clear that many blacks voted in the GOP runoff, which state law allowed (provided they had not participated in the Democratic primary in the first round).

The McDaniel campaign was indignant: "We must be absolutely certain that our Republican primary was won by Republican voters. In the coming days, our team will look into the irregularities to determine whether a challenge is warranted." The challengers offered rewards to anyone who could prove voter fraud. A few Democrats may have slipped through the system, but it appeared that Cochran's camp had played by the rules and had legally convinced enough African Americans that their interest was in defeating the Tea Party, no matter what the means. McDaniel's lawsuit was dismissed.

The Cochran campaign model is not easily replicated. It relies on rules with no party registration and a one-party constituency to motivate voters that align with the minority party to participate in the dominant party's primary out of self-interest. Had Democratic voters believed they could actually have defeated McDaniel, their strategic move may have been to vote *for* McDaniel, so the Democrats could pick up the seat in November. But the stunning Mississippi outcome reveals opportunities to reduce – though not eliminate – the partisan polarization that has overtaken congressional campaigns and politics.

The Cochran model rewards moderation and the ability to work across party lines to compromise and represent everyone. The McDaniel model rewards ideological consistency and standing one's ground while not caving in to the other party. Ultimately, black voters may not have gotten everything they wanted by voting for Cochran, but they got the lesser of two perceived evils. Perhaps they got more. Although the vast majority of Cochran's voters were solidly white Republicans, it was black voters who made the difference in the election. This strategy could be replicated under similar circumstances in other elections.

In fact, as Senator John Warner's campaign chairman in 1996, Tom faced a similar dilemma. Warner was unpopular with a vast segment of the GOP because he had refused to endorse Colonel Oliver North, the Republican Senate candidate in 1994. Many Republicans, particularly the most activist elements of the party, wanted retribution. They had a well-financed challenger in Jim Miller, who was formerly the management and budget director under Reagan. Miller was a conservative economist who had also opposed North for the nomination in 1994 but had supported him in the general election.

Tom was a freshman congressman in an area of the state where Senator Warner was strong and North had been defeated by a wide margin. Since Virginia has an open primary and no party registration (similar to Mississippi), his plan was to motivate as many voters as possible to vote in the GOP primary, even if it meant they had to leave their partisan comfort zone.

Tom and other Warner supporters mobilized many nontraditional Republican voters to participate in the primary process. This included a wide array of voters who felt they "owed" John Warner for his courage in standing against Oliver North. They also had a substantial number of GOP regulars who liked the senator's record and felt he was a potent leader for the Commonwealth. However, it was clear that the activist wing of the party wanted to teach the senator a lesson, even if it meant the election of a Democrat in November.

Tom and other supporters organized current and retired federal employees, ethnic leaders, suburban moderates, and other first-time GOP primary voters to help John Warner. The Democrats opted for a convention to nominate their candidate that year (an unknown businessman at the time, Mark Warner), freeing Democratic-aligned voters to participate in the Republican primary. (If the GOP leadership had had its choice, John Warner would have faced a convention and almost certain defeat, but Virginia law allows incumbents, once nominated by primary, to continue to do so if they so choose.)

The end result was a massive turnout and win for John Warner, with nearly half a million votes cast. He received 65.5% of the vote, in the largest primary turnout in history. Senator Warner went on to defeat Mark Warner (who spent $12 million of his own money in the general election) by a relatively close 52.5% to 47.5% margin.

Part of Mark Warner's vote in November came from Republicans in south and southwest Virginia casting a protest vote against John Warner. And some of John Warner's majority voters were Democrats and independents in the urban areas, particularly Tom's home in northern Virginia, rewarding him for his independence. John Warner's coalition was unlike any other GOP coalition in the state, and his primary ushered in a return by Republicans to nominating conventions, when possible. But the Cochran-Warner model, where applicable, produces a more inclusive, moderate brand of politics – in contrast to the recent trend of polarization.

The examples of Cochran and Warner are exceptions to the current political climate. Whether these strategies emerge, either institutionally (as states rewrite election laws) or behaviorally (as in Mississippi), as a counterforce to the continued polarization of the body politic remains to be seen.

By building on the influence of moderate and independent voters, these isolated developments may be the canary in the coal mine, showing alternatives to our polarized politics.

The irony of the Cochran coalition is that it runs counter to the central thesis of traditional southern politics. In his classic book *Southern Politics*, V.O. Key wrote that a political coalition of poorer whites from the upcountry and blacks could form an economic coalition that could supplant the white plantation owners in the Delta. However, it was the Mississippi establishment that recruited black voters to join them in defeating the Tea Party, whose base was with poorer whites and Memphis exurbanites. Their candidate, McDaniel, hailed from Jones County, once dubbed "the free state of Jones" because of its resistance to secession during the Civil War. Jones County had had the fewest slaves of any county in Mississippi at the time of the Civil War, and its yeoman farmers and ranchers were not eager to fight the plantation owners' war.

So, a century and a half later, instead of having developed economic coalitions within the state, Mississippi was essentially two one-party states. Blacks were Democrats and controlled counties where African American voters were in a majority – chiefly in the Delta and along the Mississippi River. White Republicans, still dominated by the plantation owners and professional class, controlled the GOP. The Tea Party was an anti-establishment uprising within the Republican Party and was denied victory by black voters in the Delta in a GOP primary runoff.

It is not yet clear what the long-term ramifications of these dissonant establishment white and Democratic black coalitions mean, either within or beyond Mississippi's borders. The angry reaction of McDaniel and his Tea Party allies, both national and local, showed that they would pursue their own remedies. But in the short term, it meant that the establishment and its candidate, Thad Cochran, had once again prevailed in the most historically ironic election in the history of one of the nation's most polarized states. For Senate Republicans, the outcome was an enormous – and perhaps a unique – switch from their internal politics of 2010 and 2012.

13

WHEN CONGRESS WAS FUN...
AND PRODUCTIVE

By Tom Davis and Martin Frost

There was a time when serving in Congress was fun and often involved initiatives undertaken on a bipartisan basis. In this chapter, Tom will recount two of his most memorable House experiences, a controversial investigation of professional sports and what could have been a contentious financial bailout. Martin will follow with his own – one overseas, and two that were Texas-based but with national legislative implications.

TOM'S VIEW

A decade after entering Congress, as chairman of the Committee on Government Reform and Oversight, I took on a front-burner issue that became "newsworthy" nationally. That was the use of steroids in professional sports.

The first time I observed the intersection of steroid use and politics was when President George W. Bush addressed the issue during his 2003 State of the Union speech. The press widely lambasted this mention, questioning why it would merit any consideration as a national priority. I didn't give the issue much thought, personally, until it came up again in a meeting with Congressman Henry Waxman, the ranking member of my committee, two years later. His aide, Phil Schiliro, brought up the subject as a health issue that was growing in epidemic proportions among high school and college athletes. It was included in Waxman's laundry list of his priorities for the committee. Of course, most of his list consisted of items that were non-starters for my Republican colleagues. But there were always some areas he would suggest that deserved an honest evaluation. I was intrigued by this one and set it aside for us to examine.

Before we proceeded, we both decided it would be important to hear what Major League Baseball had to say, so we invited MLB representatives to the Capitol to meet with us. They gave their usual song and dance about this being a baseball matter for the owners and union to discuss and told us they had some rules in place that were meant to address the problem. They asked us to give them some time to see if these rules resolved the issue.

Meanwhile, Waxman's and my staffs had been doing their own investigation and determined that steroid use by young athletes was getting out of hand. High school athletes were using them to bulk up to win scholarships to college, college players were using them to win professional contracts, and the pros were using them to remain competitive. One major leaguer went from 15 home runs to 50 and back to 15; this was attributed to going on and off steroids (although this was never proven).

We met with Don Hooton, who had set up a foundation to educate coaches, parents, and families about the potential dangers from steroid use after his son, Taylor, had committed suicide after extensive steroid use. We talked to medical experts and to prominent home run hitter Jose Canseco, whose book, *Juiced*, alleged widespread steroid use among professional baseball players.

Waxman, our staffs, and I decided to move ahead with an investigation. The reaction was swift and furious. National sports columnists came to the league's defense. George Will, whom I admire as a writer, wrote a damning column about our efforts. Members outside our committee became outraged. They alleged that this was simply a "press play" to get ourselves on television. The Energy and Commerce Committee claimed this was its jurisdiction and not ours, and said it was working quietly "behind the scenes" to fix the problem.

I informed the Speaker, Denny Hastert, a former high school wrestling coach, what I intended to do and he never tried to interfere in the process, even though several MLB team owners who were big campaign contributors were asking him to get us to back off.

Democratic leadership was experiencing the same pressure from team owners who were Democratic mega-donors. Even the players' union weighed in. At one meeting it complained to Henry that our move would "hurt the union." Waxman, a staunch labor supporter, responded, "Then maybe the union deserves to be hurt." I was proud of him and happy to have him as a partner because it was clear this was a full committee investigation and not a partisan one.

We received additional pushback, initially, from Senator John McCain, who had made a previous effort to push Major League Baseball into banning steroid use. At his insistence, MLB had allegedly adopted a policy against the use of performance-enhancing drugs, and he was not entirely pleased we were encroaching on his domain.

We caught a public relations break when we requested that MLB produce a copy of its steroid policy and found out it had never actually been put into writing. That discovery turned Senator McCain's initial skepticism into support. He and Senator Jim Bunning, a baseball hall of famer, joined our bandwagon. The Republican and Democratic committee staff coordinated every step forward together, realizing that the committee itself was under a microscope and our destinies were intertwined.

The committee issued initial subpoenas to several major league stars who had been widely linked to the steroid conversation: Rafael Palmeiro, Sammy Sosa, Curt Schilling, Mark McGwire, and Jose Canseco. At the request of the Department of Justice, we did not call Barry Bonds. We also arranged for Don Hooton and the parent of another young athlete who had committed suicide while using steroids to act as leadoff witnesses. Senator Bunning, MLB commissioner Bud Selig, and medical experts rounded out the panels.

Waxman and I appeared on the Sunday talk shows together after some players opined that they had more important things to do than appear before our committee. "What if they don't show up?" we were asked by Bob Schieffer on CBS's *Face the Nation*. I replied that they would be in contempt of Congress, but Waxman, ever the statesman, said, "We have every expectation they will show up."

The truth was that a contempt motion would have had to be voted out of committee and would then have had to be voted on by the full House. We certainly had the votes in our committee, but we had not checked with House leaders to see if they would even put that motion on the floor, let alone whip members to ask if they would support it. We were on shaky ground, but we proceeded boldly, together, as if there were no contingencies.

After interviewing Canseco and McGwire, it was clear this would be a high-stakes hearing with tremendous media coverage. McGwire was one of the most honest people I have ever interrogated. Our conversation was off the record and he was willing to tell all (but not implicate other players) if we could give him transactional immunity from prosecution, as there was a five-year statute of limitations and he had only been out of the game for four years. He had a wife and family and was willing to put his baseball legacy on the line, but he did not want to jeopardize his family.

I called U.S. Attorney General Alberto Gonzalez, whose permission I would need to invoke immunity for McGwire, and he declined. I reminded him that he had no investigations of McGwire pending and that getting the facts out could really shine a light on what we were trying to accomplish. But he wouldn't budge. It was not the department's policy to grant immunities in this manner and he did not have the inclination to break with that tradition.

In meeting with McGwire, we were astounded at his honesty and forthrightness. We also saw no reason to "throw him to the wolves," so we agreed he'd take a gentle Fifth Amendment refusal to self-incriminate and note, for the record, that he wanted to talk about a baseball future devoid of steroid use. It was awkward, but it helped fulfill our goal of getting MLB to create a written policy against the players' use of steroids.

Canseco was so radioactive with the other players that we couldn't have them wait in the same anteroom. We arranged for Canseco to wait down the hall in the office of Congresswoman Ileana Ros-Lehtinen, who represented the Miami area and was of Cuban descent. She represented the congressional district where both Canseco and Palmeiro had been raised.

(Though those two had grown up together, they were not friendly going into the hearing, as I'm sure Palmeiro was not pleased with having to testify and it was Canseco's mention of him in *Juiced* that precipitated our sending him a subpoena.)

The hearings turned out to be a success. The committee members, who were usually at each others' partisan throats, were thrilled to be a part of history, and both MLB and the players' union agreed to create a written policy forbidding the use of steroids. I'll leave it to others to judge the effectiveness of the outcome. All that we did accomplish was a result of the committee members taking our partisan insignia off our uniforms and working together.

A few years later, we urged MLB (at Waxman's request) to investigate itself on this issue, and it hired former Senate majority leader George Mitchell to lead the investigation. Mitchell named over 70 players who had used performance-enhancing drugs; and only one, Roger Clemens, took exception. Again, with the integrity of the report under question, we jointly invited (but did not compel) Roger Clemens to come to the committee to state his case. The rest is history, including the federal indictment of Clemens for perjury and making false statements to Congress. He ultimately was found not guilty.

Commissioner Bud Selig called me after the hearings to thank me, noting that the process had been neither smooth nor pretty. But by forcing the issue, he said, we had provided him an opportunity to clean up the whole sordid mess. In addition to cleaning up Major League Baseball, Waxman and I also took solace in knowing that we might just have saved the lives of teenage athletes, who are no longer compelled to use steroids to bulk up in order to compete for athletic college scholarships.

The main takeaway from this drama is very simple. Though parties play a unique and important role in the political process, most major changes are accomplished when the partisanship is put aside and the best of both sides are brought together. This used to be the way Congress operated in critical times. And though Congress still has a stable of extremely intelligent, accomplished, and dedicated members who want to do right by the American people, bipartisanship is now the exception and not the rule, as members fear retribution from their respective party bases when they choose to compromise for the greater good.

Another prominent issue that I managed generated little national attention but was vital locally – for my constituents and those in neighboring congressional districts.

I entered the house in 1995 as the chairman of the newly-created District of Columbia Subcommittee under the jurisdiction of the Government Reform and Oversight Committee. I was placed there as a freshman congressman for several reasons. Firstly, no one else was clamoring for the position. Secondly, it offered me the opportunity to have a gavel that would ensure a multitude of local press coverage (and thereby potentially help my reelection in a swing district). And thirdly, I was uniquely qualified, having been the president of the Washington Metropolitan Council of Governments (COG) and the elected leader of the largest jurisdiction in the region (Fairfax County).

I will let a passage in the 1996 edition of *The Almanac of American Politics* speak for me about this appointment:

As soon as he arrived on Capitol Hill, Davis was handed by Speaker Newt Gingrich one of the hottest potatoes to fall into the hands of the new Congress: staunching the District of Columbia's ever-deepening river of red ink. As chairman of the House Government Reform and Oversight Committee's District of Columbia subcommittee, Davis first rejected D.C. Mayor Marion Barry's request for massive federal aid, insisting instead on a specific plan to cut District spending and payrolls. In this he worked closely with Gingrich and District Delegate Eleanor Holmes Norton; together they backed in March 1995 a law creating a five-member financial control board to oversee District of Columbia finances.

That is the 50-cent version. The facts are far more complex. When Speaker Gingrich and the full committee chairman, Bill Clinger, appointed me chairman, the role looked like a cakewalk. The subcommittee had been a full standing committee in previous Congresses, but had produced little legislation. It had been rolled into the Government Reform and Oversight Committee, along with the Post Office and Civil Service Committee.

Within two weeks of the announcement of my appointment, the city's finances collapsed. Its bonds went to junk status and the eyes of the country were on a failed nation's capital.

As a white Republican overseeing a heavily Democratic city that was majority black, I was viewed with great suspicion. Sharing the same media market as the city presented me with both a challenge and an opportunity. Unlike previous Republicans who had served on the committee and made their reputation beating up on the city, I would pay a political price for doing so. Many of my top political advisors thought that accepting the chairmanship was a stupid move that could only end badly for me. But I viewed it differently. What good is political office if you can't solve problems? At any rate, running away from the difficulty was not an option.

Confrontation was not my style, but many elements in the city wanted exactly that. The Reverend Willy Wilson, an outspoken African American leader, labeled Newt Gingrich, Representative Jim Walsh of New York (the D.C. Appropriations chair), and me "Ku, Klux, and Klan." I didn't help myself when I told a reporter the subcommittee was going to be "a real tar baby," a reference to the very sticky Uncle Remus character. No racial offense was intended – it was an offhand comment about this being a sticky situation – but for many city advocates who were not happy with congressional interference, particularly by a Republican from a suburban county, it was a free shot.

I recognized early that I would get lots of criticism, no matter what decisions I made. Many D.C. advocates saw any congressional intervention as a violation of their "home rule" rights. Many conservatives wanted to do away with home rule altogether, feeling that the city had blown it and was not deserving of another chance.

There was also a lot of suspicion on the part of congressional Democrats regarding how Republicans would approach solving the city's financial woes. At that time, D.C. was a Democratic city on the brink of financial disaster with a dwindling tax base and prone to corruption. With the subpoena power of our chairmanships, we had the ability to investigate violations of the fiscal-control Anti-Deficiency Act, mismanagement, and poor planning, with the blame going to the past Democratic Congresses that had looked the other way rather than fulfilling their oversight responsibilities. For the

new sheriff in town (the Republican Congress), the situation offered up a
buffet of opportunities to investigate and embarrass the Democrats.

But I quickly moved to dispel the Democrats' fears. I was able to convince Eleanor Holmes Norton, the District's non-voting delegate to Congress, that I needed her input and assistance if I was to ward off more
aggressive action by my Republican colleagues. I had an able and experienced partner in Dr. Alice Rivlin, who was both the Clinton administration's OMB director and a District resident. It was also helpful that Speaker
Gingrich understood the downside of beating up on the city and stood
behind our efforts to fix the problem in a congenial manner.

Together, we worked to establish a control board that was constituted of
D.C. residents appointed by President Clinton and took over most of the
city's functions. Without everyone working together in earnest to solve a
difficult financial problem and an even more difficult political challenge, we
never would have succeeded. Under my sponsorship but with much input
from all sides and the smartest experts we could find, the legislation I introduced was passed by both chambers and signed by the president within two
weeks of being filed.

I was also fortunate that my Senate partners – Bill Cohen from Maine as
the authorizer and Jim Jeffords of Vermont as the appropriator (both were
moderate Republicans at the time) – liked what we were doing and made
only a couple substantive changes to the legislation that we had introduced.
In the end, the bill passed nearly unanimously, the city accepted the legislation with a minimum of negativity, and press accounts were very supportive.

I had not only survived my first congressional challenge, I had turned it
into a big political victory. My experience in local government, where partisanship generally took a back seat to problem solving, had served me well, as
had my understanding of municipal corporations. And, I must admit, I was
too focused on solving the problem and too afraid to fail to play politics.

Twenty years later, Washington, D.C., was enjoying the largest surplus of
any city in the country. The independent chief financial officer we established made a huge difference in the city's financial operations and the tax
base continued to expand.

Looking back, identifying the solution and working through the political
traps was downright fun! Making a difference and solving problems was

what I had been sent to Washington to do; and even decades later, our work has withstood the test of time.

To have been given the chance to make a significant legislative mark as a freshman member of Congress was a rare and exhilarating opportunity. I'm not sure that if the same situation occurred today, the same players could achieve the same result. We had no blogs to contend with. The local media was supportive. And there was no cable news to fan the ideological flames and frighten members into rejecting the agreement. Moreover, no super PACs existed to threaten members of Congress who voted for the compromise.

MARTIN'S VIEW

One of the most dramatic events in my adult life was when the Berlin Wall came down. We had all grown up assuming that Communist domination of Eastern Europe was permanent. And then all of a sudden the world changed.

I was so struck by the turn of events that I asked to be included in the first congressional delegation (CODEL) to Berlin. Speaker Tom Foley granted my request and off I went in early December of 1989, part of a delegation headed by my colleague Steny Hoyer of Maryland. I had a personal interest in this region; my father's family emigrated from Berlin to the United States in the 19th century and my mother's family was originally from Lithuania.

While in Berlin, we visited with the East Berliners who were the driving force in pulling East Germany away from the Soviet orbit. As members of Congress often do in these circumstances, we asked, "What can we do to be helpful?" Their response was very direct. East Germany had not had any experience with operating a democratic parliament since well before World War II. These people needed someone to teach them about democracy and to provide computer and other electronic equipment – such as fax machines – that the communists had denied their "show" parliament, which had only met once a year.

Upon our return, I went to see Speaker Foley and suggested that the House should provide technical and material help to East Germany as well as other countries in the region that quickly executed their own nonviolent revolutions, like Czechoslovakia and Hungary. We also determined that the Senate had lost interest in doing anything further for Poland, so we added that country to the list. Then West Germany announced the merging of East and West Germany, so the East Germans were taken off our list.

There are moments in history when the planets are in alignment. Most House Speakers are primarily concerned about domestic policy and don't focus on foreign policy. Speaker Foley was different. He had a longstanding interest in foreign policy – in fact, he later became the United States ambassador to Japan – and had his own foreign policy adviser, Werner Brandt. Speaker Foley quickly decided this was something the House should undertake and asked me to head a special bipartisan task force to help the parliaments of Eastern and Central Europe. Also, it just so happened that the new Librarian of Congress, James Billington, was a scholar on Russia and had accompanied a Foley CODEL to the Soviet Union in 1983 as head of the Woodrow Wilson Center for International Scholars. I had been the junior member of that CODEL. Once the task force was set up, I went to Dr. Billington, who made the resources of Congressional Research Service (CRS) fully at our disposal.

It was clear to me from the beginning that the task force had to be fully bipartisan and that we had to actively involve the Bush administration if we were to be successful. Three very thoughtful Republicans were recruited for our efforts: Jerry Solomon of New York, Jim Leach of Iowa, and Doug Bereuter of Nebraska. Democratic Members included Bart Gordon of Tennessee and Bob Mrazek from New York. We convened regular meetings of these members and representatives from the State Department, USAID, and CRS. Since Congress cannot appropriate money to itself to run programs, we arranged for an initial appropriation to be made to the State Department, which agreed to subcontract with CRS, with the work being supervised by our task force. We traveled on the signature of the Speaker so that our travel expenses did not need to come out of the appropriated funds, which would be used to purchase equipment for the parliaments.

Our first task force CODEL was to Hungary, Czechoslovakia, and Poland. In addition to the members, we now had a parliamentary library specialist from CRS, an Eastern European specialist from CRS, and former Michigan congressman Lucien Nedzi, who traced his family origins to

Poland. Serving as staff director was my Rules Committee staffer Kristi Walseth, who turned out to be an inspired choice and devoted much of the next
five years to making this project a success.

The leaders and staffs of these newly-democratized parliaments welcomed us with open arms. In Poland and Czechoslovakia, for example, we
worked closely with people who had been banished from important positions by the communist government. The head librarian of the Czechoslo-
vakian parliamentary library was a trained librarian who had been relegated
to a job as a traveling salesman. He was especially eager to develop library
and research services for his government, knowing firsthand how important
free access to information is to the democratic process.

We quickly learned that these leaders had been getting a lot of verbal
encouragement from various Western European parliaments but that no
one was actually doing anything concrete for them. When we told them we
would supply computers and fax machines, they were overjoyed and gave us
a shopping list of what they needed. They also appreciated our offer to help
them establish modern parliamentary libraries and to conduct training sessions – both in Washington, D.C., and in their own countries – for parliamentary members and key staff. In fact, members of the Hungarian government told us that our assistance had moved them forward by 10 years in the
space of two.

We made some threshold decisions: (1) we would only move into additional countries when our State Department told us those countries were
ready; (2) we would insist that all assistance be provided equally to all parties (majority and minority) in the parliaments; and (3) we would limit our
activities to Eastern and Central Europe – we didn't have the staff or
resources to focus on Russia or other large parts of the old Soviet Union,
such as Ukraine. We ultimately expanded our work to Latvia, Lithuania,
Estonia, Bulgaria, Romania, Albania, and the Slovak Republic (when Czechoslovakia split into two countries).

Our work was a tremendous success and our task force made numerous
trips back into the region to deliver equipment and meet with parliamentary
leaders from 1990 to 1994. When Newt Gingrich became Speaker in 1995,
he wanted to disband the task force, seeing it as an unnecessary project and
expense. However, Gerry Solomon, who became the chairman of the task

force when the Republicans took control of the House, eventually convinced Speaker Gingrich of the importance of the project, and it was allowed to finish its work in Romania and Albania. Ten years later, Speaker Dennis Hastert revived the project as the House Democracy Partnership at the urging of Republican congressmen Doug Bereuter of Nebraska and David Dreier of California, and Democratic congressman David Price of North Carolina.

This work was absolutely one of the most rewarding things I did as a member of Congress, though it had little or no political benefit to me back home in my district. I believe that our work contributed significantly to those new democracies' becoming allies of the United States. In 2010, 20 years after the work had begun, my staff and I were invited to Poland, where the Polish government honored us for our efforts. I have continued my interest in pro-democracy work and in the spring of 2013 was named board chairman of the bipartisan National Endowment for Democracy (NED).

One of the other side benefits of my work on the task force was that I got to visit Jewish historical sites in each of these countries and to meet with the handful of remaining Jewish legislators elected to these parliaments. I will long remember a Passover Seder in Warsaw with the remnants of the local Jewish community in the early 1990s and our side trip to the Auschwitz concentration camp.

Another classic example of working across party lines to accomplish something that was important involved the AMBER Alert.

In 1996, a little girl in my congressional district was tragically kidnapped, molested, and murdered. Her name was Amber Hagerman.

Once this became public, I went to see her family and neighbors in a blue-collar section of Arlington, not too far from Six Flags Over Texas. I expressed my condolences and then, just as we had when we visited Berlin, asked, "What can I do to help?"

Their answer was very direct: "Congressman, pass a law to make sure this doesn't happen to anyone else's little girl." What they wanted was a federal law to increase criminal penalties against child predators.

I returned to Washington and drafted what became known as the Amber Hagerman Child Protection Act, which would apply to any predator who crossed states lines to commit such an offense – the only cases that could be tried in federal rather than state courts. That bill also created a national sex offender registry. It was ultimately passed by Congress with both Democratic and Republican support. I escorted Amber's parents to the White House, where we witnessed President Clinton sign the bill.

But the story didn't end there. Local law enforcement and media in the Dallas-Ft. Worth area created what became known as the "AMBER Alert," designed to immediately publicize child abduction under the theory that the chances of recovering a child alive significantly drop after the first 24 hours. Texas was the first state to create a system with the alerts.

I then invited Dallas-Ft. Worth law enforcement and media representatives to come to Washington and brief members of Congress about the AMBER Alert with the hope that they would take this back to their home districts and get a similar program started. A number did, and AMBER Alerts began popping up around the country.

Ultimately, I worked with Texas Republican senator Kay Bailey Hutchinson to introduce a national AMBER Alert law. That law is formally known as the PROTECT (Prosecutorial Remedies and Other Tools to End the Exploitation of Children Today) Act. It established an office in the U.S. Justice Department to oversee AMBER Alerts around the country and provided for federal grants to localities to put up electronic signs on interstate highways publicizing AMBER Alerts and take other steps to develop notification systems.

However, nothing in Washington is ever simple. The AMBER Alert legislation was referred to the House Judiciary Committee chaired by Republican congressman Jim Sensenbrenner of Wisconsin. Congressman Sensenbrenner was working on a comprehensive criminal justice bill that contained many controversial sections. Unfortunately, he attached the AMBER Alert to this bill, and the entire measure was deadlocked in committee.

Sensenbrenner testified before the Rules Committee on an unrelated bill and I asked him why he didn't just strip out the AMBER Alert and send it to the floor as a separate bill. He simply refused.

And then an extraordinary thing happened. While this was all taking place, I had been seeking out the support of other advocates of legislation to protect children to brief them on the AMBER Alert bill and to ask for their help. One of these was Ed Smart, the father of Elizabeth Smart, who had been kidnapped nine months previously in Utah. Miraculously, Elizabeth Smart finally escaped her captors and was returned to her family.

Ed Smart held a press conference the night she was found. He first thanked local law enforcement officials for never giving up. Then he did something unbelievable. Though obviously overcome with emotion about the safe return of his daughter, he called out Jim Sensenbrenner on live national television for bottling up the AMBER Alert, which could help other children like his daughter.

The effect was monumental. Even Jim Sensenbrenner, a very tough committee chairman, could not take this kind of heat; and the AMBER Alert bill became law in 2003, when it was signed by President George W. Bush, who coincidentally had been Texas governor when Amber had been killed. Since then, AMBER Alert plans have been created in all 50 states and have assisted in the search and recovery of hundreds of children.

By the way, Ed Smart is a Republican.

Another local example of getting things accomplished on a bipartisan basis involved the construction of a veterans cemetery in my district in north Texas. The project spanned three presidential administrations – two Republican and one Democratic – and periods of time when the Democrats and Republicans each controlled the House.

The Veterans Department reported to Congress in 1987 the findings of a congressionally mandated study identifying the 10 metropolitan areas in the country with the largest concentration of veterans not conveniently served by the national cemetery system. The Dallas-Ft. Worth area was high on this list, as was Albany, New York (which turned out to be a critical link in the process).

The leaders of all the national veterans organizations with a significant presence in north Texas came to see me and asked that I take the lead on getting a veterans cemetery for our area.

I agreed to help. In addition to wanting to serve my district, I had a personal interest in this issue. I served in the Army Reserves during the Vietnam era. My father had served in the Navy during World War II, and my grandfather had been an enlisted man in the Army during World War I. My mother's only brother was an Army officer during World War II, taking part in a number of landings in the Pacific; and my uncle Joe had survived the Japanese attack on Pearl Harbor while stationed on the USS *Pennsyl-vania*. Three of my male first cousins had completed ROTC while in college and had served as Army officers. Also, Texas is a very patriotic state, and Texas A&M – which several of my cousins attended – provided more offi-cers for the Army during World War II than West Point did.

The first thing I did was call in officials from the Veterans Department and ask why there was nothing in the president's budget to implement their own recommendation. They replied that they wanted a veterans cemetery for north Texas, but the Office of Management and Budget would not let them make the request because of the tight budget. And then they told me, "Congressman, if you can get the money, we will be happy to build the cem-etery."

I then began the long process of obtaining funding, which stretched through the administrations of George H. W. Bush and Bill Clinton and a Democratically-controlled (1987-1994) and Republican-controlled (1995 until the cemetery was opened in 2000) House. My first step was to appear before the House Appropriations subcommittee with jurisdiction over the Veterans Department. I brought with me a local veteran, Cloyde Pinson, whose son had been killed in Vietnam. Pinson was a Republican, but he wanted this cemetery built and was more than happy to work with a Demo-cratic congressman to get it done. He told the subcommittee about his son's death in Vietnam and there wasn't a dry eye in the room.

I was able to get initial funding for an environmental impact study (EIS; the first step for building the cemetery), which identified the preferred site, which happened to be in my district. Once the site was identified, I got funding for the design, then for land acquisition costs, and finally for con-struction. Funding for the EIS, site design, and land acquisition occurred while Democrats still controlled the House. Construction funding came while the Republicans controlled it. The cemetery was dedicated during the closing days of the administration of President Bill Clinton.

It just so happened that a Republican congressman from upstate New York, Jerry Solomon, was also seeking funding for a local veterans cemetery, in the Albany area. Solomon had been one of the Republicans who'd served on my task force to help the parliaments of Eastern and Central Europe, and by the time we needed construction funding he had become chairman of the House Rules Committee. Even though money was tight, Solomon made sure that the annual appropriations bills contained sufficient funding for both the New York and Texas cemeteries. We were colleagues on the Rules Committee, and while we didn't agree philosophically on a number of issues, he was my friend. We worked together and both projects were completed. I'm not sure that such bipartisan cooperation would be possible today, even on projects as worthy as a last resting place for the men and women who served our country.

Also, Solomon and I obtained funding for our projects long before the House decided to end earmarks. Ending earmarks for a member's own district has greatly contributed to a breakdown in bipartisan cooperation and will be explored later in this book.

14

COMMITTEE SELECTIONS AND LEADERSHIP ELECTIONS

By Tom Davis

The confluence of safe party districts, polarized media, and independent super PACs brings pressure on members to cater to their parties' primary voters rather than focusing on their general elections. This can often pull them in directions opposite those of their leadership, especially on important votes. The processes of committee selection and promoting members to key committee chairmanships are tools leaders still have in their tool boxes to discipline and reward members.

Leaders view the protection of their majority as one of their primary obligations. That involves a tightrope walk between keeping their more ideological members happy (and protected from primary challenges) and holding competitive districts that are necessary in order to maintain a minimum of 218 seats in the House.

Seniority in the House was king for determining committee leadership positions for a very long time, but both parties – the Republicans somewhat more so than the Democrats – have taken significant steps in recent years to open up the process, and party leaders now play a determining role.

It all started in 1974 with the election of 75 "Watergate babies" to the Democratic Caucus. This large number of reform-minded new members demanded a change in House rules to end the strict seniority system that had resulted in a number of chairmen in their late 70s and 80s who were not always responsive to the membership as a whole.

One of the changes adopted that year required a yes/no secret ballot by the entire caucus on the continuation of a given senior member as chairman of a full committee. Three chairmen were rejected on this secret ballot in the organizing caucus following the 1974 elections, and a fourth stepped down under pressure.

Republicans likewise adopted further rules changes following the 1994 election, when they took control of the House for the first time in 40 years. They instituted a six-year term limit on full committee chairmanship and permitted the new Speaker, Newt Gingrich, to bypass senior members when recommending full committee chairs. The latter reform was to ensure that Republicans had their more capable members serving as chairs of key committees in order to protect their newly-won majority.

The precise procedures for implementing these changes (which differ in the Republican and Democratic caucuses) will be discussed in full later in this chapter.

Among the most secretive and mysterious aspects of House procedures are the members' assignments to committees and the order of seniority on those committees, as well as the selection of the committee and subcommittee chairmen. While these determinations are generally seniority-based in the Senate, the House operates under "jungle rules," where seniority is but one factor in assigning members to committees and selecting chairmen. The House also changes its selection processes periodically so that precedent constantly evolves, along with changes in leadership. And there are significant differences between the two parties.

Over the course of time, the methods have shifted from strong Speakers (such as Tom Reed, Joe Cannon, and Nicholas Longworth) to strong committee powers (such as the Ways and Means Committee, the Rules Committee, and the Steering Committee) to seniority-based rule to party caucus votes. Seniority after the assignment of committee slots has had varying degrees of relevance. Each of these methods had its strengths and weaknesses and when things went badly, the system would change.

During our government's first 100 years, House members rarely made Congress a career. Being a member of Congress was not a full-time job, members were paid a per diem, and four terms was considered a long tenure. Henry Clay was elected Speaker in his first term in the House! A freshman committee chair was not a rarity and the electorate was volatile in its voter preferences.

In 1910, the House rebelled against the dictatorial rule of Speaker Cannon and implemented a seniority-based system for committee chairmen. Eventually, that resulted in powerful autocrats who were not responsive to the House or their parties. Starting in the 1960s, many Democrats objected to the conservative Democratic chairmen – mostly from the South – who resisted the majority of the Democratic Caucus and the activist agendas of Democratic presidents.

After a series of incremental steps, the dam burst in 1974, when the huge Watergate class joined the Democratic reformers to create a solid majority of the party caucus. This group removed chairmen who not only were out of step with their party's ideology, but also made little effort to solicit the views of other members. The result replaced four veteran and influential committee chairmen and increased the influence of the caucus, which in turn led to attacks on "King Caucus." Most Democratic chairmen subsequently became responsive to party leaders and other members.

But there have been occasional instances since 1974 when Democratic chairmen were ousted. An example came after the 2008 election, when Henry Waxman of California successfully challenged John Dingell of Michigan, the veteran chairman of the Energy and Commerce Committee. Waxman and Dingell had some major differences on issues such as energy and the environment, and some members also believed that incoming president Barack Obama needed a more aggressive ally to handle his health care proposal. Waxman also benefited from the tacit support of Speaker Nancy Pelosi.

The current system for committee rule on the Republican side evolved from the 1994 "Gingrich revolution" election. House Republicans had been out of power for 40 years. Democrats, it was felt, abused their power (this was the GOP narrative) by bottling up Republican bills and popular legislation through strong committee chairs, some of whom had literally held their positions for decades.

Sensing the general electorate's growing frustration with Congress, Republicans ran on a platform called the Contract With America, which called for, among other things, reforming Congress. The platform included:

1. Calls to abolish proxy voting in both subcommittees and full committees, which reflected Republican frustration with Democratic chairmen holding the proxy votes of absent Democratic members so that Republican amendments could be defeated at the chairmen's whims. Majority members would not have to be bogged down in committee markups to debate or even hear Republican amendments or arguments. They could simply leave their proxy vote with the chairman, who would vote the way he or she saw fit, always carrying the day.

2. The decision to apply the rules and laws Congress passed for the rest of the country to Congress itself. For years, Congress had exempted itself from major legislation, including the National Labor Relations Act, the Americans for Disabilities Act, the Occupational Safety and Health Act, and the Fair Labor Standards Act.

3. A three-term limit on committee chairs. This was a reaction to entrenched committee chairs, many of whom utilized committee staff as personal staff and campaign aides and offered little sunshine to the public.

As a newly-elected member of that 104th Congress, in 1995 I dutifully joined all Republicans in voting for all of these reforms my first day on the job. We believed we were involved in a revolution to alter the culture of Congress, which would enable us to change the direction of the country for the better.

Proxy Voting

It didn't take long for us to understand why the Democrats hadn't put these rules in place when they were in the majority. Although greater transparency and term limits have their benefits, they also have their disadvantages. For example, eliminating proxy voting was fairer and gave interested members, particularly minority members, better opportunities to affect legislation; but it also made the legislative process more cumbersome and less efficient. Most members served on multiple committees, and if two of those committees marked up legislation at the same time (not a rare occurrence), it was impossible to be in two places at once and be in attendance at both committee meetings – particularly if the committees met in different buildings (also not a rare occurrence).

The minority members learned to strategize to determine which amendments they would prioritize, and made sure they were in their seats for votes at those committee meetings. The Republicans often had no clue where the Democrats would take their fight, and we had to scurry to keep a majority in place. This was not a problem on key committees, where the partisan ratios were apportioned to supermajority status. But on some committees, the ratios were much closer (for instance, 24 to 20, which was the Oversight Committee's ratio when I became chairman in 2003), and a few absent Republican members plus a planned Democratic ambush could yield unfavorable results.

Alas, we had put ourselves in this position and had to learn to live with it. I remember chairing one committee markup on my bill to vouchers for private schools to students in the District of Columbia who attended public schools that were failing. The vote was going to be close, and I needed every Republican on the committee because the Democrats were unanimously opposed.

I knew I would lose two of my members, who had cut deals with their teachers' unions back home to oppose any voucher bill, so the margin of error was zero. This was an important bill to John Boehner (the chairman of the Education and Workforce Committee) and me. Because Boehner's committee had narrow party ratios and a disproportionate number of more moderate Republicans, he couldn't pass it through his committee. So it fell to me to pull together a positive committee vote and move it to the floor. Unfortunately, the morning of the vote, one of my members flipped on me and said he could not support the measure. My count indicated that if every Democrat turned up at the committee meeting, I would lose the vote.

I asked this member if he could "take a walk" and not be present for the vote. He was on board with that idea until he was revisited by the national teachers' group (National Education Association) and told if the bill passed by one vote, it would cost him their endorsement and subsequent PAC money in his next election. Nevertheless, he agreed to stay in the back room and vote late if I needed him. But he could not be seen as taking a walk by the union.

When the roll was called, it went according to plan – except that one Democrat, Major Owens from New York, did not show up. When I asked Henry Waxman, my ranking Democratic member, where he was, he responded that Owens was in the hospital in New York City and couldn't make it. At that point, I sent a note to my member in the back room and told him I didn't need his vote and he could come out and vote no. He did and I won by one vote!

The bill then went to the House floor for a vote. Boehner and I managed the legislation. Although we lost several Republicans, we picked up four Democrats. (I had personally solicited about a dozen, but they were nervous about the NEA and the American Federation of Teachers pulling their support in their next elections.) Still, when the votes were in, it looked like we were going to lose the bill by one vote. I went to Tom DeLay, the Majority Leader, and asked him to hold the vote open so we could try to get one member to switch or two members who had voted no to abstain.

After a half hour of arm-twisting, we got DeLay to agree, and we descended on Ernie Fletcher, a Kentucky Republican who had voted no. He explained that he was running for governor and a yes vote would hurt him with his public school supporters and the black vote in Louisville. He had no illusions about an NEA endorsement but was concerned about spiking the opposition's intensity. We explained to him that the legislation was supported by the black mayor and black school board chairman in D.C. and, though we couldn't tell him this was a majority position in the black community, there certainly was a constituency for it. I asked Ernie, "What percentage of the African American vote do you need?" and he said, "About 10%." After some thoughtful interchange about the importance of the vote, Ernie went down to the House well and changed his vote to yes, which put us up by one vote. The Speaker's gavel immediately came down before the Democratic leaders could get one of their four back in line, and the bill was passed.

We never could get the 60 votes we needed to force a vote to pass the bill in the Senate. But with the help of Democrats Joe Lieberman and Dianne Feinstein, we rolled it into an appropriations bill. In the ever-secretive exchanges in the conference between the House and Senate, we were able to have the measure included in a larger measure, which passed and was signed into law. As a footnote, Ernie Fletcher went on to win his governor's race and used the voucher issue effectively in the black community, garnering 16% of the black vote in Louisville.

In this case, having eliminated the proxy rule worked in our favor. Had Waxman held Owens's proxy, it would have tied up the vote in committee and we would have been unable to move the bill to the floor.

The no-proxy rules have remained in effect in the House – even under Democratic control – despite the continued grumbling of some senior members. This is an example of how the Republicans' takeover of the House in 1994 led to some wide-ranging changes that leaders of both parties ultimately embraced.

TERM LIMITS

Under House Republican rules, term limits for committee chairs have allowed new blood to come in and rejuvenate committees and offered some upward mobility for more junior members. They have also helped Republican campaign committee fundraising, since when a chairmanship becomes open and available, several members audition for the part and an important part of the audition is demonstrating one's fundraising prowess. Thus, chairman aspirants redouble their efforts in raising campaign money for "the team" to impress upon Steering Committee members that their fundraising base will be enhanced by granting them a chairmanship. This has proven to be a financial bonanza for the campaign committee.

However, this change has also had a downside. After members have completed their six-year tenures as committee chair and are term-limited out of that position, they must decide if they want to rotate to the backbenches or leave Congress on top, with their portrait on the committee room wall and an opportunity to earn a significant income in the private sector. Many Republicans in this position who represented swing districts have chosen to retire, putting their seats at risk of switching to Democratic representation at the next election.

Democratic rules do not include committee chair term limits. Many Democrats remain distinctly unenthusiastic about such rules. For example, the Congressional Black Caucus – ironically, like conservative southern Democrats of earlier times – opposes them because many of its members represent secure districts and have benefited from seniority.

To the dismay of these and some other Democrats, Speaker Pelosi left intact the Republican term limit rules when Democrats gained House control in 2007. In effect, Democratic chairmen were given a six-year reprieve, with the possibility that they could change the rule before the guillotine came down in 2013. That became a moot point when Republicans regained House control in 2011. The term limits have not restricted the tenure of senior House Democrats while they have been in the minority.

COMMITTEE SELECTION

Before the start of every Congress, each party meets in caucus, elects its leaders, and proceeds to elect a Steering Committee (also known as a Committee on Committees), which will organize caucus members and designate their committee assignments. The Steering Committee's members and structure vary from Congress to Congress, but it always has a leadership influence within its structure.

Democratic Caucus procedures for electing House committee and subcommittee chairs are much more formalized than Republican procedures. They give heavy weight to the wishes of the Democratic leader but do provide for an easier challenge in the full caucus.

For full committee chairs or ranking members, the initial decision is made by the Steering and Policy Committee, which has 53 members. Of these members, 13 are at-large appointees of the Democratic leader and four are co-chairs and vice-chairs appointed by the leader. Because these individuals can be expected to follow their leader's lead, the leader typically has 17 votes in addition to his or her own. If the Steering and Policy Committee nominates someone other than the senior member of a committee, that person is automatically entitled to a vote in the full caucus if he or she receives at least 14 votes in the Steering and Policy Committee. If the Steering and Policy Committee nominates the senior member, a member who gets 50 other members to sign a petition can challenge that person in the full caucus. Otherwise, all names are sent to the caucus for a yes/no secret ballot. If the full caucus rejects someone, the floor is then open for nominations, which may include the member rejected.

Here's how it works for subcommittee chairs (or ranking members). Appropriations has its own procedure, which recognizes subcommittee seniority. For all other committees, members bid in full committee seniority order for subcommittee chair/ranking member positions. Someone may challenge the person who bids for a position, in which case there is a vote of the full committee. Subcommittee chairs of exclusive committees – whose members typically don't sit on any other committees; for instance, Ways and Means, Appropriations, Energy and Commerce, and Financial Services – are subject to a yes/no secret ballot in the full caucus. If someone is rejected, the decision goes back to full committee for further proceedings, though as a practical matter this never happens.

One of the most sought-after committee assignments for both parties is to the Ways and Means Committee because its jurisdiction includes tax law and trade preferences. From this perch, a member can raise a lot of campaign money. Although tax laws are not written every year, one-year extensions of tax preferences worth billions of dollars to American industry are enacted annually. They are invisible to the average voter, devoid of partisan animus, and worth thousands of individual PAC contributions; this is a most notable abuse of the tax system. These preferences are clothed in "job creation" cloth, literally, as everyone from mink ranchers to oil producers to technology companies ante up millions of dollars in contributions to ensure billions of dollars in tax savings annually.

Competition for this coveted committee is keen, with prospective members raising money for the campaign committees of each party and showing leadership loyalty in their voting to gain favor and win a coveted slot.

Steering Committee members weigh the prospects' dedication to the "team." How much did they raise? How much did they contribute to vulnerable candidates? Did they vote with the leadership on a tough vote? Most importantly, on the Republican side at least, will they support free trade agreements? Trade agreements are an absolute must for committee members to be able to move trade legislation. A bad trade vote has vetoed many a prospective Ways and Means Committee member. On occasion, vulnerable members will be assigned to the committee to help them raise money to keep their seats. This has proven a persuasive argument so long as the other criteria are also met.

Committee chairs also have considerable influence and a blackball over their respective committees' membership. The majority party also gives a ratio boost to its "A-list" committees so the leadership will still prevail on votes even if a couple of its members have to buck the party due to local political survival concerns. This is particularly true of the Rules Committee, through which all legislation must pass and where the majority party has held a nine-to-four edge for decades.

At the beginning of the 113th Congress (2013-14), when the GOP held a 234 to 201 edge, the Ways and Means ratio was 23 to 16. Compare that with the Science, Space and Technology Committee, one from which very little money can be raised, where the ratio was 22 to 18, or the Agriculture and Foreign Affairs Committees, each with a 25 to 21 ratio.

Other sought-after committee assignments are Financial Services, which regulates banking, housing, and insurance and attracts mega-PAC money; and Energy and Commerce, which has jurisdiction over health care, energy, and telecom policy and attracts a lot of PAC money from regulated industries in those areas. For these A-list committees, along with Appropriations (which spends tax dollars), the competition for slots is intense.

As a rule, a member who sits on an A-list committee cannot serve on another committee, while members who serve on the B-list committees – particularly members of the majority party – serve on two or three committees. There is certainly nothing negative about the B-list committees, except that they are not particularly advantageous for fundraising. For example, the Agriculture Committee is critical to members from farming districts. The Judiciary Committee involves many interesting and high-profile pieces of legislation, from immigration to patent reform to constitutional amendments. If guns and abortions are your top issues, than Judiciary is your committee.

Transportation is another committee that may not raise members a lot of money but can certainly help their reelections. Whether it's a bridge, road, or water project, the committee traditionally has been a bipartisan magnet for members who like to "bring home the bacon" and show voters they, at least, are getting something done.

And if a member has a military base to protect, the Armed Services Committee is where it's at. Every year for five decades, a defense bill has passed Congress and been signed into law. This legislation, which sets defense policy for the next year, is largely written in the committee. Moreover, letters to the Pentagon from the committee's members receive a quicker and more thorough response than those from other individuals do.

But though these committees are important to certain constituencies, they do not have the demand and fundraising potential of the A-list committees.

My strategy when I was elected to Congress was fairly simple. Aside from signing the Contract for America, I wanted to be reelected, gain some seniority, and work to be in a place where I could make a real difference for my northern Virginia district. The stars appeared to align for me as far as committee assignments were concerned. The Gingrich revolutionaries decided to cut back on the number of committees from previous Congresses; and as a part of their reorganization, they combined three B-list committees – the Post Office and Civil Service Committee, the District of Columbia Committee, and the Government Operations Committee – into one committee. It was still a B-list committee and not one that had much attraction for the average member. But for me it was the trifecta.

My district was in the suburbs of the District of Columbia and I had served as the president of the Metropolitan Washington Council of Governments while serving as the chairman of the Fairfax County Board of Supervisors. Moreover, this new committee, not the Transportation Committee, had jurisdiction over the Washington Metropolitan Area Transit Authority, which oversaw the local bus and subway service that ventured into my district.

The Civil Service Committee set policy for federal employees, of which some 56,000 were among my constituency. And the Government Operations Committee oversaw federal contracting. I had over 500 federal contractors scattered throughout my district. Being able to put in a good word here or add a helpful amendment there couldn't hurt.

So I listed this newly-formed committee as my first choice. Only one other freshman, Congressman Dave McIntosh of Indiana, who was a government management geek, did the same. We both were assigned to the committee ahead of other freshmen in seniority. Because the committee was most members' second or third, we became subcommittee chairs in our first year in Congress.

It seemed that Speaker Gingrich, dealing with a caucus that was nearly one-third freshmen in makeup, wanted to throw out a few bones to the newcomers, so some of the A-list committee slots and three subcommittee chairmanships went to the freshman class. As an acknowledgement that I had been given a prized gavel and six patronage slots to staff it (even though the District of Columbia subcommittee was probably the least sought-after assignment in the House), I took the Science Committee for my second committee. This was an interesting committee if you had an interest in the space program or more esoteric research issues, but it was a public relations and fundraising dud. Still, wielding a gavel over matters concerning the District of Columbia guaranteed me high-level press coverage in my home county of Fairfax.

PARTY LOYALTY

Under Republican rules, the committee chairman generally chooses House subcommittee chairmen on a seniority basis. My Government Reform Committee chair, Bill Clinger of Pennsylvania, was a fellow moderate and University of Virginia Law School alumnus. We bonded immediately.

However, this GOP selection process is not a hard and fast rule, and a committee chair may pass over a more senior member if that member is not acceptable for reasons of party loyalty or reliability. A prime example is Walter Jones of North Carolina, a very senior member of the Armed Services Committee who was repeatedly passed over as a subcommittee chair because of his vote against the Iraq War and independent voting record on key issues in the committee.

Jones came to Congress in 1994 as one of my class in the Gingrich revolution. He had run before, in 1992, and was defeated in a Democratic primary for the seat his father had held for a generation in coastal North Carolina. His father had been a Democrat. But the state legislature, in drawing the lines in the redistricting following the 1990 census, had produced a district that was majority African American. Jones had led the initial primary but under North Carolina's runoff provisions faced Eva Clayton, a soft-spoken black state legislator, in the runoff; he was defeated, 54% to 46%.

Not to be deterred, Walter came back in 1994, running as a Republican in the neighboring 3rd district, which was a white majority district and also contained several counties from his father's previous district. In a strong Republican year, the Jones name and the anti-Clinton trend propelled Walter to a 53% to 47% victory. At the same time, three other Democratic seats in the state shifted to the Republicans; and Jones, a self-described conservative, was on his way to Washington.

Jones wore his Christianity and conservatism on his sleeve, but party loyalty took on a new twist in this district. Jones had come to believe that the Iraq War was wrong, after having first embraced it and having had the French fries in the members' dining room relabeled "freedom fries." His alienation from the Bush administration carried into other areas, such as government contracting; and he soon made himself persona non grata on a committee that was very pro-military on the Republican side. His acts of conscience cost him a chairmanship. But if it was intended to intimidate Jones, it had the opposite effect, and he continued to work the church groups and was repeatedly nominated in his party's primaries. This same pass-over occurred with his Financial Services Committee slot as well, when Speaker John Boehner in 2013 removed him from his senior position on the committee for being insufficiently supportive of leadership.

There have been several other members who have gotten so out of line with their parties' positions that they too have not reaped the benefits of their seniority in the House. The leadership uses its clout to enforce loyalty so it can continue to pass legislation.

COMMITTEE CHAIRMEN

Especially for Republicans, selecting committee chairs in the House is even more subjective and is the result of Steering Committee deliberations in which seniority is again but one factor. The Senate has a more predictive process, whereby seniority is rarely subjugated in the selection process. This has resulted in more amicable transfers of power and more independent voting in that body.

In the House, the primary criterion for the selection of a chair is ability to utilize the gavel to raise money for "the team." As one leader put it in a Steering Committee deliberation, "A gavel is a terrible thing to waste." Thus, as a chairman's six-year tenure draws to a close, the other members of the committee audition with the leadership (and, to a lesser extent, the total membership) by chairing party fundraisers, giving large chunks of campaign cash to the NRCC, and donating to marginal members of the team. This avenue is not available to those members from marginal districts who must raise large amounts of money just to survive. Thus, the advantage goes to members from relatively safe districts who are not as tempted to stray from the party line.

Of course, the Steering Committee must also take a myriad of other considerations into account. In the 113th Congress, the committee chairmen turned out to be all males. That left the leadership scrambling to fill the House Administration Committee chairmanship with Candice Miller from Michigan, as that committee (along with the Rules Committee) is not chosen by the Steering Committee. As it turns out, Representative Miller had served as Secretary of State in Michigan for eight years, supervising state elections among other things; the House Administration Committee had jurisdiction over federal election law. Miller, having been passed over for chair of the Homeland Security Committee, landed another assignment for which she was highly qualified and that aided the GOP in the optics of its chairmanships.

The Democratic side undoubtedly gives more consideration to diversity, ensuring an appropriate balance of Hispanic, black, and female chairs. Geographic balance is also a consideration. In the 113th Congress, there were five blacks and four women among the ranking committee members. Maxine Waters of California (Financial Services) and Eddie Bernice Johnson of Texas (Science) were twofers. Two Hispanic women also held ranking committee positions: Linda Sanchez of California (Ethics) and Nydia Velazquez of New York (Small Business).

Another factor in choosing a chairman is loyalty to the leadership. Has the member been reliable in carrying out the priorities of the leadership, or does he or she act independently? It is important to leaders that they can depend on their chairmen to carry out the priorities of the caucus.

Republican Chris Smith of New Jersey was chair of the Veterans Affairs Committee in the 107th Congress (2001-02). However, he teamed with his Democratic ranking member to authorize benefit programs that far exceeded budget caps imposed by the Republican leadership and the Budget Committee. This put Republican members in the embarrassing position of having to either hike federal spending and break the budget caps or vote against veterans, a group that generally had a Republican lean.

The Steering Committee made its call at the start of the following Congress when it replaced Smith (who, although a staunch advocate for veterans, had never served in the armed forces) with Steve Buyer of Indiana, a veteran of Operation Desert Storm and a leadership loyalist. Smith's demotion was controversial within the Steering Committee, as he was well-liked by members; but the leadership put its foot down and he was replaced.

The leadership can ill afford a noncompliant committee chair when it is in pitched battles to move legislation and drive home the party's message.

I had my own issues with leadership on a regular basis once I became a committee chair. On the day of one of the hearings on steroid use in Major League Baseball – the most widely-viewed hearings in our committee's history – I returned to my office about 6 PM, having "outed" the widespread use of steroids in major league sports. The hearing had been bipartisan. Major League Baseball had been exposed as a haven for performance-enhancing drugs and the committee had been vindicated for its investigation. I felt tired and relieved but self-confident as I returned to my office. I was surprised to see the majority whip, Tom DeLay, waiting for me in my reception area, as leadership never went to members' offices. Rather, we were summoned to the leaders' offices. But there he was!

He greeted me with, "We've got a problem and we need your help." I ushered him into my private office, closed the door, and asked what I could do. He said to me, "Terri Schiavo." I asked him what on Earth Terri Schiavo had to do with me. After all, this was a woman who had been in a comatose state for several years, in Florida, with feeding tubes keeping her alive. Her husband, who was living with and had children with another woman, had decided to move on, seeing no chance for his wife's recovery. He had requested the feeding tubes be removed. Her family had objected and a court suit had ensued with the husband, under Florida law, prevailing.

The case had become a cause celebre in Florida and across the nation, as pro-life groups rallied to Schiavo's defense while pro-choice groups supported the husband. The pro-life forces had prevailed on Congress to intervene. Both the House and Senate had passed legislation to keep her alive and give her family another appeal. The problem was that the two chambers had passed differing legislation and the differences, given the congressional schedule, could not be resolved until after the weekend. In the meantime, the Florida authorities were going to remove the feeding tubes, which would weaken or kill Schiavo before the House could accept the Senate version of the legislation. DeLay asked me to subpoena the feeding tubes so that Florida could not act.

"Why me?" I asked. After all, this was not an issue for which I thought legislative interference was particularly appropriate, and there were many other chairmen who embraced these issues and stood to gain politically from such action. But in my case, not only was I hesitant to support it, I knew it would be a political loser in my upscale congressional district. DeLay replied that I was the only member of the House who had subpoena power under my own signature without a committee vote or agreement with his ranking member, and time was of the essence. Would I do it?

Recognizing that committee chairs were the representatives of the conference and that the leadership had given me great flexibility to run the committee as I saw fit, I agreed to do it.

I subpoenaed the tubes, the Florida Court refused to honor the subpoena, the House voted on a Sunday evening to agree to the Senate bill (which had passed by unanimous consent – any member could have objected, but hadn't), and Terri Schiavo was granted a new hearing in which a new judge ruled in the husband's favor. The feeding tubes were removed and she died a short time later.

After agreeing to issue the subpoena, I immediately called my Democratic ranking member, Henry Waxman, with whom I had worked so closely on the steroid hearings, to explain what I was doing and why. He said he understood my position but would have to issue a press release strongly condemning my actions. I told him I understood and we all went back to our corners. The House vote was overwhelmingly in favor of agreeing to the

Senate bill, with Democrats splitting almost evenly and Republicans approving overwhelmingly.

As I had feared when originally confronted by Tom DeLay, the public reaction was swift and overwhelmingly against us. However, although the issue clearly did not help me in my reelection race (it was raised in every public forum), I did what was expected of a chair who gets power from the Steering Committee. When the leadership needs you, it is important to comply. To have done otherwise would have jeopardized my ability to do other things that were critical to my constituents and me and could have cost me the gavel.

John Donne wrote, "No man is an island." In the House, at least, no chairman is an independent agent. The memories of Chris Smith's ouster and the leverage of leadership cast a strong shadow over a chairman's and a member's actions.

In 2013, John Boehner, through the Steering Committee, removed four recalcitrant Republicans (including Walter Jones) from committees, relegating them to less important posts for voting against leadership on a continuing basis. These members didn't become more obedient to the leadership after their ouster. On the contrary, they became more defiant. On one occasion the Speaker approached Walter Jones on a critical vote and said, "I need you on this one, Walter." Jones reportedly told him, "You should have thought of that before you removed me from Financial Services." However, to dozens of other members of the Republican Conference, the removal of these four was a necessary lesson that fealty to leadership would be rewarded and recalcitrance punished.

The assignment of committees and the selection of chairmen are among the few tools the leadership has to reward and discipline members. This system grew out of bad experiences in which blind seniority advanced chairmen who owed nothing to leadership, making advancing legislation difficult. Today, the committee structure runs congruent with leadership demands. But the increasing volatility of primary voters often tugs rank-and-file members in a different direction, removing any clarity in the legislative process and making it harder for Congress to govern.

15

THE BIG PUNT

By Martin Frost and Rich Cohen

There is an old saying that two wrongs don't make a right. President Obama and Congress really put this old saw to the test.

A deadlocked Congress found it impossible to enact significant legislation on a range of issues including climate change, workplace discrimination against gays, immigration reform, and improving Obamacare. On a bipartisan basis, Congress continued failing to address the budget deficit and national energy policy.

The House and Senate barely spoke to each other, with each chamber passing meaningless legislation it knew had no chance across the Capitol and shying away from tough votes that could cost the majority its control.

And into this breach stepped President Obama, issuing a number of executive orders and agency regulations that attempt to implement changes in law without consulting Congress. That's not how our separation of powers system was designed to work, no matter how much anyone may approve of the president's unilateral actions on the merits.

Congress punted the ball to Obama and he has run down the field time after time. It's what we call the "big punt."

Members of Congress, who refused to act on major issues facing the country, assumed the posture of the child who kills his parents and then throws himself on the mercy of the court because he is an orphan.

The president pushed the envelope in addressing major problems through unilateral action by the executive branch; and whether or not the judiciary branch put some brakes on this runaway train, Congress had no one to blame but itself.

The State of the Union message is the annual celebration of our constitutional system in which presidents ceremonially appear before Congress to request the legislation they want in the coming year. But in his January 2014 speech, President Barack Obama's message was one of confrontation, not cooperation. In effect, he told the lawmakers that he planned to go his own way.

Following a year in which Congress had acted on few of his proposals (or anything else, for that matter), Obama illustrated how the breakdown in Congress was affecting other parts of the federal government. He told the senators and House members seated in front of him that he would take action – with or without them. "America does not stand still – and neither will I," the president said defiantly. "So wherever and whenever I can take steps without legislation to expand opportunity for more American families, that's what I'm going to do."

White House aides called the new strategy his "pen and phone" initiative. The president would use his pen to sign executive actions that did not require congressional approval and his phone to call private-sector leaders to encourage them to adopt his policies. "I wouldn't tell you that executive action is a substitute for major bipartisan legislation; it's not," White House adviser Dan Pfeiffer told USA Today. "But what we're not going to do is wait around for Congress to act. We're going to try every day to move the ball forward with what executive authority the president has."[54]

Not many years before Obama's presidency, presidents – such as George H. W. Bush and Bill Clinton – did business with Congresses that were controlled by the other party. But Obama threw in the towel, even though his own party had the Senate majority. Three years before the end of his presidency, he seemed to abandon the possibility that he could find common ground with Congress.

Republicans were more dismissive than disappointed. "With few bipartisan proposals, Americans heard a president more interested in advancing ideology than in solving the problems regular folks are talking about," House Speaker John Boehner responded. "Instead of our areas of common ground, the president focused too much on the things that divide us – many we've heard before – and warnings of unilateral action."

If there were any lingering doubts, this rhetorical exchange was proof that the policy-making process between the White House and Capitol Hill had broken down. Standard procedures for doing business no longer applied. Some of these collapses across government have resulted directly from the changes in Congress that we have described in this book; others have reflected problems in the executive branch or, to some extent, paralysis in the private sector. But they all added to the mess on Capitol Hill.

Amid mounting frustration over his inability to gain approval of his chief priorities, Obama sought to circumvent Congress by taking executive action, sometimes with sweeping regulations. Probably the most controversial was the Environmental Protection Administration's initiative responding to the threat of climate change by regulating power plant emissions. Several states, utilities, and other industrial interests prepared lawsuits to challenge the agency's authority to issue the regulations – the likely result being years of litigation.

The EPA regulations would become the initial major battleground for Obama's efforts to achieve through executive action what he could not enact legislatively. Working behind the scenes with White House officials and sympathetic environmental groups, the agency crafted an initiative to slow climate change and the spread of greenhouse gases from carbon emissions. Its specific focus was to reduce the pollution from hundreds of coal-fired power plants across the nation, many of which were aging and inefficient. Obama aides were not shy in highlighting the significance of their initiative. "We have an obligation to leave our children a planet that's not polluted or damaged," was the top claim in the talking points issued by the White House prior to the EPA's announcement.

Virtually all Republicans were strongly opposed. Some Democrats objected too, especially those from states – such as West Virginia or Kentucky – with abundant coal mining or with utilities that relied heavily on coal rather than natural gas or renewable fuels. Not coincidentally, the states that objected most vehemently to the plan tended to be those that had voted against Obama, while those that welcomed the proposed changes in environmental policy – chiefly the states on the East and West Coasts – had been most supportive of him. Thus, his proposal deepened the conflict between red states and blue states. Among other things, that stiffened the reelection challenges facing congressional Democrats from battleground states hostile to Obama.

In fact, Obama's ambition was hardly new. In 2009, the Democratic-controlled House passed – with a handful of Republican votes – sweeping legislation that was designed to reduce global warming. But a comparable proposal died in the Senate, which at the time had 60 Democratic senators (including two Independents who caucused with the majority party). The bill never reached the Senate floor during that Congress or during the subsequent four years when Democrats controlled the chamber. Senators from states that produced or relied heavily on coal for their utilities objected to the measure. Obama sought to accomplish by regulation what he had failed to achieve with legislation.

EPA administrator Gina McCarthy unveiled the proposed executive action four months after Obama's State of the Union, which was rapid movement for such a complex policy initiative. "June 2 is the most important day of Obama's second term," Vox, a public affairs website, headlined. But this would be far from the final hurdle in a regulatory and judicial marathon that was expected to extend for several years. Short-circuiting Congress may have been Obama's only option to address climate change. But in our constitutional system, attempting to set new policy without legislative collaboration has its limitations and raises many additional obstacles.

In this case, the EPA was relying on a little-known provision in the Clean Air Act of 1970. That law had been passed long before climate change had been identified as a national – and international – problem. The administration's strategy to rely on each of the 50 states to develop a plan to help meet the objective of a 30% pollution reduction (from a 2005 baseline) by 2030 raised many uncertainties – not least the prospect that a subsequent president might decide to change these regulations, with or without Congress. Some environmentalists, in fact, criticized Obama's plan as too modest.

Other critics pointed out that the increased carbon emissions from third-world and other developing nations would swamp any benefits from United States cutbacks.

Even Obama allies conceded that his jerry-rigged regulatory approach might not succeed. "This is the sad reality of climate policy in the United States, circa 2014," Harvard law professor Jody Freeman, who had been Obama's counselor for energy and climate change in 2009-10, wrote on the *New York Times* op-ed page. "With Congress paralyzed on the issue, the country's climate and energy policy is being made in arcane legal battles over the meaning of single phrases in statutes written long ago, leaving government and industry to duke it out in court ... . This is how policy is made when Congress abdicates its role."[55]

In Congress, many members contended that they had not abdicated their responsibility. Instead, their view of environmental policy differed from that of the president – and of many others in Congress, too. In decades past, the competing interests might have sought common ground on at least some facet of the sweeping problem. That is known as the "deliberative process" for consensus-building. Historically, in this diverse nation with many competing economic, social, and business perspectives, no single faction has gotten everything that it wants. But recently the search for common ground has become not only a forgotten art, but also undesirable: as we have written, various factions have decreed that centrism is unacceptable.

There are no textbook rules or scientific formulas for how Congress and the president engage most effectively with each other to address public problems. When it comes to governing, some approaches work better than others. But especially since the 1990s, we have seen a head-spinning variety of approaches to leadership and policymaking – both at the White House and on Capitol Hill.

Within Congress, occasionally each party has sought alternatives to break the deadlock. But those efforts have often proved counterproductive. That's particularly been the case with the federal budget. Republicans have insisted on reducing the huge federal deficit, but without tax increases. Democrats have opposed big cuts in domestic spending, and they advocate higher taxes on the wealthy. Occasionally, President Obama and other top White House officials have joined those negotiations – but with little, if any, success. The mutual mistrust between House Speaker John Boehner on the one side and Obama and Senate Democratic leader Harry Reid on the other has grown so high that those individuals have said that they no longer want to meet with each other.

Although there have been some legislative successes, the public has endured in the recent past continuing showdowns, partisan slugfests, and constant failures. Depending on your perspective, it's easy to assign blame to one party or the other. But the outcome understandably has caused many people to cast a pox on both parties and all of Washington. Senator John McCain has joked that public approval of Congress has dropped so low that only family members support what he does, and he's been losing their confidence too. Some prominent politicians seemed to relish the hostility of the Capitol crowd. "I hope we see leaders who are willing to suffer the scorn of Washington," Senator Ted Cruz told a gathering of Texas Republicans in 2014.

Starting in 2011, Congress faced the challenge of divided party control: a Republican-controlled House and a Democrat-controlled Senate. This has been a relatively rare phenomenon in American history, though in the more distant past it hasn't necessarily resulted in such gridlock. But more recently, the difficulty of finding common ground was exacerbated by the increased polarization in both parties. As a result, both chambers often found themselves on separate legislative tracks that never met. Often, prominent bills that passed one chamber piled up at the doorstep of the other, where they were largely ignored: House-passed bills to repeal the Affordable Care Act, for example, and Senate measures to make sweeping changes in immigration policy. With few exceptions, there was a breakdown of communications across Capitol Hill among members and staff in party leadership and at committees.

With these deadlocks, climate change was not the only issue on which Obama decided to go it alone. The divisions on immigration legislation led him to call for implementing parts of that agenda by regulatory actions such as the Dream Act, which provided a road to citizenship for illegal aliens who attended college or served in the military. If Congress failed to act, Obama said, he might also reduce deportations of illegal immigrants; that stricter enforcement had stirred objections from many Hispanic groups.

In reality, the legislative picture here was more mixed. The Democrat-controlled Senate in 2013 passed 68-32 a sweeping bipartisan bill that included an eventual path to citizenship for millions of unauthorized immigrants, an expanded guest worker program, and intensified border security. Under pressure to go along coming from some sympathetic Republicans and business groups, Speaker Boehner said that he was open to legislative action, though with a more incremental approach that might mollify the objections of Tea Party groups.

But many Republicans complained that the unilateral initiatives by the Obama administration – whether real or just threatened – poisoned the water for congressional action on immigration and other issues. They threatened to retaliate against Boehner if he made a deal with Democrats. The more Obama talked about going his own way, they contended, the more they couldn't trust him to stick with the terms of a possible legislative deal. Democratic leaders responded that they had run out of patience with Republican delays.

Obama critics added that – as with climate change – Democrats had failed to act on immigration in 2009-10 when they'd had solid control of both the House and Senate. The debate was compounded by divisions within each party and concerns over the implications for the increasingly powerful Hispanic vote.

President Obama took on another social issue when he ordered agencies to require that federal contractors in the private sector not discriminate against workers based on their sexual orientations. Gay-rights leaders hailed the action for promoting more equitable workplaces across the nation. And Democratic leaders like Nancy Pelosi said that it was "disappointing that House Republicans continue to stand on the wrong side of history" by blocking a vote on similar Senate-passed legislation. Republicans, for their part, became more cautious in commenting on the broad topic, given the shifts in public opinion. But social-conservative groups complained that the executive order was overreaching.

Another source of partisan battles was the implementation of the Affordable Care Act, which Republicans had unanimously opposed during congressional debate. Those conflicts seemed to grow, even after the bill was enacted in 2010 and the Supreme Court – on a 5-4 vote – upheld its constitutionality.₅₆ Republican objections were fueled, in part, by grassroots opposition from Tea Party groups that launched local protests and challenged the Obama administration's implementation of the law.

The president's practice of making significant enforcement changes following enactment of the expanded health insurance law added to the conflicts, especially with the botched rollout of signups on the Department of Health and Human Services website. His shifts of deadlines and exemption of groups from coverage, for example, were steps that should have required new legislation, Republicans complained. In the bitter political battle, even sensible legislative fixes such as a technical corrections bill – typically approved following the passage of massive legislation – became unlikely to gain the requisite bipartisan support without broader changes in the new program that would have been unacceptable to Obama and other supporters. Republicans continued to hope to eventually repeal the law, while discussing its merits became the centerpiece of the Democrats' agenda.

These seemingly endless battles and other regulatory initiatives by Obama to singlehandedly impose his policy views have been comparable to actions by President George W. Bush that stirred the ire of Democrats. He had a frequent practice of issuing "signing statements" to accompany laws that Congress had enacted. With a military spending bill that limited his flexibility with Iraq, for example, his statement instructed federal agencies to ignore what he termed unconstitutional restraints. In some cases, he redefined congressional actions in ways that were inconsistent with the original intent, his critics said. Or the statements caused ambiguity about how such laws should be enforced by the executive branch or interpreted by the courts. Ultimately such uncertainties can be confusing or burdensome for many citizens or businesses.

When Obama signed a defense bill that included restrictions on his authority to transfer detainees from the U.S. military prison in Guantanamo Bay, Cuba, he included a statement that he had the constitutional authority to override those limits. This unilateralist approach is politically risky and exposed the president "to accusations that he is concentrating too much power in the White House," according to *New York Times* reporter Charlie Savage, who during the Bush administration wrote a book on the topic (*Takeover: The Return of the Imperial Presidency and the Subversion of Amer-*

ican Democracy).₅₇ Some firebrands in Congress contended that the president's actions warranted impeachment, but that seemed unlikely.

The conflict over signing statements intensified during the controversy over Obama's decision to release five senior Taliban commanders – who had been held without trial for more than a dozen years at Guantanamo – in exchange for Sergeant Beau Bergdahl, who had abandoned his base in Afghanistan and been held captive for five years by Taliban groups. Many congressional leaders – including Senate Intelligence Committee chairwoman Dianne Feinstein, a California Democrat – were infuriated that Obama had ignored a provision that they had added in 2013 to a military funding law, which required 30 days' notice to congressional leaders if the president was planning a release of detainees.

When he'd signed the bill, Obama had issued a statement that the executive branch needed "flexibility ... to act swiftly in conducting negotiations with foreign countries regarding the circumstances of detainee transfers." But Feinstein criticized the White House's failure to notify Congress – especially Intelligence Committee leaders – in advance of the detainees' release. "It's very disappointing that there was not a level of trust sufficient to justify alerting us," she said. "There certainly was time to pick up the phone and call and say, 'I know you all had concerns about this, we consulted in the past, we want you to know we have renewed these negotiations.'"

Not surprisingly, congressional reactions to such signing statements have always depended partly on which party controlled the White House when they were issued.

Occasionally, these standoffs between the president and Congress have led to efforts by well-intentioned outside groups to kick-start their own solutions. In some cases, these initiatives have included members who were appointed by top government officials. An example was the budget plan prepared by a group of private citizens and members of Congress, led by former Republican senator Alan Simpson and Clinton administration budget official Erskine Bowles. That commission offered what seemed to be commonsense centrist proposals that included painful political steps for each side. As it turned out, neither Obama nor congressional Republicans were willing to stand behind the group that they had originally created.

Unfortunately, the "regular order" for legislative action has become the exception, rather than the rule, for our public officials to take the requisite steps to find common ground.

The continuing gridlock and bold assertions of presidential prerogatives inevitably have created new sets of problems. Prompted by Boehner, the House in July 2014 approved a resolution supporting a lawsuit to challenge Obama's alleged excesses. Despite his usual objections to litigation, Boehner said that the House's action was required because Obama was "creating his own laws and excusing himself from executing statutes he is sworn to enforce ... . This shifts the balance of power decisively and dangerously in favor of the presidency, giving the president king-like authority at the expense of the American people and their elected legislators."

Punting to the judiciary branch the conflict between Congress and the presidency, rather than finding some common ground, has its own consequences. The nine Supreme Court Justices are appointed, not elected, and they hold their seats for life. They are lawyers and typically have scant expertise in policy or politics. Partly for those reasons, justices have often been reluctant to intervene in battles over "checks and balances" in our constitutional system.

Still, the Supreme Court unanimously sided with Senate prerogatives in a June 2014 ruling that Obama lacked the authority to make three "recess appointments" to the National Labor Relations Board in January 2012.[58] Obama's action violated the constitutional provision on the president's recess authority, wrote Justice Stephen Breyer, who had been nominated to the Court by President Clinton and previously served as a top aide to Senator Ted Kennedy. White House officials responded that they were "deeply disappointed." But Obama, who once taught constitutional law classes, had overreached, with an outcome that may have limited long-established presidential prerogatives.

But even conservatives on the Court recognized that presidents and their top officials retain broad regulatory authority – which has grown substantially in recent decades. In a decision a few days earlier, Justice Antonin Scalia upheld the EPA's rulemaking power to limit air pollution from industrial facilities – so long as the regulatory action was clearly intended by Congress.[59] While he cautioned, "An agency has no power to 'tailor' legislation to bureaucratic policy goals by rewriting unambiguous statutory terms," Scalia said that the EPA in this case would be able to regulate 83% of the emissions that result instead of the 86% that it originally sought; two other conservative justices dissented from that part of his decision.

In many ways, the Washington paralysis reflects the narrow divisions within the public at large. Occasionally, election outcomes in the past two decades have produced what expert political analyst Michael Barone termed a "49% nation." As he wrote in the 2002 edition of the *Almanac of American Politics*, recent presidential and congressional election results had left both parties short of a convincing majority. Since then, election waves have given a temporary boost to one party or the other. But typically those outcomes have been followed by quick shifts in the opposite direction.

The following data are relevant to our broader discussion. In their four successive presidential elections, Bill Clinton and George W. Bush never exceeded 51% of the popular vote. Barack Obama won 53% and 51% of the popular vote in his two victories and had larger Electoral College margins than his two predecessors. But as they did with Clinton, Democrats suffered major setbacks during Obama's first midterm election and never regained House control during his presidency. For various reasons, Democrats in 2010 and 2012 were more successful in the Senate. But Republicans prepared for big Senate gains in the 2014 election. Regardless of party control, the sharper partisan lines in the Senate and smaller majorities have resulted in continuing and often intense conflict in that chamber.

During their 40-year House control that ended in 1994, Democrats held at least 243 seats in each Congress except for the first four years of that period. By contrast, only once in the past 20 years has the majority party in the House controlled more than 243 seats. That was the Obama-Pelosi Congress in 2009-10, which was successful legislatively but lost 63 Democratic seats in November 2010 in the biggest party loss of House seats since 1948.

The sharp divisions between the two parties and their supporters, plus the large centrist block of independent voters who move back and forth, have produced frequent cases of divided government and shifts of political power in the past 20 years, resulting in an unusual instability. These changes in partisan control are not inherently problematic, and could have been productive if accompanied by decisive presidential and congressional actions. But in too many cases, the majority has been unprepared or has overplayed its hand. These factors help to explain the legislative failures that have become so prevalent.

As we discussed earlier, the split-party control of the House and Senate that began in 2011 compounded these problems. And yet, the longest recent parallel to this state of play – the Democrat-controlled House and Republican-controlled Senate from 1981-86 – was far more legislatively manageable. In part, that can be attributed to President Reagan's popularity, his skillful advisers, and his relatively modest agenda following his legislative successes during his initial six months in office. But another factor in the relative harmony at the time was the political skill of the chief congressional leaders at the time: House Speaker Tip O'Neill (a Democrat) and Senate majority leaders Howard Baker and Bob Dole (both Republicans); they also benefited from the deal-making skills of several of their committee chairmen.

Presidential leadership is essential to our constitutional separation of powers. But Congress is the "first branch" in our Constitution, and its vibrancy is vital to democracy. When it doesn't function well, as we have recently seen, that increases presidential prerogatives and can trigger occasional abuses.

In the past century, the most productive outcomes for governance resulted when the president ran on a clear agenda that was embraced during the campaign by members of Congress and other candidates from his own party and then received broad support from voters. The two most successful recent examples have been from the opposite ends of the ideological spectrum: Lyndon Johnson in 1964 and Ronald Reagan in 1980.

Johnson ran on his Great Society platform, which featured Medicare coverage of health care for senior citizens, education, fighting poverty, and voting rights protection. He won 44 states, and Democrats took two-thirds control of both the House and Senate. Reagan's platform 16 years later pledged steep cuts in taxes and spending. He also won 44 states, and Republicans took control of the Senate for the first time in 26 years. As it had in 1964, the winning party gained more than 30 House seats. Even with nominal Democratic control of the House, Reagan had a working majority – at the start.

Both presidents had a successful record of working with Congress during their next two years. Even though they suffered significant setbacks in the subsequent midterm elections, especially in the House, they had achieved most of their campaign objectives.

In hindsight, both the Johnson and Reagan programs had some rough edges that needed to be trimmed back or clarified in later legislation. But each president seized his opportunities and used his electoral mandate to place his imprint on government. Each presidency began with an agenda that unified the president's party and subsequently garnered the support of some – but hardly all – members of the opposing party. In each case, the president's party understood that single-party rule is usually not sustainable; the minority party found a balance between encouraging conciliation and serving as the loyal opposition.

These examples of presidential leadership and coattails have become the exception in recent years. Bill Clinton, for example, found his 1993 plan to reform health care bogged down due to its complexity and his advisers' failure to work with the Democrat-controlled Congress on the details. That led, in turn, to the Republican takeover of the House and Senate and Speaker Newt Gingrich's largely unsuccessful efforts to lead as though he were commanding a parliamentary form of government.

Next, George W. Bush's 2000 narrow election victory was marred by the Supreme Court's resolution of the Florida vote count and Republicans' loss of Senate control. The 9/11 attacks gave him a second chance to assert leadership, but that eventually led to the extended wars in Afghanistan and Iraq, where the United States ultimately failed to achieve its objectives. His second-term efforts to reform Social Security failed in part because of his insufficient collaboration with Republicans in Congress.

Barack Obama displayed great political skill and success in 2008. Once elected, he largely deferred to congressional Democrats on the details of health care reform. But the results were too complex for most members – and the public – to comprehend. The Republicans' 2010 takeover of the House left a divided Congress that struggled to find common ground. The continuing focus on steps to boost the weak economy and reduce the huge deficit met stiff headwinds. The legislative scorecards during the next four years were among the least productive in modern United States history.

These showdowns have often been accompanied by threats to shut down the federal government or doubts about the government's commitment to pay its debts. That has resulted in such spectacles as the failure of a congressional "supercommittee" – composed of senior lawmakers and with broad powers – to reach a budget deal, and frantic New Year's Eve negotiations and late-night votes to avoid a big tax hike. In a particularly embarrassing outcome, a "sequester" of both domestic and Pentagon spending – which leaders of both parties had agreed would be disastrous – took effect and led to big budget cuts. Beneficiaries suffered for two years, though there was less disruption than many had initially forecast.

Like Clinton's and George W. Bush's before him, Obama's political skills helped navigate a reelection. His second term also followed Clinton's and Bush's pattern of limited legislative success plus increased conflict with Congress. Such political cycles are not inevitable. But these three presidencies – with the presidents' varied personalities and skills – have both become a reflection of the nation's increased polarization and added to the dysfunction.

Consequently, Obama – like his immediate predecessors – failed to resolve numerous pressing issues facing the nation. These include:

1. The domestic economy remains weak, and the nation has fallen behind in its international competitiveness.

2. Crucial fiscal problems continue to be deferred, with adverse economic consequences. These include large deficits that are projected to increase further, inadequately-funded retirement programs, and inequities in the tax code.

3. Even with discoveries of new energy resources and the technologies to deliver them to markets, the nation lacks coherent energy and environmental policies – either for domestic purposes or as part of the international efforts to address climate change.

4. Many millions of immigrants who arrived illegally and lack proper documentation live and work across the nation in ways that violate the law and cause both tensions with other low-income groups and hardships for themselves and their families.

These shortcomings help to explain why many people – not only the Tea Party groups – tell public-opinion surveys that they continue to seek change and that the nation is on the wrong track.

Congress didn't create all of these problems. But it bears some responsibility for the failure to fix them. Constructive solutions are available that could attract bipartisan support. When lawmakers are unable to work together in a deliberative process, that has significant adverse consequences.

A legislator's job can be demanding, and the answers are not always obvious. Former representative Barney Frank of Massachusetts astutely observed that often the public is not a bargain, partly because people are insufficiently informed or unskillful at communicating. It's also true that elected officials have deeper resources of information, and they are expected to apply their best judgment in addressing problems. But that can be more difficult when there is so much noise in the public dialogue. Much of it confuses rather than enlightens.

For Congress to function well, the public must provide clear direction. That can happen through elections at the macro level and through interest groups and lobbying at the micro level. The influence of factions is at the heart of our constitutional framework. But in recent years, the voice of the people has become muddled or quick to change due to various factors in politics and changes in the media.

Each branch of the government must remain mindful of both its responsibilities and its limits, and of democratic imperatives. When the president as chief executive or commander in chief doesn't engage sufficiently with Congress or the general public, it complicates the challenge of finding and delivering coherent policy solutions.

An independent judiciary, likewise, remains influential – and essential. Even the Supreme Court has found itself sharply divided on ideological lines, with constant 5-4 decisions on key issues. Regardless of which side the majority takes, those divisions can increase the public's confusion and lack of confidence in the justices.

All of these government leaders, with their various approaches, must remain mindful of and attentive to the "bases" in each political camp. They too have their responsibilities as public officials. In a diverse and demanding nation, skillful and bold leadership remains essential to find common ground.

TOM'S RESPONSE

I agree with Rich and Martin that the abrogation of leadership by Congress (in its failure to produce a work product) and the president has been a major contributor to the current congressional inertia. To put the current circumstances into perspective, though, that is exactly what the voters elected them to do.

For President Obama's first two years, Democrats had the 60 senators needed for absolute control for a period of six months (commencing when Al Franken of Minnesota was sworn into office in July 2009 and ending with the election of Scott Brown of Massachusetts in January 2010). During the two-year period, they passed a massive stimulus bill, the Affordable Care Act (Obamacare), and the Dodd-Frank financial reform bill. They passed a controversial cap and trade bill in the House as well. These initiatives were not without controversy and passed with little or no Republican support.

As often happens after times of great legislative activity, there ensued plenty of opposition to the changes from affected groups. In the same context, unemployment stayed high and societal changes – including affirmative action and the redefinition of marriage – were taking place.

Energy companies and coal country erupted against cap and trade. Taxpayer groups fought Obamacare. Financial institutions rallied against Dodd-Frank. While most Americans (and probably most members of Congress) never even read the laws, cable TV, talk radio, and the Internet buzzed with sound bites either deifying or demonizing these legislative initiatives.

The Tea Party was born from Obamacare, and the voters put Republicans back in charge in the House (and, save a few dysfunctional GOP nominees, could have flipped the Senate too). What is important to understand is that the voters were not voting in a Republican agenda; they were simply putting a check on the Democrats. After all, the voters had thrown congressional Republicans out of power in 2006, and Obama's 2008 victory was in large part a repudiation of the Bush years (particularly the war in Iraq and the economic meltdown). It would have been the height of hubris to think that voters were lamenting the demise of Republican rule and wanted to put us back in charge.

And yet, noteworthily and predictably, many of my fellow GOP leaders felt that the voters were giving us a mandate. In fact, the voters in the midterm, given two undesirable choices, opted to put a check on President Obama rather than give him a blank check for two more years. The fact that general election voters rejected more ideological Republican nominees in swing states – notably Colorado, Nevada, and Delaware – is proof positive that voters were more centered and strategic in their checks-and-balances approach than most pundits gave them credit for.

In solidly red states like Utah, the GOP label was enough to elect a Mike Lee; but in swing states (where independents still matter), voters offered some discretion as to the type of Republican that would be acceptable as a legislative backstop to the president.

Two years later, many Republicans were declaring a premature victory over Barack Obama, as the economy was still stalled and his agenda appeared dead in the water. But voters were still not enamored with Republicans; and to the surprise of the Romney camp, Karl Rove, and many conservative commentators, they returned Obama to the White House with a substantial, albeit reduced, margin.

Voters had, in fact, collectively and institutionally opted for divided government. I say institutionally because, as discussed in previous chapters, the House districting process has a solid Republican bias to its boundary-making and the Electoral College now has a Democratic advantage in its distribution. But it is that diminishing but still viable swath of independent voters, who neither mistrust nor hold allegiances to either party, that helped to determine this split verdict. They would rather have no legislation pass than see bad or unbalanced legislation. Not content with either party, it is they, as much as the institutional parameters discussed, who opted for divided government.

As the checks and balances between the executive, legislative, and judicial branches envisioned by our founders have mutated into a semi-parliamentary system, it is the voters themselves that have created a newer "checks and balances" on government through the election process – by dividing power between the parties.

The resulting gridlock is not a popular outcome, but is what these swing voters prefer to one-party government and the ideological, unbalanced outcomes that result.

16

THE WAY FORWARD

By Tom Davis and Martin Frost

The late Congressman Bill Lehman (D-FL, 1973-93) had been a used-car dealer in Miami doing business under the name of Alabama Bill before he was elected to Congress. He used to joke that he didn't think he could fall any lower in public esteem. Then he was elected to Congress.

Lehman, who died in 2005, didn't live long enough to see exactly how far Congress could fall in public esteem. In the summer of 2014, Congress dropped to a 7% approval rating.[60]

Various scholars and politicians have looked at the current state of Congress and tried to make suggestions on what should be done to restore public confidence in the institutions of government. The most serious effort to date has been an 18-month study conducted by the Bipartisan Policy Center's Commission on Political Reform.

This bipartisan commission included 29 members and had a distinguished group of co-chairs – Former Senate majority leader Tom Daschle of South Dakota, former congressman Dan Glickman of Kansas, former governor Dirk Kempthorne of Idaho, former Senate majority leader Trent Lott of Mississippi, and former senator Olympia Snowe of Maine. The commission announced its recommendations at a public rollout in Washington,

D.C., on June 24, 2014, in a report entitled, "Governing in a Polarized America: A Bipartisan Blueprint to Strengthen our Democracy."

In the language of the Supreme Court, we "concur in part and dissent in part" with the commission's report. We will note the commission's recommendations with the designation "BPC commission" whenever they appear in this chapter.

Our recommendations are not limited to the items outlined by the BPC commission, and we will focus on the biggest issues rather than deal with a laundry list of items such as congressional schedules.

CAMPAIGN FINANCE

Let's start with the 1,000-pound gorilla in the room: campaign finance.

As a result of actions by Congress and the U.S. Supreme Court (as discussed in Chapter 6), we have a campaign finance system that is totally out of control and is a major contributor to gridlock in our country.

Basically, anyone – individuals, corporations, and unions – can spend unlimited amounts of money to influence federal elections in the United States, with only limited disclosure. This is far worse than the situation was before campaign finance reform was enacted. Defenders of McCain-Feingold will blame it on the *Citizens United* court decision in 2010, but the system had already begun unraveling by then.

As members of the House, we both raised serious objections to Congress's enactment of the McCain-Feingold campaign finance reform legislation in 2002. Our primary concern was that the legislation took money away from political parties (funds that, at that time, were fully disclosed as to contributors and amounts) and put it into the hands of outside groups, many of which have extreme ideological agendas and are not subject to adequate disclosure. Political parties have traditionally been centering forces in American politics. Congress, at the urging of the "reform" community, neutered the major parties.

Prior to the passage of McCain-Feingold, political parties could accept unlimited amounts of "soft money" (contributions from individuals, corporations, and unions). The parties used this money for get-out-the-vote activities and for issue ads promoting or opposing positions taken by federal candidates. These contributions had to be fully disclosed to the Federal Election Commission (FEC). McCain-Feingold totally eliminated "soft money" contributions to the national party committees.

Our first recommendation would be to restore the right of individuals, corporations, and unions to make unlimited contributions to national party committees – contributions that would be fully disclosed as to contributors and amounts. As the law has developed since the passage of McCain-Feingold, these individuals, corporations, and unions can make unlimited "soft money" contributions to various entities such as super PACs and 501(c)(4) and (c)(6) nonprofit organizations. Some, but not all, expenditures by nonprofits must be disclosed to the FEC, but no donor information is required to be revealed.

We do not believe that you can fully restore the status quo ante (put the genie back in the bottle). Significant contributions will continue to flow to outside groups. But at least political parties would be on a somewhat level playing field.

Speaking to one billionaire financier of super PACs, Tom asked, "Wouldn't you rather give your millions through a political party than through a super PAC?" The answer was quick and candid: "Of course." By giving his money to a political party committee, the billionaire was making a contribution that was public and transparent. Thus, any favors derived therein would be disclosed and subject to media and public interpretation that the contribution was a quid-pro-quo. That is the disadvantage of giving directly to a political party. However, the disadvantage is outweighed by the benefits and recognition a party can give a donor, such as preferred seating at conventions, intimate meetings with party elders, and recognition by elected leaders that those dollars are spread across the spectrum "for the whole team" and not just for a faction or sub-faction.

Also, for super PACs that delve into primaries, an "outed" contributor can make as many enemies as friends *within his or her own party*!

Under current law and FEC regulations, super PACs (entities organized to support the work of a particular party committee, or supporting or opposing a particular candidate) must disclose all their independent expenditures and contributors to the FEC. However, 501(c)(4) and (c)(6) nonprofits are subject only to limited disclosure. If they buy express advocacy ads ("vote for" or "vote against"), they must disclose to the FEC their expenditures but not their contributors.

If they purchase ads deemed to be election communications (mentioning a federal candidate by name, but without a direct request to vote for or against a candidate), they must disclose any expenditures within 60 days of a general election or 30 days of a primary; but they are not required to disclose any contributor information. If they purchase ads outside the 60-day/30-day window, they don't even have to disclose their expenditures to the FEC.

We would change this by requiring full disclosure by nonprofit organizations of all expenditures and contributions above a low threshold amount – regardless of when during the two-year election cycle the expenditure is made – if the expenditure mentions a federal candidate by name.

The BPC commission recommended the following: "Political contributions, including those made to outside and independent groups, should be disclosed so that citizens have full information about who is paying for the political messages they see." But then they seemed to back away from implementation of their recommendation by proposing, "Congress should establish a Bipartisan National Task Force on Campaign Finance whose structure is modeled after that of the 9/11 Commission." This commission would be appointed by March 2015 and issue a report no later than nine months after its first meeting.

We would bypass appointing another commission and go straight to legislation. The problem in getting any traction in campaign finance legislation is that each stakeholder's position is determined by how the reform will affect his or her chances of winning the election. Reforms that are perceived to advantage one side will be strongly resisted by the other side. It reminds us of the political "Golden Rule": "He who has the gold makes the rules."

There are a number of other BPC commission recommendations on campaign finance worthy of consideration, such as limiting "leadership PACs" to the top three leaders of each party in each house rather than permitting all freshman congressmen and senators to establish them as soon as they enter office.

And then there is the question of establishing aggregate limits on how much money can be raised and spent by a candidate for the House or

Senate. Congress tried to establish aggregate limits in 1974, but these limits were struck down by the Supreme Court in the 1976 *Buckley vs. Valeo* case as a violation of the First Amendment. There is general consensus that establishing such limits could only be accomplished by an amendment to the Constitution giving Congress the authority to legislate in this area.

Gaining two-thirds votes in both the House and Senate, plus ratification by three-fourths of the states for a constitutional amendment, is very difficult but it is worthy of consideration. Any such amendment would be meaningless if it didn't also limit the amount of money corporations, unions, and individuals can spend directly on express advocacy or give to outside nonprofit groups supporting or opposing a particular candidate. This right was established by the Supreme Court in the *Citizens United* case and by subsequent FEC rules and lower court decisions. Any action to address this issue would also require a constitutional amendment that would authorize Congress and the states to impose fundraising or spending restrictions that would overturn the Court rulings.

Although a constitutional amendment could override the unintended overreach of *Buckley vs. Valeo* and *Citizens United,* we consider the prospects highly unlikely, so long as one party considers those changes as detrimental to its political prospects.

GERRYMANDERING

The next major issue that should be confronted is partisan gerrymandering by state legislatures when drawing congressional districts. The Supreme Court has taken the position that political motivation can be taken into account by legislatures when drawing lines as long as the legislatures don't engage in racial discrimination in violation of the Voting Rights Act.

The result of all this is that the vast majority of districts are no longer competitive in general elections. As a result, many incumbents are sensitive to the primary voters who elect them and can ignore the general electorate. Members move to secure their bases to ward off a challenge in their own party primaries. Primary voters tend to punish compromisers, so we have continuing gridlock.

Moving to a nonpartisan commission to redraw congressional lines would certainly help, although it doesn't solve the problem. Single-party districts (as discussed in Chapter 3) are the result of three major factors, of which gerrymandering is but one. Residential sorting patterns still create vast swaths of deep blue and red districts. Also, the GOP's skillful use of the Voting Rights Act to pack blacks in the South into a relatively small number of safe minority districts and to bleach surrounding areas into heavily white districts contributed to the problem. Commissions are not something Martin originally supported. However, based on his experience in 2003, when Tom DeLay convinced the Republican Texas Legislature to divide Martin's district into five pieces to prevent any realistic chance of his reelection, he has changed his mind.

Moving to a system whereby congressional districts would be drawn by commissions rather than state legislatures would not be easy. Currently, there are only five states – Arizona, California, Iowa, New Jersey, and Washington – with a significant number of districts that use this approach.

The BPC commission recommended moving to commissions but then, unrealistically, said that the decision should be made on a state-by-state basis.

It is possible for Congress to pass national legislation requiring this approach, though such legislation might be challenged in the courts. In fact, Congress in the 19th century enacted several laws that dictated to the states how they should handle congressional redistricting. According to a report by the Congressional Research Service of the Library of Congress, these actions included standards providing that districts be compact, contiguous, and essentially equal in population. Congress then switched course in 1929, when it repealed those standards. But that changed again in the 1960s, when the Supreme Court handed down a series of landmark rulings on redistricting, starting with *Baker vs. Carr*, which required the "one man, one vote" standard for equal population in congressional districts.

In recent years, a handful of members of Congress have filed legislation to create independent national or state commissions to draw redistricting maps for each state, with federal guidelines.

Article I, Section 4 of the United States Constitution reads as follows: "The Times, Places and Manner of holding Elections for Senators and Representatives shall be prescribed in each State by the Legislature thereof; but the Congress may at any time by Law make or alter such Regulations ... . "

Congress relied on this authority to pass a national "motor voter" law in 1993, which provides that citizens can register to vote when they apply for or renew their driver's licenses.

Constitutional scholars we have consulted believe that Congress could pass legislation requiring states to draw congressional (though not state legislative) lines by using a bipartisan or non-partisan commission. Congress, of course, would need to be prepared to defend any such law in the federal courts.

PRIMARIES

Another interesting idea recommended by the BPC commission deals with having one uniform national primary day in June rather than having primaries for Congress held over a period of months from March to September (as is the current practice). The rationale for having a uniform national date is that this would increase voter turnout, which is often very low in primaries, because the national media would focus on this date and make it into something of national consequence. Increasing primary turnout is important because that reduces the influence of well-organized fringe elements in determining the parties' nominees. Reducing the power of these groups would also make it more likely that Democrats and Republicans could work together once elected, without facing the same level of primary retribution.

Once again, however, the BPC commission, unrealistically, would leave it to the states to voluntarily agree on such a national date.

Under Article I, Section 4, Congress clearly could pass legislation establishing a uniform national primary date, according to scholars we have consulted.

There would be some practical difficulties if such a law were enacted. First, it could only apply to federal elections; though to save money, most states would undoubtedly conform their primaries for state and local office to this date. Also, there is the issue of presidential primaries held by many states every four years. States could continue to hold presidential primaries on different dates from congressional primaries; though, again, they might choose to conform their presidential primaries to the same date as the congressional/state/local primary in order to save money. Congress would need to leave that decision to the states.

California's redistricting changes have been accompanied by election runoff provisions that allow the top two candidates in an open "jungle primary" to proceed to the November election regardless of party. This results occasionally in unconventional faceoffs in the general election. In contrast to the recent trend toward polarization, under these circumstances the minority party's voters play a significant role in selecting the eventual winners.

The California procedure was passed by voter initiative over the objections of the dominant political party, the Democrats. Although the long-term effects of this initiative will not be known for years, the early reports show a moderation in political behavior by both parties' incumbents. In the 2012 congressional election, the first held under these new rules, the runoffs produced two Republican vs. Republican, one Republican vs. Independent, five Democrat vs. Democrat, and one Democrat vs. Independent contests in the general election. This effectively mandates that should candidates become too partisan, they risk losing votes in a runoff because the other party's voters participate in making the decision.

Take the case of Pete Stark, a 40-year incumbent from the East Bay. Elected in 1972, his very partisan and often acerbic style played well with the Democratic base, but over time it became tiresome to some. A young Democratic challenger, Eric Swalwell, decided to take him on in the jungle primary in 2012. Stark narrowly led Swalwell in the primary. But it was clear from the returns in November that independents and Republicans, thoroughly tired of the ultra-partisan Stark, gave the bulk of their support to Swalwell, a 32-year-old Dublin councilman. Although Swalwell will generally toe the Democratic line, he and others in California's safe partisan districts know that the minority parties in their districts cannot be ignored.

Other states – notably Louisiana and Washington, with their vastly different local politics – have used varying forms of jungle primaries.

We encourage such procedures, but with two caveats: (1) any candidate who gets 50% of the total vote in the first round should be the automatic winner, and (2) the runoff election in each state should be held on the national election day in November.

FEDERAL DEFICITS

This brings us to another big idea – not dealt with by the BPC commission – that could significantly contribute to restoring public confidence in Congress.

Few issues highlight Congress's incompetence more than its inability to deal with the long-term fiscal issues facing our nation. We recommend that Congress pass legislation establishing a new Simpson-Bowles type of commission to deal with the issue of reducing federal deficits, but with some significant differences this time.

Legislation creating the original Simpson-Bowles Commission was weakened at the last minute when Republicans in the Senate inserted language eliminating an automatic vote by Congress on Simpson-Bowles proposals unless they were adopted by a supermajority of the commission. Their recommendations received majority support but not the requisite supermajority.

If controversial proposals like the ones generated by a Simpson-Bowles type of commission are to have any chances for enactment, there must be automatic up-or-down votes in both the House and Senate within a specified time period once the proposals are approved by a simple majority of the commission. If the commission has gone too far in its recommendations, they will not pass both houses of Congress. This will encourage compromise within the commission and guarantee the public that Congress will actually take up its proposals. A similar approach was taken when the bipartisan commission to reform Social Security made its report to Congress in the early 1980s.

Another aspect of any such commission is that the executive branch (read: President Obama or his successor) must drop the ludicrous requirement imposed by President Obama that no registered lobbyists be appointed to the commission. There are scores of former members of the House and Senate – from both parties – who would gladly donate hundreds of hours of their time to such an endeavor without any thought of compensation. They would bring wide experience to any such effort. Certainly, they could be required to recuse themselves from votes on any recommendation affecting one of their current or past clients.

Speaker of the House Nancy Pelosi asked the president to appoint Martin to the Simpson-Bowles Commission. Martin had served six years (the maximum permitted under House rules) on the House Budget Committee in the 1980s and 26 years on the House Rules Committee, the committee that has original jurisdiction over any changes in the Budget Act. Obama's staff summarily rejected Speaker Pelosi's recommendation because Martin was a registered lobbyist. Of course, the administration did end up picking lobbyists for many high-profile executive positions, after finding that Washington experience was at a premium and that to run a government meant utilizing the best talent pool available. Many of these experts have spent some time lobbying for one cause or another.[61]

FINAL THOUGHTS

This brings us to some thoughts on the general situation in Washington.

We believe that leaders of both houses of Congress are people of goodwill who want to do what's best for our country. Speaker Boehner has found it difficult to handle the warring factions within his own Republican Conference at some key junctures on issues such as the budget and immigration reform. Both House Democratic Leader Pelosi and Senate Majority Leader Reid have had great difficulty dealing with the issue of entitlements such as Social Security and Medicare because of strong liberal voices in their respective caucuses.

We often hear lamentations by political commentators that Congress and the president need to work together better. On the 50th anniversary of the signing of the Civil Rights Act, we were reminded of how bipartisanship and presidential leadership overcame huge odds and changed the country. Also cited was the great bipartisan relationship that used to exist between Tip O'Neill and Ronald Reagan. Even the late Senate Foreign Relations Committee chairman Arthur Vandenberg heeded the axiom that "politics stops at the water's edge," meaning that in an international crisis, partisanship ceases and we all stand behind the commander in chief.

But as the saying goes, that was then and this is now. Imagine how an LBJ would react to what's going on today. Parties are ideologically sorted, the news media have highly polarizing business models, and super PACs rule the day. Members respond to their primary voters and the country has devolved into parliamentary behavior, both in its voting habits and its legis-lative behavior. LBJ couldn't have had secret meetings. The news media would have been all over members who strayed from the party line and super PACs would have been raising money from true believers on all sides. We also forget that LBJ would have had a difficult time being re-nominated in 1968. Think of the pressures he would have to endure today!

Tom recently heard the learned historian Doris Kearns Goodwin try to explain the differences between the 1960s-70s and today. Goodwin noted that today's money chase and congressional schedules do not allow the poker games, informal dinners, and after-hour drinks that once allowed members to get to know one another, which made working together less impersonal and more productive. And it's true; Congress's schedule is set to maximize members' time away from Washington, back home with the folks who elected them. Weeknights are filled with fundraisers. The CODELs – foreign trips where members and their spouses travel together and get to know one another and the world – are now rare.

The bipartisan retreats we started in 1995 that allowed members and their families to interact, discuss policies, and get to know one another are now gone, victims of tighter ethics rules that will not allow charitable groups to sponsor such events.

Gone, too, are the earmarks, whereby members could obtain project-spe-cific funding for their districts in consideration of voting for the "package," be it an appropriation or an authorization bill. With no such projects mem-bers can point to, these bills have become hard to pass, resulting in gridlock, short-term stopgap measures, and continuing resolutions. This sad state of things evolved because a few members, such as San Diego's Duke Cun-ningham, began "selling" earmarks for campaign contributions or bribes. Congress, in an adverse political environment, banned all earmarks rather than adding metrics and transparency to the process. The results have not been good.

In fact, someone somewhere in government always "earmarks" where money is to be spent. For example, following the enactment of the 2009 stimulus package, the Department of Energy designated billions of dollars for clean energy projects that went bankrupt. These projects were heavily lobbied by political contributors to the administration. Many other projects were designated by local politicians to reward their political constituencies. There are, in fact, no studies that show that the abolition of earmarks has resulted in a more efficient distribution of dollars. What it has unquestionably done is make legislation in the public interest – e.g., appropriations bills and highway funding bills – nearly impossible to pass. The result is more gridlock.

Two suggestions for Congress: (1) bring back earmarks for designated public projects with accompanying metrics and transparency to eliminate abuses, and (2) accommodate more bipartisan fraternization.

The first is easily done. Members want it. Earmarks, at their peak, were less than 1% of appropriated funds. The greater good is accomplished by having a timely, predictable appropriations process. The same goes for infrastructure funding for highways and other public works. Stopgap measures do not provide for long-term planning, economies of scale, or consistent polices. More money is literally wasted in contracts being shut down, restarted, and shut down again than is spent on earmarks. Agency planning and operations freeze when the budget is not determined until six months into the fiscal year. Moreover, our crumbling infrastructure is not repaired efficiently when no long-term contracts on major projects are allowed.

The second suggestion is equally important. There are currently few opportunities for members of the two parties to interact informally and socially. Bipartisan settings such as the House gym or the congressional baseball game are hardly ideal for successfully integrating members and their families. Each party holds caucus or conference meetings on a weekly basis when its respective chamber is in session. In addition, each party holds a retreat every year to develop strategy and messaging. We would suggest that at the start of every Congress, the leaders of both parties hold a bipartisan retreat – free of media and interest groups – where the members and their families can come together, in work sessions with recognized experts, to discuss the problems facing the nation.

Boards of Directors and other entities often use retreats to formulate policy goals and flesh out issues before they flare up. Tom recalls when he served on his local Board of Supervisors, holding such retreats after the election to fully discuss the issues facing Fairfax County. These retreats served as sounding boards for the members who came with different agendas, reality checks for some of our campaign promises, and validators of the facts we would be dealing with. They helped establish positive working relationships between members with different ideologies and from different parties.

Today, the members of Congress often don't even agree on basic facts, relying instead on talking points given to them by interest groups or party-messaging masters to drive a point of view. Members often talk past each other, using their time on cable news to drive a message rather than genuinely dialogue. Little time is spent communicating and listening to the other side. With time a limited commodity for our elected leaders, with pressure to raise money either for their own reelections or for the team, and with their political future largely decided by primary voters, who can blame them? But institutionalizing bipartisan retreats or monthly discussion groups can be helpful in adding comity, mutual understanding, and respect to the legislative process.

In our experience, most members – even those in safe one-party seats – are interested in getting things done and working together. However, their leaders, who control the schedule and tempo, feel they have a responsibility to win majorities and get their members reelected. So an us-versus-them, red-versus-blue mentality takes hold instead. Bipartisan meetings can bring the discussion back to the reality zone and contribute to a more productive legislative process.

However, these changes – from redistricting reform to campaign finance reform to basic congressional reforms – still beg the question of parliamentary tendencies. As voter behavior has become less about the people and more about the parties, and as the parties have continued to be ideologically sorted, we have become parliamentary in our behavior (as discussed in previous chapters). Parliamentary systems, which our founders discussed and dismissed for America, have their advantages and disadvantages. The Founding Fathers gave us a government with balance of powers, where each branch – legislative, judicial and executive – would place a check on the others. Parliamentary behavior in a balance-of-powers structure does not work!

Today, the House and Senate operate along predictable partisan lines. The Senate Democrats, believing their collective destinies are intertwined with President Obama, act as an agent of the executive branch, keeping controversy from the president's desk, failing to investigate the administration's mishaps and scandals, and carrying out the president's agenda where possible. This was demonstrated by the Senate's "nuclear option" rule change to allow a simple majority to bring up appointments of the president for confirmation votes. Although the move was understandable, it broke decades of Senate precedent, changed the role of minority senators, and added to the distrust of party leadership.

House Republicans, on the other hand, overcompensate for the Senate's deference to the president by over-investigating and sensationalizing every mishap that befalls the executive branch. House Democrats, recognizing that a president's falling public approval number jeopardizes some of their colleagues' seats, immediately rush to the president's defense, while the polarizing media allies of each side go into overdrive to sell their respective positions.

In effect, the president's party in Congress has become simply an appendage of the executive branch, rarely exercising its constitutional checks and balances on its president. The "out" party responds by reflexively opposing presidential initiatives. A couple of decades ago, the congressional wing of the "out" party would act like a minority partner and have a voice in shaping, molding, and sometimes tamping down presidential initiatives. Today's climate, barring strong public opinion to the contrary, turns the "out" party into straight-out opposition.

The good news for Americans is that, in times of crisis, the parties will pull together. Tom was a whip for the Troubled Asset Relief Program (TARP), designed to prevent a further meltdown of our banking system in 2008. When Lehman Brothers failed and the markets went into a panic, Republican president George W. Bush decided the only way out of the crisis was to allow the Treasury to buy the troubled assets (subprime mortgages) that had flooded the market and had inflated the major banks' balance sheets. Administration officials believed that to calm the markets and prevent a literal run on the banks, they had to step in and backstop the major financial institutions.

Although the action itself was fraught with controversy and will be debated for years, the tension was palpable. An outgoing Republican president was asking a Democratic Congress to make an unpopular vote to save the financial system. If Congress did not act, Democrats would be blamed if the system collapsed. If Congress did act, Democrats would be taking an unpopular vote to prop up the "big boys on Wall Street." To add another layer of suspense, a presidential election still too close to call was a few weeks away.

Democratic leaders were wary of passing a Republican president's controversial initiative with Democratic votes, so an informal deal was reached with House GOP leaders. The Democrats would deliver a majority of their caucus if the Republicans would do the same. After all, they reasoned, it was President Bush's neglect of the economy that had led to this crisis. Why should the Democrats pay the price at the polls? To their credit, the major presidential candidates (who were both members of the Senate) supported the measure, with Republican John McCain suggesting that the matter was so serious both senators should suspend their campaigns, return to Washington, and ensure its passage.

As we know, the measure failed in the House on the first vote, with 65 Republicans voting yes and 133 voting no. The Democratic tally was 140 voting yes and 95 voting no. At that point, the Dow Jones Industrial Average dropped 700 points in less than one hour, the Senate leaders announced they would pass TARP and send it back to the House, and the markets stabilized. Four days later, sanity prevailed and the House passed a similar measure with 172 Democrats and 91 Republicans voting in favor.

Politically, the entire fiasco undid whatever chance John McCain had of winning, as this was viewed as a Bush- (read: Republican-) caused problem. But what if the Democratic Congress had *not* passed TARP, or what if it had passed it without GOP help? Both scenarios would have incurred unpleasant consequences for the Democrats. Instead, the leaders acted responsibly (albeit clumsily), rose above the politics of the moment, and passed the legislation.

One vignette from the backroom was a discussion with a Republican member from a conservative district who said, "I hope you guys pass this." Tom replied, "Great, we are glad to have your vote. This is close." He replied, "Oh, I can't vote for this. I just hope it passes. I could never explain this back home." Tom responded, "Why are you here if you can't take a tough vote for the country?" But we all knew better.

The member had calculated that he would let the rest of us do the heavy lifting and take the criticism, and he would have deniability and distance from the action. He would not have to face the consequences of allowing the markets and banks to melt down because others had made the votes to prevent it. And those of us who voted yes would never be able to convince most of the country that the worst would have happened had we not voted in favor. The public would never see it as anything other than a Wall Street bailout.

Somehow, people of goodwill must find ways to dialogue with one another and to stand up to loud voices in their own parties when the national interest is at stake. We are not asking them to do the impossible, but we are asking that they talk to each other regularly and explore serious compromise on key issues.

There are outside groups, such as the business community and organized labor, that could reinforce efforts at compromise by supporting these leaders publicly when they make difficult decisions.

We remain optimistic about our country, but we firmly believe that changes need to be made so that political compromise is not a dirty word. Let's get started.

ENDNOTES

Chapter 1

1. Jimmy Breslin chronicled this incident in his 1963 book, *Can't Anyone Here Play this Game? The Improbable Saga of the New York Mets' First Year*, Viking Press, 1963. According to Breslin, the remark was made by Stengel after a few drinks at a party celebrating his 72nd birthday on July 30, 1962.

Chapter 2

2. Martin's role in helping the DLC in its early days is described by Al From in his book, *The New Democrats and the Return to Power*, Palgrave MacMillan, 2013, pp. 33 and 65.

Chapter 3

3. The exact figure is 1,443,595. This was calculated using state-by-state figures from a table created by the Federal Election Commission for 2012 congressional election returns (eliminating the totals for the District of Columbia, which has three electoral votes but no voting member of Congress, and the five other territories that have neither electoral votes nor a voting member of Congress). Under this calculation, the Democratic vote for Congress was 59,967,096 and the Republican vote for Congress was 58,523,501.

4. These numbers are supplied by the *Almanac of American Politics 2014*, Michael Barone and Chuck McCutcheon, University of Chicago Press, 2014.

5. The more remarkable swing was in the Connecticut state legislature, where the 1956 electorate gave the GOP a 31-5 margin in the State Senate and a 249-30 edge in the State House. Two years later, Democratic sweep changed the State Senate to 29-7 Democratic and the State House to 141-138 Democratic. Straight-party voter levers also turned around the New Hampshire legislative as recently as 2010, when they were abolished.

New Hampshire Legislature

	Senate		House		
	R	D	R	D	Other
2004	16	8	253	147	
2006	10	14	161	239	
2008	10	14	176	222	
2010	19	5	293	101	2
2012	13	11	179	218	3

6. See *Almanac of American Politics*, 2014.

7. "Mid-term voters: Older, whiter, righter," *The Economist*, May 17, 2014.

8. Ibid.

Chapter 4

9. This chart was compiled from data for each presidential year published in "US Elections – How Groups Voted" by the Roper Center, Public Opinion Archives, University of Connecticut.

10. "U.S. Seniors Have Realigned With the Republican Party," Jeffrey M. Jones, March 26, 2014, www.gallup.com.

11. This chart was compiled from data for each presidential year published in "US Elections – How Groups Voted" by the Roper Center, Public Opinion Archives, University of Connecticut.

12. Ibid.

13. Key, Valdimer Orlando. *Southern Politics in State and Nation*. University of Tennessee Press, 1984, p. 15.

14. "Black Americans in Congress," prepared by the House Administration Committee, 2007.

15. Ibid.

16. Ibid.

17. "African American Precincts," America Votes (1956, 1960, 1964).

Chapter 5

18. "Republicans Win Congress as Democrats Get Most Votes," Greg Giroux, March 18, 2013, www.bloomberg.com.

19. *Baker vs. Carr*, 369 U.S. 186 (1962)

20. "The Great Election Grab: When does gerrymandering become a threat to democracy?" Jeffrey Toobin, *The New Yorker*, Dec. 8, 2003.

21. "Justice Staff Saw Texas Districting as Illegal – Voting Rights Finding on Map Pushed by DeLay Was Overruled," Dan Eggen, *Washington Post*, Dec. 2, 2005. Text of entire internal Justice Department memo available from authors on request.

22. Chart compiled by authors by reviewing district-by-district returns from each year cited. The year 2004 was used instead of 2002 because it took into account results of mid-decade redistricting in Texas.

23. This chart was compiled using election returns published for 2012 by the Federal Election Commission. For the best discussion of the effect of 2010 state legislative elections on line-drawing for 2012 and the rest of the decade, see "The Lessons of 2010: Why that election put Democrats at a disadvantage for a decade," Charlie Cook, *National Journal*, Aug. 2, 2014, p. 15.

24. These maps are for districts created over several redistricting cycles and appeared in "Modern Gerrymanders: 10 Most Contorted Congressional Districts," Peter Bell, *National Journal*, March 20, 2012.

Chapter 6

25. For excellent discussions on the unintended consequences of the passage of the McCain-Feingold campaign reform legislation, see "A Decade of McCain-Feingold: The good, the bad and the ugly," Neil Reiff and Don McGahn, *Campaigns and Elections*, May 2014; and "McCain-Feingold's devastating legacy," Robert Helner and Raymond La Raja, *Washington Post*, April 11, 2014.

26. For two detailed discussions of how all this works, see *Corporate Political Activities 2012: Complying with Campaign Finance, Lobbying and Ethics Laws*, Kenneth A. Gross, Chip Nielsen, and Jan Witold Baran, Practicing Law Institute, Corporate Law and Practice Course Handbook Series; and "Independent Expenditures: What are they and what are the rules," Alliance for Justice Action Campaign, www.afjactioncampaign.org.

27. "Kochs launch new super PAC for midterm fight," Kenneth P. Vogel and Darren Goode, *Politico*, June 16, 2014. See also, "Koch Brothers Unveil New Strategy at Big Donor Retreat," *The Daily Beast*, June 13, 2014.

28. Independent Expenditure Table 2, Committees/Persons Reporting Independent Expenditures Jan. 1, 2011 through Dec. 31, 2012, cited in FEC press release "FEC Summarizes Campaign Activity of the 2011-2012 Election Cycle," April 19, 2013.

29. Press release, "FEC Summarizes Campaign Activity of the 2011-12 Election Cycle," April 19, 2013.

30. Press release, "FEC Summarizes Campaign Activity of the 2011-12 Election Cycle, " Section V – Independent Expenditures, April 19, 2013.

31. Discussed in Ira Berkow's review of *Playing for Keeps – Michael Jordan and the World He Made*, David Halberstam, New York Times, Jan. 31, 1999.

32. "A History of the Committee on House Administration, 1947-2012," published by the House Administration Committee, 2012, p. 98.

33. *McCutcheon vs. Federal Election Commission*, 572 U.S. ___ (2014) (slip opinion)

34. *Buckley vs. Valeo*, 424 U.S. 1 (1976)

35. "A History of the Committee on House Administration, 1947-2012," p. 105.

36. Ibid.

37. *McConnell vs. Federal Election Commission*, 540 U.S. 93 (2003)

38. *Federal Election Commission vs. Wisconsin Right to Life, Inc.*, 551 U.S. 449 (2007)

39. *Citizens United vs. FEC*, 558 U.S. 310 (2010)

40. "The Long-Suffering Super PAC," Calvin Trillin, *New York Times Sunday Review* (Opinion Page), Feb. 25, 2012.

41. "Some candidates' super PACs are a family affair," Fredreka Schouten and Christopher Schnaars, *USA Today*, July 18, 2014.

42. "Mrs. Grossman's Contribution? $100,000!" Lindsay Kalter and Matt Stout, *Boston Herald*, August 6, 2014.

43. "Must-have accessory for House candidates in 2014: The personalized super PAC," Matea Gold and Tom Hamburger, *Washington Post*, July 18, 2014.

Chapter 7

44. *Almanac of American Politics*, 2014.

45. Ibid.

46. *National Journal* annual vote ratings.

47. This graph was created using data from two sources: for 1952-2008, "Vital Statistics on American Politics 2011-2012" (CQ Press/Sage Publishing); and for 2012, "Presidential results by congressional districts: Obama is reelected but Romney carries a majority of districts," Clark Bensen, Polidata, April 2013.

Chapter 9

48. "Where Political Lines Are, and Aren't, Being Drawn," Wonkblog, *Washington Post*, May 16, 2014.

Chapter 10

49. "How the Presidential Candidates Use the Web and Social Media," Pew Research Center's Journalism Project staff, Aug. 15, 2012.

Chapter 11

50. "High schools that have produced the most NFL draft picks," May 15, 2014, www.maxpreps.com. The study showed that DeSoto (Texas) High School had produced seven top NFL draft picks in the period between 1997 and 2012.

Chapter 12

51. "The Gingrich Senators and Party Polarization in the U.S. Senate," Sean M. Theriault and David W. Rohde, *The Journal of Politics*, Oct. 2011, pp. 1011-1024.

52. "Taking Stock of House-Senate Differences," Donald Wolfensberger, The Congress Project, Woodrow Wilson Center, March 21, 2012.

Chapter 15

53. "State of the Union analysis: What a difference a year makes," Susan Page, *USA Today*, Jan. 29, 2014.

54. The barring of Democratic voters from the first primary from participating in the GOP runoff is not explicit in the underlying statute, but relies on an opinion of the state's attorney general. The issue has never been formally litigated.

55. "Teaching an Old Law New Tricks," Jody Freeman, *New York Times*, May 29, 2014.

56. *National Federation of Independent Business vs. Sebelius*, 132 S.Ct. 2566 (2012)

57. *Takeover: The Return of the Imperial Presidency and the Subversion of American Democracy*, Charlie Savage, Little Brown and Company, 2007.

58. *National Labor Relations Board vs. Noel Canning*, 573 U.S. ____ (2014) (slip opinion)

59. *Utility Air Regulatory Group vs. Environmental Protection Agency*, 573 U.S. ____ (2014) (slip opinion)

Chapter 16

60. "Public Faith in Congress Falls Again, Hits Historic Low," Rebecca Riffkin, www.gallup.com, June 19, 2014.

61. The Obama Administration took initial steps to permit registered lobbyists to serve on government boards and commissions in August of 2014. See "W.H. to reverse part of lobbyist ban," by Byron Tau, *Politico*, Aug. 12, 2014.

ABOUT THE AUTHORS

Tom Davis served in Congress from 1994 to 2008 representing Virginia's 11th district. During that time, he served as House GOP campaign chairman for two cycles (2000 and 2002), and chairman of the House Committee on Government Reform and Oversight before retiring, undefeated, in 2008. He is a graduate of Amherst College and the University of Virginia Law School. He currently serves as a Director at Deloitte LLP and resides in Vienna, VA. He is also a co-founder of *"No Labels."*

Martin Frost served 26 years in Congress representing the Dallas–Ft. Worth area in North Texas. During that time he served four years as chair of the Democratic Congressional Campaign Committee and four years as Chair of the House Democratic Caucus. He has undergraduate degrees in journalism and history from the University of Missouri and a law degree from the Georgetown University Law Center. He is a senior partner in the Washington office of the Polsinelli law firm and resides in Alexandria, VA.

Richard Cohen has written about Congress for *National Journal*, Politico and *Congressional Quarterly*. He is the author of several books, including *Washington at Work: Back Rooms and Clean Air* and *Rostenkowski: The Pursuit of Power and The End of the Old Politics*. He received his undergraduate degree from Brown University and a law degree from Georgetown University Law Center. He resides in McLean, VA.

David Eisenhower, grandson of general and President Dwight
D. Eisenhower, is an historian and the Director of the Institute
for Public Service at the Annenberg Public Policy Center.
He serves as a senior research fellow at the University of
Pennsylvania's Annenberg School of Communication and
is a fellow in the International Relations Department at the
University. Eisenhower is the author of *Eisenhower: At War*,
which was a finalist for the Pulitzer Prize in history in 1986. He
is the co-author, with wife Julie Nixon Eisenhower, of *Going
Home to Glory*. David resides in the Philadelphia, PA, area.

INDEX

5

501(c)(4),
76–79, 84–87, 210, 211, 273
501(c)(6),
76–78, 89, 273

9

9/11,
24, 84, 265, 274

A

abortion,
3, 24, 33, 42, 51, 56, 79, 100, 106,
152, 162, 244
Adelson, Sheldon,
77
affirmative action,
56, 268
Affordable Care Act,
105, 258, 259, 268. See Obamacare
Afghanistan,
261, 265
AFL-CIO,
105, 169, 213
African American,
39, 53, 55, 57–60, 66, 156, 202, 212,
214, 216, 218, 225, 240, 246, 289

Agriculture Committee,
167, 244
Ailes, Roger,
173
Alabama Bill,
271. *See* Lehman, Bill
Alaska,
37, 184, 200
Albania,
229, 230
Alioto, Joe,
12
Alito, Samuel,
86
All Citizens for Mississippi,
214
Allen, George,
101, 169
Allen, Ray,
144
Almanac of American Politics, The,
xvi, 5, 27, 224, 263, 287, 288, 291
AMBER Alert,
230–232. *See* Hagerman, Amber
Amber Hagerman Child Protection
Act,
230
American Chemistry Council,
145

American Conservative Union,
213
American Crossroads,
77, 78, 87
American Federation of Teachers,
240
American League,
2
American Revolution,
175
Americans for Democratic Action,
213
Americans for Prosperity,
76, 88
Americans with Disabilities Act,
238
America the Super,
90
America Votes,
14, 289
Amherst College,
ix, 15
Angle, Matt,
x, 13, 69, 196
Anti-Deficiency Act,
225
AP,
13
Appalachia,
41–43, 98
Arkansas,
56, 63, 160, 163, 164, 200, 202, 206,
210, 213
Arlington,
40, 230
Arlington County,
15
Army Reserves,
232
Armed Services Committee,
96, 98, 245, 246
Asia, Asian,
50, 51, 58

Auschwitz,
230
Austin, Texas,
69

B

Baca, Joe,
190
Baldwin, Tammy,
13
Baghdad,
173
Baker, Howard,
264
Baker vs. Carr,
61, 276, 289
Baltimore,
39, 108, 151, 161
Baltimore Orioles,
2
Barry, Marion,
224
baseball steroid hearings,
xvi, 2, 219–23, 249, 250
Battle of Quebec,
70
Bay Area,
39
Bass, Ross,
53
Barone, Michael,
xvi, 263, 287
Bayne, Floyd,
144
Baucus, Max,
200
BCRA,
84, 85. *See* Bipartisan Campaign
Reform Act
Beaumont,
67
Beauprez, Bob,
190

Bentsen, Lloyd,
201
Bereuter, Doug,
228, 230
Berg, Rick,
204, 205
Bergdahl, Beau,
261
Berlin Wall,
12, 227
Berkley, Shelley,
204
Best Financially Managed County in
America,
20
Bethesda,
40
Biden, Joe,
203
Big Government website,
176
Billington, James,
228
bipartisan, bipartisanship,
iv, v, x, 2, 3, 26, 32, 33, 45, 65, 72,
80, 83, 84, 91, 106, 173, 178, 208, 213,
219, 223, 228, 230, 232, 234, 244, 249,
253–55, 259, 260, 267, 271, 272, 274,
277, 279, 280–83
Bipartisan Campaign Reform Act
(BCRA),
84
Bipartisan Policy Center,
x, 208, 271
black vote/voters,
53–55, 57, 59, 62–64, 66, 161, 168,
212, 216, 218, 240, 241
black(s),
3, 5, 9, 10, 13, 22, 39, 41, 47, 48,
50–64, 66, 67, 79, 160, 161, 166–68,
191, 192, 197, 201, 202, 212, 214, 215,
218, 225, 240–42, 247, 248, 276, 288
Black Caucus,
242
Blitzer, Wolf,
173
Bloomberg, Michael,
77, 190, 289
"Blue Dog" Democrat,
103

Boehner, John,
23, 27, 110, 239, 240, 247, 251, 255,
258, 259, 262, 280
Bolling, Dick,
11
Bonds, Barry,
221. *See* baseball steroid hearings
Bonilla, Henry,
69
Boston Herald,
91, 291
Boston Red Sox,
5
Boucher, Rick,
43, 98, 99
Bowles, Erskine,
261, 279, 280
BPC, BPC commission,
272, 274, 276, 277, 279. *See* Bipartisan Policy Center
Brandt, Werner,
228
Brault, Abe,
16
Breitbart, Andrew,
176
Brewer, Mark D.,
148
Breyer, Stephen,
262
Brooke, Edward,
26, 162
Brown, Scott,
209, 268
Bryant, John,
67
Brachfield, Charlie,
7
Brat, David,
109, 144–46
Brazile, Donna,
vi, 168
Brooks, Jack,
67

Brownstein, Ron,
56
Brown Daily Herald,
25
Brown University,
25
Buckley, James,
81
Buckley, William F.,
81
Buckley v. Valeo,
81–83, 89, 275, 290
Budget Committee,
98, 249, 280
Bulgaria,
229
Bunning, Jim,
221. *See* baseball steroid hearings
Bush, George H.W.,
27, 39, 67, 108, 228, 233, 254
Bush, George W.,
24, 32, 33, 40–42, 51, 57, 84, 100, 102,
103, 154, 168, 170, 188, 189, 204, 219,
232
Buyer, Steve,
249
Byrd, Harry,
4, 54
Byrne, Leslie,
20–22

C
Cairo,
175
California,
12, 15, 39, 62, 65, 98, 108, 190, 210,
230, 237, 248, 261, 276, 278
Calhoun, Credell,
214
Camden Yards,
2
campaign finance law,
3, 75, 89
Camp David,
146
Canada,
165
Cantor, Eric,
109, 110, 143–46, 212

Campbell, Courtney,
187
Cannon, Joe,
236, 237
Canseco, Jose,
220–223. *See* baseball steroid hearings
Cao, Joseph,
98
Capital Beltway,
40
Capitol Hill,
iii, 4, 27, 29, 224, 255, 257, 258
Capitol Page School,
15
Caraway, Hattie,
202
Caray, Harry,
1
Cardin, Ben,
204
Carey, Thomas,
213
Carrico, Bill,
98
Carter, Jimmy,
iv, 9, 10, 57, 58, 67
Cartwright, Matt,
105
Case, Clifford,
162
Castle, Mike,
90
Catholic,
51, 160
Census Bureau,
45
Center for Responsible Politics,
187
Central Europe,
12, 228, 229, 233
Chapman, Jim,
67
Charlottesville,
15
checks and balances,
xiii, xv, 262, 284
Cherrydale precinct,
16

Chicago,
  39, 53, 55, 84, 151, 161
Childers, Travis,
  214
China,
  175, 200
Citizens United vs. FEC,
  86–89, 92, 210, 272, 275, 290
City and State (now *Governing*)
magazine,
  20
civil rights,
  xiv, 4, 14, 47, 52–57, 160, 161, 212, 280
Civil Rights Act of 1964,
  52–55, 160, 161, 280
Civil Service Committee,
  224, 245
Civil War,
  xiv, 55, 106, 160, 218
Clay, Henry,
  237
Clayton, Eva,
  247
Clean Air Act of 1970,
  256
Clean Air Act of 1990,
  27
Clemens, Roger,
  223. *See* baseball steroid hearings
Cleveland,
  39
Clinger, Bill,
  224, 246
Clinton administration,
  201, 226, 261
Clinton, Bill,
  iv, 5, 13, 14, 22, 24, 32, 33, 45, 51, 52,
  57, 53, 83, 87, 96, 146, 172, 226, 231,
  233, 247, 254, 262–66
Clinton, Hillary,
  51, 86
Club for Growth,
  90, 211
Clyburn, Jim,
  48
CNN,
  vi, 172–74
Cochran, Thad,
  59, 211–18

CODEL,
  227, 228, 281. *See* congressional
  delegation
Cohen, Bill,
  226
Cold War,
  25
Coleman, Marshall,
  21
college-educated, single suburban
women,
  51
Collins, Susan,
  37
Colorado,
  103, 165, 190, 195, 196, 202, 269
Columbia Journalism Review,
  26
Commission on Political Reform,
  x, 271. *See* Bipartisan Policy Center
Committee on Government Reform
and Oversight,
  21, 219
compromise,
  xiii–xvii, 4, 32, 33, 44, 45, 71, 90, 92,
  110, 143, 144, 146, 149, 150, 159, 162,
  163, 165, 166, 178, 180, 183, 194, 207,
  216, 224, 227, 275, 279, 286
Confederate, confederacy,
  56, 63, 160, 162
congressional delegation,
  3, 62, 65, 70, 205, 227
Congressional Quarterly,
  8, 27
*Congressional Quarterly Weekly
Report*,
  171
Congressional Research Service,
  228, 276
Connecticut,
  38, 108, 288
Connolly, Gerry,
  40
Constitution, constitutional,
  55, 81, 82, 84, 88, 889, 106, 178, 184,
  200, 244, 254, 256, 260, 262, 264, 267,
  275–77, 284
Contract With America,
  238

Cornyn, John,
203
County Board of Supervisors,
16, 18, 19, 40, 245
Cramer, Bill,
187
Crossroads GPS,
78, 87. *See* American Crossroads
Cruz, Ted,
163, 174, 204, 258
CRS.
See Congressional Research Service
crybaby,
14
C-SPAN,
172, 177
Cuba,
107, 192, 222, 260
Cuccinelli, Ken,
156, 157
Cudrup, Ronnie C., Sr.,
214
Cunningham, Duke,
281
Czechoslovakia,
228, 229

D
Dallas,
8–11, 61, 66, 67, 70, 151, 160, 167,
171, 177, 197, 202, 231, 232
Dallas Love Field,
8
Dallas-Ft. Worth,
9, 10, 61, 66, 70, 177, 231, 232
dark money,
77
Daschle, Tom,
185, 271
Davis-Bacon wage legislation,
169
D.C.,
2, 22, 24, 87, 146, 151, 171, 177, 185,
193, 205, 213, 224–26, 229, 240 *See*
District of Columbia

DCCC,
xvi, 12, 13, 49, 168, 171, 186–88,
195–97, 209
D.C. Circuit Court,
87
Deeds, Creigh,
156, 157, 164
DeLay, Tom,
14, 23, 68–70, 185, 240, 249–51, 276,
289
Delaware,
8, 90, 103, 171, 202, 203, 269
Delta,
215, 218
Democratic Caucus Rules Committee,
11
Democratic Congressional Campaign
Committee,
x, xvi, 12, 62, 186. *See* DCCC
Democratic Leadership Council,
11
Democratic National Committee,
vi, 8, 10, 65, 83
Dent, Harry,
15
Department of Defense,
179
Department of Energy,
281
Department of Health and Human
Services,
260
Depression,
xiv, 53
De Priest, Oscar,
53, 55
Detroit,
39, 161
Dewhurst, David,
204
digital campaigning,
176. *See* Facebook, Twitter, YouTube

DINKs,
41
Dingell, John,
237
"Disclose" bill,
87
District of Columbia,
2, 22, 34, 224, 245, 246, 287
District of Columbia Committee,
245
District of Columbia Subcommittee,
22, 224, 246
Djou, Charles,
98
DNC,
179. *See* Democratic National Committee
Dole, Bob,
203, 206, 207, 264
Dream Act,
258
Dreier, David,
230
Duffy, Jim,
167
Dukakis, Michael,
39, 58
Duke University,
207
Dumfries,
40
Dunklau, Rupert,
91
Durbin, Dick,
203
dysfunction,
vi, 29, 207, 266, 268

E
earmarks,
143, 234, 281, 282
East Berliners,
227

Eastern Europe,
227, 228
East Germany,
227
Economist,
45, 288
Edwards, Chet,
67, 68, 98
Eisenhower administration,
14
Eisenhower, David,
iv, ix, xiii, xvii, 15
Eisenhower, Dwight D.,
xvii, 15, 160, 187
Eisenhower, Julie Nixon,
xvii
Egyptian,
175
Ehrlich, Bob,
98
Ehrlich, Jessica,
188
EIS,
233. *See* environmental impact study
Electoral College,
34, 102, 263, 269
Emancipation Proclamation,
55
Energy and Commerce Committee,
220, 237
Ensuring a Conservative Nebraska,
91
environmental impact study,
233
environmental movement,
14, 186
Estonia,
229
Etheridge, Bobby,
176
Evanston,
40
express advocacy,
76, 78, 86–89, 273, 275

F

Facebook,
174–77

Face the Nation,
v, 221

Fairfax County Board of Supervisors,
16, 40, 245

Fairfax County Republican Committee,
15

Fair Labor Standards Act,
238

Fazio, Vic,
62

FEC,
75, 76, 78, 86–88, 273–75, 290. *See* Federal Election Commission

Federal Election Campaign Act of 1974,
80

Federal Election Commission,
75, 273

Federal Election Commission vs. Wisconsin Right to Life, Inc.,
86, 290

Feingold, Russ,
65, 83, 85–88, 92, 272, 273, 289

Feinstein, Dianne,
240, 261

Fenway Park,
193

filibuster,
43, 55, 86, 87, 207

Financial Services Committee,
247

Fiorina, Carly,
98

First Amendment,
81, 82, 86, 88, 89, 275

Fletcher, Ernie,
240, 241

Florida,
4, 24, 57, 63, 65, 66, 91, 160, 162, 175, 187, 189, 192, 210, 249, 250, 265

Foley, Tom,
227, 228

Ford, Gerald,
57, 81

Foreign Affairs Committee,
244

Fort Worth Star-Telegram,
177

Founding Fathers,
44, 208, 283

Fox News,
173, 179

Frank, Barney,
267

Freedom Partners Action Fund,
76

Freedom Works,
90

Freeman, Jody,
257, 292

Frelinghuysen, Rodney,
107

French and Indian War,
70

Ft. Worth Press,
171

Ft. Worth, Texas,
1, 8–11, 47, 61, 66, 67, 69, 70, 146, 166, 167, 171, 177, 231, 232

G

Gallup polling,
49, 50, 288, 292

Gantt, Harvey,
79

gay(s),
5, 13, 42, 51, 79, 156, 165, 166, 168, 169, 253, 259

gay marriage,
79, 156, 165, 166, 169

gay rights,
42, 79, 259
Gekas, George,
105
gender gap,
52
general election(s),
13, 19, 33, 53, 54, 70, 76, 80, 81, 85,
88, 105, 106, 108, 151, 154, 155, 158,
163, 165–67, 174, 184, 189, 195, 196,
204, 207, 213, 214, 216, 217, 235,
269, 274, 275, 278
Georgetown Law School,
8, 26
Georgia,
9, 23, 54, 57, 63, 64, 66, 161, 204
Gephardt, Dick,
vii, x, 12, 27, 85, 97
Geren, Pete,
67
gerrymander, gerrymandering,
xv, 3, 14, 24, 34, 37, 38, 43, 61, 68,
71, 72, 101, 105, 108, 147, 159, 161,
162, 184, 200, 275, 276, 289
Gersh, Mark,
64
Gettysburg,
53
Gilligan, John,
108
Gingrich, Newt,
12–14, 21–23, 27, 33, 45, 77, 100,
172, 207, 208, 224–26, 229, 230, 236,
237, 245, 246, 265, 292
Ginsburg, Ben,
64, 65
Glickman, Dan,
271
Gold, Jeff,
90, 91
Goldwater, Barry,
54, 56, 57
Gonzalez, Alberto,
222

Goodwin, Doris Kearns,
281
Gordon, Bart,
228
Gore, Al,
12, 24, 51, 57, 58, 102, 188
Government Operations Committee,
245
Government Reform and Oversight
Committee,
224
Government Reform Committee,
vi, xvi, 246
Great Society,
264
Green, Bill,
39
Green Party,
144
Griffith, Morgan,
99
Grossman, Shirley,
91, 291
Grossman, Steve,
91
Gulf Coast,
96, 215
gun control,
3, 33, 77

H
Hall, Ralph,
3, 68
Hagan, Kay,
163, 206
Hagerman, Amber,
230
Harding, Warren G.,
207
hard money,
78, 79
Harrison, Ed,
197

Harvard Law School,
14, 204
Hastert, Denny,
v, 23, 24, 100, 189, 221, 230
Hatch, Orrin,
163
Hawaii,
98, 152
health care,
33, 96, 98, 237, 244, 264, 265
Heitkamp, Heidi,
37, 204, 205
Helms, Jesse,
57
Henderson, Texas,
7
Heritage Action,
90
Hinkle, Betsy,
18
Holden, Tim,
105
Holt, Rush,
107, 196
Hooton, Don,
220, 221
Hoover, Herbert,
160
Hoyer, Steny,
x, 227
Hillarycare,
33
Hispanic(s),
3, 5, 14, 45, 49–52, 57, 58, 63, 64, 66, 67, 69, 70
Hispanic vote,
14, 50, 57, 64, 69, 70, 259
Homeland Security Committee,
248
House Administration Committee,
248, 288, 290
House Appropriations Committee,
13, 188

House Committee on Government Reform and Oversight,
25
House Democracy Partnership,
230. *See* CODEL
House Democratic Caucus,
xvi, 48, 146
House Government Reform Committee,
xvi
House Judiciary Committee,
26, 231
House Majority Leader,
11, 68
House Majority PAC,
77, 88
House of Representatives,
v, 21, 31, 34, 37, 42, 44, 172, 183, 195, 199
House Rules Committee,
4, 11, 196, 208, 234, 280
House Ways and Means Committee,
27
Houston,
8, 39, 67, 151, 185
Hughes, Sarah T.,
8, 9, 11
Human Rights Campaign Fund,
100
Hume, Brit,
173
Humphrey, Hubert,
56
Hungary,
228
Hurricane Katrina,
96, 213, 215
Hutchinson, Kay Bailey,
201, 231

I

ideological sorting,
xiv, 101

Illinois,
27, 37, 55, 65, 184, 202
immigrant(s),
59, 107, 258, 259, 266
immigration,
32, 45, 51, 107, 109, 110, 166, 180,
244, 253, 258, 259, 280
Independence USA PAC,
77
independent,
xiv, xv, xvii, 25, 28, 33, 44, 76–80,
82, 87, 88, 106, 107, 145, 147, 149–
57, 164, 170, 186, 189, 190, 204, 205,
209, 217, 218, 226, 235, 246–48, 251,
263, 267, 269, 273, 274, 276, 278
Indiana,
90, 185, 202, 245, 249,
Indianapolis,
151
Intelligence Committee,
261
Internal Revenue Service,
75
Internet,
xv, 172, 174, 179, 180, 189, 268
Iowa,
12, 108, 228, 276
Iowa Caucuses,
12
Iraq,
246, 247, 260, 265, 268
IRS,
75, 76, 78. *See* Internal Revenue
Service

J
Japan,
228, 233
Javits, Jacob,
162
Jeb Stuart High School,
17
Jeffords, Jim,
24, 25, 226

Jewish voters,
5
Jews,
51
Jim Crow,
55
Johnson, Lyndon B.,
8, 26, 54, 58, 161, 203, 207, 264
Johnson, Eddie Bernice,
67, 248
Johnson, Ron,
37
joint fundraising committees,
89
Jolly, Dave,
187–89
Jones County,
211, 215, 218
Jones, free state of,
218
Jones, Walter,
246, 247, 251
Jordan, B. Everett,
53, 211
Jordan, Michael,
79, 290
Journal of Politics,
207, 292
Judiciary Committee,
26, 231, 244
Juiced,
220, 223. *See* baseball steroid hearings
jungle primary,
190, 278
jungle rules,
180, 236
Justice Department,
67, 69, 231, 289

K
Kansas,
176, 108, 163, 196, 271

Kansas City, Missouri,
 11, 196, 201
Keating, Ken,
 15
Kempthorne, Dirk,
 271
Kennedy, Bud,
 177
Kennedy, John F.,
 25, 57, 177, 207
Kennedy, Robert F.,
 55
Kennedy, Ted,
 262
Kentucky,
 162, 163, 191, 240, 255
Kerry, John,
 51, 57, 58, 103, 188, 204, 207
Keystone Pipeline,
 165
Key, V.O.,
 66, 53, 153, 218, 288. *See* Southern
 Politics
Kiev Maidan protests,
 175
Kilgore, Terry,
 98
King, Angus,
 37
King, Martin Luther, Jr.,
 26, 57, 146
Kirk, Mark,
 37
Kirk, Ron,
 201, 202
Koch brothers,
 76, 88, 290
Korean American,
 169
Ku Klux Klan,
 7, 55
Kyl, Jon,
 108

L
labor union(s),
 77, 79, 81, 86, 166
Lake Barcroft,
 18
Lampson, Nick,
 68
Landrieu, Mary,
 163, 206
Latvia,
 229
Laughlin, Greg,
 185
Law School Young Republicans,
 15
Leach, Jim,
 228
leadership PAC,
 82, 274
League of Conservation Voters,
 105
Lee, Mike,
 63, 204, 269
Lee, Robert E.,
 53
Lehman, Bill,
 271
Lehman Brothers,
 284
Lehrer, Jim,
 9, 171
Leland, Mickey,
 39
Lewinsky, Monica,
 22
Lewis, John,
 48, 64
liberal Republicans,
 104
Library of Congress,
 276
Lieberman, Joe,
 57, 240
Limbaugh, Rush,
 153, 174
Lincoln, Abraham,
 53, 55

Lincoln-Douglas debates,
184
Lincoln, Blanche,
164
Linder, John,
23
Lithuania,
227, 229
Livingston, Bob,
13, 23
Lombardi, Vince,
195
Longworth House Office Building,
177
Longworth, Nicholas,
192, 236
Los Angeles,
8, 39, 143, 151
Los Angeles Times,
84
Lott, Trent,
v, 172, 203, 271
Louisiana,
13, 54, 63, 98, 163, 189, 200, 206, 210,
278
Love, Mia,
59
Lugar, Richard,
90, 185

M
Maddow, Rachel,
180
Madison, Wisconsin,
13
Magazine, Alan,
16, 18
Maine,
37, 205, 226, 271
Maisel, L. Sandy,
148
Majority PAC,
77, 88
Major League Baseball,
220, 221, 223, 249
Man of the House,
95
marginalize, marginalization,
xv, 151, 155, 190, 192, 248

Markey, Ed,
204
Marwil, Mose,
7
Maryland,
60, 98, 100, 152, 202, 204, 227
Mason, Virginia,
16, 18–22
Massachusetts,
5, 25, 40, 91, 152, 162, 202, 204, 209,
267, 268
Mass Forward PAC,
91
Matheson,
102
Matthews, Chris,
180
Mayer, William G.,
150
Mayors Against Illegal Guns,
190
McAuliffe, Terry,
32, 156, 157, 164
McCain-Feingold campaign finance
reform law,
65, 85–88, 92, 272,, 273, 289
McCain, John,
83, 207, 221, 258, 285
McCarthy, Eugene,
26
McCarthy, Gina,
256
McCarver, Tim,
1
McClellan, John,
213
McConnell, Mitch,
143, 203
McCutcheon vs. FEC,
88
McDaniel, Chris,
211–16, 218
McDaniels, Wayne,
214, 215. *See* NAACP
McDonnell, Bob,
156
McGovern, George,
57, 58
McGwire, Mark,
221, 222. *See* baseball steroid hearings

McIntosh, Dave,
  245
McIntyre,
  102
McLeod, Gloria Negrete,
  190
McMillian, John,
  53
McNeil-Lehrer Report,
  9, 171
Medicare,
  52, 264, 280
Meehan, Marty,
  83, 92
Meinrath, Sascha,
  175
Merrifield, Virginia,
  40, 41
Metro,
  41
Metropolitan Washington Council of
Governments,
  245
Michigan,
  55, 60, 66, 228, 237, 248
Midwest,
  14, 65, 160, 162, 163, ,187, 201
Mikulski, Barbara,
  202
Milford, Dale,
  9, 10
Miller,
  102
Miller, Candice,
  248
Miller, Jim,
  216
minorities,
  44, 48, 49, 64, 69, 71
minority vote, voters,
  48, 58, 69, 154, 156, 165
minority women,
  52
Mississippi,
  13, 54, 63, 64, 96, 161, 189, 211–18,
  271
Mississippi Delta,
  215
Mississippi River,
  218

Mitchell, Andrea,
  173
Mitchell, Arthur,
  55
Missouri,
  8, 9, 11, 64, 98, 162, 171, 201, 202
Mitchell, George,
  223
MLB,
  220–223. *See* Major League Baseball
Mollohan, Alan,
  196
Mondale, Walter,
  58, 197
Montreal,
  2
Moore, Audrey,
  19, 20
Moore, Dennis,
  196
Morella, Connie,
  100, 101
Morning Joe,
  173
Mrazek, Bob,
  228
MSNBC,
  173, 174, 180
Mubarak, Hosni,
  175
mugwump,
  53
multi-candidate PACs,
  79, 81
Murphy, Patrick,
  192

N
NAACP,
  20, 167, 214
Nader, Ralph,
  102, 188
NARAL,
  100
Nassau County,
  40
National Committee for an Effective
Congress (NCEC),
  64

National Conference of State Legislatures,
184
National Education Association,
239
National Endowment for Democracy,
230
national health care,
33
National Journal,
vi, 26, 27, 56, 104, 289, 291
National Labor Relations Act,
238
National League,
2
National Republican Campaign Committee,
23, 186. *See* NRCC
National Rifle Association,
23
National Right to Life,
23
national sex offender registry,
231
NBC,
iv, 173
NCEC,
64. *See* National Committee for an Effective Congress
NEA,
240. *See* National Education Association
Nebraska,
14, 17, 91, 228, 230
NED.
See National Endowment for Democracy
Nedzi, Lucien,
228
Nevada,
103, 202, 204, 205, 269
New America Foundation,
175
Newark, New Jersey,
39
New Deal,
3, 55
New Hampshire,
26, 107, 288

New Jersey,
107, 162, 183, 196, 249, 276
New Jersey Plan,
183
New Mexico,
89
New York,
1, 14–16, 39, 55,81, 84, 143, 151, 160, 175, 190, 197, 210, 225, 228, 232–34, 240, 248, 257, 287
New York City,
143, 190, 197, 240
New York Daily News,
14
New Yorker,
289
New York Mets,
1, 287
Neuberger, Maurine,
202
NextGen Climate Action PAC,
77
NIKE, Inc.,
79
Nixon, Richard,
15, 26, 56, 80, 81
Norpel, Dorothy,
17
Norquist, Grover,
179
Northampton, Massachusetts,
25, 26, 28
North Carolina,
53, 63, 64, 66, 160, 162, 163, 176, 200, 206, 210, 211, 230, 246, 247,
North Dakota,
37, 184, 204, 205
North, Oliver,
19, 21, 22, 216, 217
Norton, Eleanor Holmes,
22, 224, 226
NRA,
96
NRCC,
xvi, 23, 24, 97, 186, 187, 189, 190, 192, 195, 248. *See* National Republican Campaign Committee
nuclear option,
284

Nunn, Sam,
161

O

Obama administration,
110, 259, 260, 292
Obama, Barack,
4, 5, 14, 32–34, 37–39, 48–52, 58–60,
72, 77, 80, 87, 88, 96–98, 101, 103,
107, 110, 146, 156, 157, 159, 160, 165,
166, 168, 174–76, 179, 180, 188, 189,
191, 192, 202, 207, 212, 237, 253,
254–63, 265, 266, 268, 269, 279, 280,
283, 291
Obamacare,
27, 96, 105, 107, 110, 156, 162, 175,
189, 253, 268. See Affordable Care
Act
Obama for America (OFA),
179
O'Connor, Sandra Day,
86
Occupational Safety and Health Act,
238
OFA.
See Obama for America
Ohio,
56, 65, 66, 108, 154
Oklahoma,
91
O'Neill, Tip,
xv, 11, 95, 172, 264, 280
Open Technology Initiative,
175
Operation Desert Storm,
173, 249
Oregon,
202
Owens, Major,
240, 241
Oxford, Wisconsin,
27

P

PACs,
75–82, 87, 88, 90, 92, 99, 104, 106,
186, 187, 189, 195, 196, 210, 211, 227,
235, 273, 274, 280, 281, 291

Palazzo, Steve,
96, 97
Palmeiro, Rafael,
221–23. See baseball steroid hearings
Pappas, Mike,
196, 197
parliament(s), parliamentary,
xv, 12, 33, 43, 101, 103, 227–30, 233,
265, 281, 283
Parties and Elections in America,
148
partisan redistricting,
70–72
Pasadena,
40
Passover Seder,
230
Patrick, Deval,
202
Paul, Rand,
163, 204
Paul, Ron,
145, 185
PBS,
9, 171
Pearl Harbor,
233
Pelosi, Nancy,
v, 27, 96, 97, 105, 108, 163, 237, 242,
259, 263, 280
Pennsylvania,
iv, xvii, 37, 55, 60, 65 , 66, 105, 162,
246
Pentagon,
173, 245, 266
Periodical Press Gallery,
28
Perot, Ross,
48
Perry, Rick,
68
Pew,
110, 154, 155, 176
Pew Research Center,
148, 176, 291
Pfeiffer, Dan,
254
Philadelphia,
xiii, 39, 84, 107, 151, 161

Phoenix,
   151
Pine, Jeff,
   193
Pinson, Cloyde,
   233
Pittsburgh,
   39
Playboy,
   10
Poland,
   228–30
political action committee(s),
   77, 88
"Political Polarization in the American
Public",
   148
Political Science,
   15
Politico,
   27, 77, 290, 292
Post Office and Civil Service Committee,
   224, 245
Price, David,
   230
primary, primaries,
   vi, xiv, xv, 4, 9, 18, 26, 43, 44, 53,
   54, 56, 59, 67, 70, 76, 77, 80, 81, 85,
   86, 88, 90, 91, 105, 106, 108–10,
   143–47, 149–51, 154, 155, 157, 158,
   161, 163–66, 174, 175, 177, 179, 185,
   187–91, 196, 201, 202, 211–18, 228,
   235, 246–48, 251, 273–75, 277, 278,
   280, 283, 292
Priorities USA Action,
   77, 88
pro-choice,
   14, 105, 250
Professional Firefighters,
   21, 168
pro-gun,
   105
Prohibition,
   160

Project for Excellence in Journalism,
   176. *See* Pew Research Center
Project Ratfuck,
   64
pro-labor,
   105
pro-life,
   96, 105, 169, 250
Prosecutorial Remedies and Other
Tools to End the Exploitation of Children Today Act,
   231
PROTECT.
See Prosecutorial Remedies and Other
Tools to End the Exploitation of Children Today Act
Providence, Rhode Island,
   25
Pryor, David,
   213
Pryor, Mark,
   163, 206
public campaign financing,
   xv, 80

R
Rabin, Yitzhak,
   13, 14
racial,
   13, 47, 48, 50, 56–59, 63, 64, 161, 212,
   225, 275
racial vote,
   48
Rahall, Nick,
   42
Rangel, Charlie,
   48, 168
Rangers,
   1, 2
Reagan, Ronald,
   3, 32, 57, 58, 172, 177, 216, 264, 265,
   280
redistricting,
   xvii, 4, 12, 24, 25, 37 ,38, 40, 45, 61,
   64–66, 68–72, 99, 100, 105, 106, 162,
   188, 246, 276, 278, 283, 289

"red wall" states,
34
Reed, Tom,
236
Reform Judaism,
47
Rehnquist, William,
86
Reid, Harry,
143, 203, 258, 280
Republican National Committee,
65, 179
Republican Party of Virginia,
21
residential sorting,
xv, 34, 37, 39, 43, 101, 106
Reston, Virginia,
40
Restore our Future,
77, 87
Rhode Island,
25, 151, 152, 193
Richards, Ann,
67, 201
Richmond, Virginia,
4, 149
Rivlin, Alice,
22, 226
Roosevelt, Franklin D.,
55
Roberts, John,
86, 88
Roberts, Pat,
163
Robertson, A. Willis,
53
Robinson, Joe,
160
Rockefeller, Nelson,
15
Rocky Mountain West,
14
Rodriguez, Ciro,
69
Rogers, Hal,
191
Rohde, David,
207, 208, 292
Romania,
229, 230

Romney, Mitt,
34, 37–39, 49, 77, 87, 101, 145, 159, 160, 175, 176, 192, 212, 269, 291
Rostenkowski, Dan,
27
Rotary Club,
16, 18
Rothblatt, Gabriel,
91
Rothblatt, Martine,
91
Rove, Karl,
48, 58, 77, 78, 87, 212, 269
Rules Committee,
4, 11, 13, 196, 201, 208, 209, 229, 231, 234, 236, 244, 248, 280
Runyan, Jon,
102, 107

S
Sabato, Larry,
150
Salvadorian,
169
Sanchez, Linda,
248
Sanders, Bernie,
37, 152
San Diego,
151, 281
Sandlin, Max,
68
Sasse, Ben,
91
Savage, Charlie,
260, 292
Scalia, Antonin,
262, 263
Schiavo, Terri,
249, 250
Schieffer, Bob,
v, 221
Science Committee,
246
Science, Space and Technology Committee,
244
Schiliro, Phil,
220

Schilling, Curt,
221. *See* baseball steroid hearings
school busing,
56
school prayer,
162
Schumer, Chuck,
203
Schwarzenegger, Arnold,
65
Scott, Hugh,
162
Scott, Tim,
59, 202
Scranton, Pennsylvania,
105
Sebelius, Kathleen,
108, 292
Selig, Bud,
221, 223. *See* baseball steroid hearings
Senate Appropriations Committee,
211
Senate Conservative Fund,
224
Senate Foreign Relations Committee,
280
Senate Intelligence Committee,
261
Sensenbrenner, Jim,
231, 332
Serrano, Jose,
191
Seventeenth Amendment,
199
Shands, Nancy,
18
Shays, Chris,
83, 92
Shays-Meehan,
92
Shows, Ronnie,
13
Shultz, Ed,
180
Silicon Valley,
143
Simpson, Alan,
261
Simpson-Bowles,
279, 280

Simpson-Mazzoli,
32
single-party districts,
92, 144
single woman base,
165
single women,
44, 153
Sink, Alex,
187–89
Sires, Albio,
107
Skelton, Ike,
98
slave(s), slavery,
53, 55, 160, 218
Slovak Republic,
229
Smart, Ed,
231, 232
Smart, Elizabeth,
231, 232
Smith, Al,
160
Smith, Chris,
249, 251
Smith, Howard W.,
53
Smith, "Judge" Howard,
4
Snowbarger, Vince,
196
Snowe, Olympia,
271
Social Security,
52, 265, 279, 280
soft money,
65, 78, 79, 83, 85, 87, 88, 92, 272, 273
Solomon, Gerry,
229
Solomon, Jerry,
228, 233, 234
Sosa, Sammy,
221. *See* baseball steroid hearings
South Carolina,
53, 54, 59, 63, 98, 173, 174, 202
South Dakota,
37, 185, 200, 205, 271
Southern Politics,
53, 218, 288. *See* V.O. Key

South, the,
1, 4, 15, 39, 47, 53–57, 62–66, 70, 103,
106, 160–63, 167, 168, 237, 276
Soviet Union,
228, 229
Space PAC,
91
Speechnow.org vs. FEC,
87
Sports Illustrated,
2
Spratt, John,
98
Stark, Pete,
278
Starr, Ken,
196
State Department,
228, 229
State of the Union speech,
219
State Young Republicans,
15
Steering and Policy Committee,
242
Steering Committee,
236, 241–43, 247–49, 251
Stengel, Casey,
1, 287
Stenholm, Charlie,
68, 167
steroid(s),
xvi, 2, 219, 220, 223, 249, 250. *See*
baseball steroid hearings
Stevens, John Paul,
82
Stewart, Donald,
211
Steyer, Tom,
77
St. Louis,
1, 39, 151
St. Louis Cardinals,
1, 2, 5
Stone, W. Clement,
80
Straight Talk Express,
83
straight-ticket voting,
31, 32, 38, 43, 45, 153, 200

Strauss, Bob,
8, 10, 12
subprime mortgages,
284
suburban women,
5, 51, 168
Suburbia, its People and Their Politics,
40
super PACs,
75, 90, 206
Supreme Court,
24, 61, 69, 80–82, 85, 86, 89, 209,
210, 259, 262, 265, 267, 272, 275,
276
Swalwell, Eric,
278

T
Taliban,
261
Tahrir Square,
175
*Takeover: The Return of the Imperial
Presidency and the Subversion of
American Democracy*,
292
Tapper, Jake,
173
Taylor, Gene,
96–98, 101, 211
TARP,
284, 285. *See* Troubled Asset Relief
Program
tax(es),
20, 32, 33, 110, 152, 169, 179, 195, 225,
226, 243, 244, 257, 264, 266
Tea Party, 90, 104 ,107, 109, 110,
162–65, 175, 204, 211–14, 216, 218, 259,
260, 267, 268
Tennessee,
53, 63, 66, 160, 228, 288
Texas,
x, 1–4, 7–11, 14, 39, 47, 54, 57, 61–64,
66–70, 98, 160, 162–64, 167, 171,
177, 185, 197, 202–04, 207, 210, 219,
230–34, 248, 258, 276, 289, 291

Texas A&M,
233
Texas Federation of Temple Youth,
8
Texas Panhandle,
39
Texas Rangers,
1, 2
The Almanac of American Politics,
5, 224, 263, 287
The Gingrich Senators,
207, 292. *See* Theriault, Sean
The New York Times,
84, 90, 257
Theriault, Sean,
x, 207, 208, 292
The Swing Voter in American Politics,
150
The Washington Post,
20, 32, 91, 100, 161
Thompson, Bennie,
13, 48, 212
Thompson, Mike,
12
Thurmond, Strom,
15, 54, 57
ticket-splitting,
33, 37, 44, 101, 103, 108, 160
Todd, Chuck,
iv, 173
Toomey, Pat,
37
Tower, John,
203
Transportation Committee,
245
Travis County,
69
Trillin, Calvin,
90, 91, 290
Tripps precinct,
18
Troubled Asset Relief Program,
284
Truman, Harry,
161, 207
Turner, Jim,
68, 69

Turner, Mike,
91
Twitter,
174–77

U
Udall, Mark,
195, 196
Udall, Tom,
89
Ukraine,
229
Umana, Brian,
144
union members,
5, 81, 166
unions,
21, 76–79, 83, 86, 87, 89, 168, 169,
209, 239, 272, 273, 275
United Nations,
25
United States Constitution,
55, 276
University of Massachusetts,
40
University of Missouri School of
Journalism,
8
University of Texas,
x, 8, 207
University of Virginia,
15, 150, 246
University of Virginia Law School,
15, 246
upper-income whites,
5
USAID,
228
USA Today,
91, 254, 291, 292
U.S. Chamber of Commerce,
88
U.S. Fifth Circuit Court of Appeals,
8

USS *Pennsylvania*,
233
U.S. Supreme Court,
61, 81, 209, 272
Utah,
59, 149, 151, 163, 201, 232, 269

V
Valeo, Francis,
81, 89, 275, 290
Vandenberg, Arthur,
280
Veasey, Marc,
x, 177, 178
Velazquez, Nydia,
248
Vermont,
24, 152, 226
Veterans Affairs Committee,
249
Veterans Department,
232, 233
Vietnamese,
169
Vietnam War,
xiv, 12, 25, 47
Virginia,
ix, xvi, 4, 15, 16, 20, 21, 42, 43,
52–54, 57, 63, 66, 98, 99, 109, 110,
144, 149, 150, 156, 157, 160, 164,
169, 183, 184, 201, 212, 216, 217,
245, 246
Virginia Plan,
183
Voting Rights Act of 1965,
xv, 37, 39, 43, 53, 54, 56, 57, 62, 64,
106, 161, 168, 212, 275, 276

W
Waco, Texas,
67
Wallace, Chris,
175

Wallace, George,
26, 56
Walseth, Kristi,
x, 229
Walsh, Jim,
225
Walsh, John,
200
Wampler, William,
98
Wapello County,
12
Warner, John,
21, 216, 217
Warner, Mark,
157, 217
Warren, Elizabeth,
174, 209
Warsaw,
230
Washington at Work: Back Rooms and Clean Air,
27
Washington Metropolitan Area Transit Authority,
245
Washington Nationals,
2
Washington press corps,
28
Washington Senators,
2
Watergate scandal,
29, 47, 80
Waters, Maxine,
248
Watts, J.C.,
23
Waxman, Henry,
219–23, 237, 240, 241, 250
Ways and Means Committee,
27, 236, 243
Weiner, Anthony,
175

Wellstone, Paul,
84
West Germany,
228
West Virginia,
42, 43, 107, 162, 196, 200, 205, 255
Wheat, Alan,
64, 201, 202
White House,
15, 24, 33, 57, 100, 168, 206, 231,
254, 255, 257, 260–62, 269
white seniors,
49, 50, 52
white vote(rs),
48, 49, 51, 52, 58, 164, 165, 212, 214
Whitewater,
196
white women,
49, 52
Whitman, Meg,
98
Whitten, Jamie,
161
Wilkes-Barre,
105
Will, George,
220
Wilmington News-Journal,
171
Wilson, Charlie,
67
Wilson, Reverend Willy,
225
Winning Our Future,
77
Wisconsin Right to Life, Inc. (WRTL),
86, 290
Wolfensberger, Don,
208, 292
Wonkblog,
161, 291
Wood, Robert,
40

Woodrow Wilson Center for International Scholars,
228
World Series,
1, 5
World War I,
232
World War II,
40, 71, 227, 232, 233
Wright, Jim,
x, 3, 10, 11, 172
WRTL,
86, 88
Wyoming,
184

Y

Yanukovych, Victor,
175
Young, Bill,
187, 188
young people,
2, 5, 10, 40, 44
youth vote,
165
YouTube,
174–77, 206

.